Pat Hittle

Teaching Fools
Masters and Mentors

William D. Dyer

Copyright © 2023 William D. Dyer

Copyright © 2023 Salty Books Publishing, LLC

All rights reserved.

ISBN: 979-8987939321

Library of Congress Catalog Card Number: 2023910726

CONTENTS

	Acknowledgments	i
	Preface	1
Chapter 1	Enrollment in the School of Hard Knocks: An Introduction to Howard and Me	8
Chapter 2	Matriculation at the University That Is Howard	32
Chapter 3	Course Registration: Carpentry 101	49
Chapter 4	Building Howard University: The Curriculum Vitae	66
Chapter 5	Howard University's Core Curriculum: Class Convenes at the Shop	88
Chapter 6	The University Mission Statement: "Wood is a Living Thing," and Other Related but Less Vital Speculations	97
Chapter 7	An Independent Study with the Master: A Day in the Life	110
Chapter 8	Howard's Extended Campus: The Veitmeier Job	119
Chapter 9	Howard's Extended Campus: The Little House on the Prairie	129
Chapter 10	The Alumni Association: Howard's Former Students Become "Friends of the University"	141
Chapter 11	Externship I: The Sorcerer's Apprentice: From Skill-less Bankruptcy to Marginal Competence	159
Chapter 12	Externship II: From Master to Masterpiece	192
Chapter 13	Commencement (or, Let the Real Games Now Begin)	240
	Afterword: A Post-Doc Reflection	260

ACKNOWLEDGMENTS

To my daughter and soulmate Karen, who has steered me through the incalculable loss of my life-long sweetheart to Alzheimer's.

To Karen's and her husband Hunter's talented "kids" Azra and E, my son Chris, his wife Geana, and their ill-starred but brilliantly beautiful gift of a son Ronin.

To my sister Penny and her husband Jim who laughed in all the right places and thought well of this thing even when I didn't.

And, most importantly, the fiercely intrepid, beautiful Linda of the laughing face who lived the entire span of the thing, owned the only Ph.D. in the house that recognized practical skills, mastered each and every craft she put a hand to, and loved me like there was no tomorrow. The undeserved gift that will forever keep on giving.

PREFACE

"Your worships will perhaps be thinking that it an easy thing to blow up a dog?" Does your worship think it an easy thing to write a book?
—Cervantes, "Preface," *Don Quixote*

Dyer Straits
Cornucopia, Wisconsin
April 18, 2023

      Old people. A few years ago, I probably would have bunched them all together into the category of regrettable folk traveling all too slowly in front of me in the left lane with their turn signal blinking shamelessly. They would have been for me the "clapper people," they of whom the phrase "I've fallen down and I can't get up" has become the unfortunate stuff of thoughtless comic jibes. Victims of forgetfulness whose memories are stuck on "re-play." Remember Ian McKellan playing King Lear, howling in the rain as his pants slide below his knees just a little high and outside his daughter's locked castle door? No better example of full-blown second childhood. Embarrassing.
      Maybe so, but more sobering than embarrassing as I now must own up to being a bonifide old person. There's no escaping it. As of January 27th, I pushed my aged handcart into my 80th

year toward my inevitable dotage. Only ten minutes ago when I was sixty-nine and walking into what would be my final Shakespeare class, I was vaguely worried about whether my fly was zipped. But now I'm more concerned about whether my knees will support me, and for how long. Welcome to a club whose name my addled short-term memory will no longer surrender.

But that's ok. And it beats the hell out of the alternative. Besides, as Howard Bowers—skilled and wise subject of this minimum opus—told me nineteen winters ago when I visited his shop in Herbster, Wisconsin, on my last visit to my favorite place before returning to the classroom after winter break, getting to be this old has been almost criminal fun. And being old presents a matchless opportunity. For what, you might ask, besides the chance to watch your skin fold and crease, perform careful management of the sixteen hairs clinging to your head for dear life, and hear and smell the symphony of pain and bodily decay visited upon you?

As Howard so perceptively observed, old age—whenever it should arrive—is the occasion for doing what you may have always intended to do, but, because of job, family, and other time constraints, deferred until some later time. But, as Howard reminded me, that time is now. Old age, even for those beset by disabling injuries or diminishing faculties, invites one to take a continuing ed. class, go to boat-building school, learn how to sail, read that pile of books that have been gathering dust in the corner for the "right" time, travel to long dreamt-about destinations, cultivate roses, set up a 35-millimeter on a tripod by the shore and take meaningful pictures that aren't blighted by a cantankerous son's middle digit, make and (oh boy!) drink one's own wine. Even as time is running out, it's about time—using it any damned way you want for as long and as intensely as you can, while managing to sleep late and interfere semi-competently with your significant other. For Howard, who'd had a recent prostate operation, glowed in the dark a bit, and who had said, in a slight redaction of the Doors' lyric, "the time to interfere is through," there remained the chance for him to place himself seriously in the way of his wife Sally and to maintain the mostly loving war of the roses they'd been waging against each other forever.

And it's also about freedom. No more punching time cards. No more meetings. No more need to force niceness toward those who never deserved it. But, instead, the freedom to dedicate your days to whom you most love, what you most love doing, or what you've been aching to try without fear of failure.

For Howard, that has translated, until his death in 2009, into the pleasure and need to continue to ply his craft as a master carpenter and cabinet maker. Almost to the point of his decease at seventy-eight, he'd worked wood with ever-increasing expertise for over fifty-five years. Without it, I'm certain that he would have passed so much sooner, and he said as much: "when you stop getting up in the morning to do what you love, you're dead."

When I entered the side door of his shop in the gathering darkness of that late January afternoon—well beyond the normal quitting time for most professionals—he was cutting a bunch of popple planks at one-hundred inches to be carried by his fifteen-year-old part-time helper Guy McGuire for stickering and drying into his newly-fashioned kiln outside the back of the shop. Lined up like a string of low translucent icebergs sat the lower kitchen cabinets that Howard had been building for my sweetheart Linda, who has recently succumbed to the devastation of Alzheimer's and left an unmendable hole in my heart. I'd suggested that he use popple because of its near-whiteness and brightness—I could only imagine what three coats of lacquer would add to the wood's natural depth and character under the lights of the recessed cans I'd install over them in the kitchen ceiling.

Howard had been having a serious back problem over the past month—it had been diagnosed as a cracked vertebra—and, for the first several days of excruciating pain, he felt for the first time the terror that comes from running head-long into one's own fragility. Would he be able to continue to do the work that, besides providing essential money to pay expenses, he loved to wake up and do every day? Would he have to re-rig the shop to accommodate a disability? He reluctantly admitted to me that he'd had to give up lifting the heavy stuff, that he'd had to rely more on friends who could, but all of that was a most grateful trade-off for being able, with the help of pain-killers, to continue to carry on as he mended.

As I sipped some coffee he'd poured me, I told him that I'd come to some meaningful conclusions about being an old person. We're all old people, I averred. Even many of my students who thought they were going to live forever. Some were simply old in the head, no matter what actual age they'd reached; folks frozen inside a rigid mind set or prejudice (a lot of that going around). Also very young people who, regardless of their tender years, figured they knew everything despite not living a lick—I recall telling my son Chris after a frustrating go-round when he was seventeen that I looked forward to his reaching the age of his majority, at which time he'd magically become aware of how little he actually knew and how that awareness would increase exponentially with each passing year. And it happened. It's odd—most of us, when young, couldn't wait to become older. It's a rare person indeed who is happy with their chronological place on the time calendar—wishing to be older or younger, or, still better, wishing to freeze the frame.

Howard and I shared a fairly common but nonetheless secret realization about ourselves as we said good-bye to Guy and closed the lights. We both knew well that a seventeen-year-old person lived inside ourselves. That young-thinking insider carries on self-talk that defies the dilapidated state of our exteriors. It thinks vigorously about things that neither of us can actually do anymore, but thinks them nonetheless. That insider still sees its outside as young, rakishly handsome, strong, and vital. It's a wondrous magical trick that our minds continue to play on us, we agreed, because it still moves us to want to do, discover, tell off-color stories, and continue to show up. It's an insider for whom all things are still possible, that rejects sloth, and to whom each day promises change.

And it's this insider in every person, young or old, male or female or trans, that this book is intended for. Those people, like me, who want to realize an aspect of that inner self. For, like them, Howard never stopped learning—his craft; the ancient history and cultivation of roses that only he, through research and practice, could make thrive on the South Shore of Superior; his haunting photographs of Superior and its environs; and his re-invention of himself to the finite market of 200-people coastal towns within his immediate reach.

It's important to articulate what this book won't and can't be. It most decidedly is not a how-to-book. Stop right here if that's what you were looking for. I'm not equipped with the savvy or background to teach people how to build anything more sophisticated than a Shakespeare syllabus. I do spend plenty of time tracking Howard through his daily work in the shop, building cabinets and furniture, and accompanying him on some interesting site visits. But I leave that job of detailing actual construction processes to those who know better.

What I'm about here is something much more human—I'm tracking character, and a very genuine and complex character at that. Howard is both the subject and inspiration for what follows: who he was and had been; the nature of his checkered and quixotic travels that led finally and happily to a most fulfilled and productive working life in the still somewhat reclusive and undeveloped South Shore of Superior; how our drastically different lives crossed; how we became fast friends in spite of the way we met; how, along the way, he became a mentor of some consequence to one who spent forty-two years of teaching attempting to do the same for his students.

As I'll relate later on, I'm deeply in here, too, first as a curious observer of his professional doings, then as a tentative translator of some of what I'd learned from him into some (for me) challenging attempts at carpentry around my cabin on the edge of the Lake eight miles west of his shop, and, finally, as an enthusiastic informal student who applied some of Howard's semi-patient lessons to the construction of a large free-standing two-story building.

It's about process and sequence—hopefully, I've been true to the recreation of those in the re-telling—as well as the stories, both his and mine, that have led him to lead me to this stage of woodworking adequacy.

But it's also, I hope, about the character of the South Shore, the living and changing body of water that breathes silently but speaks deafeningly. There's nothing quite like it. The North Shore, the lights of which I can see twinkling through the prowed front window wall that Howard built when he was a mere kid of sixty-five, is picturesque indeed. But it's got nothing on what we have. And, unlike the North Shore, our piece of paradise is still a comparatively undiscovered treasure. I want to convey at least some glimpses of it.

And here comes one now. A year ago last April, I woke up to the most feathery snow fall. As I stepped outside to use Nature's executive washroom, sending a red fox scurrying from atop the holding tank hill just a few yards away toward the Big Lake, I saw no more than an inch had covered my old F-150. While the Twin Cities were nearly snowless, a few hours later I had to wrestle the truck through another eight inches of snow and then another two miles of an unplowed gravel road to route 13. By 4pm, after a day of writing, I looked out the upstairs gable window on a diminishing snow fall that had accumulated an additional five inches. A perfect opportunity to strap on the snowshoes that Karen and Christopher had given me for Christmas instead of the usual sweater and do a little tramping. Total silence except for the gentle rolling of the Lake. Magic. It was still snowing from a lowering sky when I emerged from the driveway and headed north up our little spur on Squaw Point. Perfect and pristine, this new and now heavily moisturized layer of snow mantled the tall pines and spruce. As I turned back toward the cabin, my only company was a solitary pair of piliated woodpeckers performing some earnest test-drilling on the bark of a dead paper birch.

Deciding, once I'd reached the cabin's big back deck, to

shed the snowshoes to trudge knee-deep over the narrow wooden flats barely discernible beneath the snow, I reached the open gazebo perched on the brownstone cliff twenty-five feet above the water. But, before I reached it, I saw what I'd never seen in twenty-nine years and several ice storms up here—a stand of young aspens, birches, and woody brush bowed to the ground, as if in silent prayer, weighed down and twisted by a thick layer of ice and snow. I'd need to tread very carefully so as not to step on and break the levelled trees that, by the spring, would return to their normal attitude. And, when I'd successfully negotiated the path to the inside of the gazebo, I glanced to the East just in time to catch a mature bald eagle rising up from the Lake's surface with talons gripping a lake trout and moving gracefully, in full shoulder flap, directly away from me toward the shelter of Myers' Beach one inlet away. Breath-taking. You can't make this stuff up.

Howard had always preached to me never to be too busy to lift my head up from my work to appreciate the joys and gifts of this special place.

And, besides, it's an integral part of enrolling in Howard University.

—Bill Dyer

CHAPTER 1

Enrollment In The School Of Hard Knocks: An Introduction To Howard And Me

Not that all architectural ornament is to be neglected even in the rudest period; but let our houses first be lined with beauty where they come in contact with our lives like the tenement of the shellfish, and not overlaid with it.
--Thoreau, *Walden*

Simplify. A prescription for a directed and fulfilled life. All the heavy and stressful accretions of what has become our everyday life—endless lawn-mowing; car commutes through the Twin Cities across the agonizing tangle of I35, 100, and 494 that would make the protocols of the computer game "Doom" seem tame; the dizzying medley of dance, sports, and social commitments to and from which we once ferried the kids just after dawn through late evening; evenings dedicated to local committee, service work, and coaching that satisfies while it numbs; a fulfilling teaching career hamstrung by blizzards of mindless memos, meeting minutes, reports, applications for promotion and tenure, class preparation, conference presentations, and papers that nearly consign the act of teaching to the status of after-thought; the ceaseless jangling of the phone,

Teaching Fools

The cliff and caves fronting the cabin

not to mention the battalion of cell phones that rudely encroach on personal space; even the mindless drone of the television and electronic hum of the personal computer screen—fall away like so many sloughed layers of skin when we're transported into a pristine natural setting.

And that's precisely where I am right now. I'm standing in a birch, aspen, and pine forest at the edge of a lake in northern Wisconsin in early August in the afterglow of sunset. But not just any lake. It's Lake Superior. Gitcheegoomie.

The Great Lake. That mammoth inland natural ice box and weather machine whose moods shift as quickly as those driven by the coastal waters of Boston's South Shore—where I grew up nearly eighty years ago. Go Red Sox.

It's a little after nine o'clock now. I'm peering north from a little gazebo my wife Linda and I built on the very edge of a twenty-five-foot cliff on Squaw Point on Superior's South Shore. The delicate chain of white and red lights that mark the ore port of Silver Bay flicker thirty-five miles across the Lake in the breathless dusk as a small freighter steams slowly toward Michigan, the vibrations of its engines pulsing like a low-level electric shock through the sandstone ledge rock I'm standing on. Alternating ribbons of purple, pink, and gray parfait the horizon, the residue of the sun's falling light burning a crimson hole through a long, low cloud like molten lava. As I thread my way through the trees that snake along the cliff on a narrow path of decked wooden platforms, the powerful but seldom-viewable beam from Split Rock Light oscillates squat on the horizon, some ten degrees to the west of little Eagle Island, seemingly suspended like an Ojibwa drum head some six miles out.

Simply amazing. Amazingly simple. Humbling.

What I see when I turn sharply south away from the Lake on the piered flats continues to be simple, but deceptively so. About sixty-five-feet up the path, and perhaps a total of eighty feet from the edge of the cliff, stand the stairs to a raised cedar deck which surrounds the window wall of a modest yet impressive cabin.

Teaching Fools

The wonderful window wall

As I look at it through the gathering gloom and remember what it has evolved from, I resist calling this structure a cabin.

There's lots of reasons not to. Beyond the short run of stairs that open on twenty feet of the double-leveled deck, two twelve-foot sections of window wall meet in a fourteen-degree prow and ascend eighteen feet to four bolted glue-laminated beams bird's-mouthed into the peak of the gabled roof. These beams span the thirty-five feet of the main structure of the building. Those prowed front walls, each containing a lower tier of three windows six feet high by three and a half feet wide and a second tier of rectangular windows ascending from five feet in height on the outside to eight feet high at the prow, create two distinctly different and strategically divided spaces. One, starting at the prow and extending back into the structure some eighteen feet, forms a broad multi-purposed vaulted space that recedes to twelve-foot sidewalls, nearly as well-windowed, from the six-twelve pitched roof. The other space rises from the floor of the original cabin to a seven-and-one-half-foot joisted floor of a loft that opens on the west to a five-foot window crowned by an eyebrow window set beneath a newly-fashioned gabled dormer, and to a similarly rectilinear five-foot wide window capped with an eyebrow under the glue-lammed beam at the rear of the building. Beneath the gabled roof to the west of the house is a small bath and shower, a service closet, a storage area where the water heater and hookups for a stackable washer-dryer unit reside, and an entrance hallway opening to the portion of the deck that wraps around the west side of the cabin.

By the standards of most, there's not much to the place—an eighteen-by-twenty-four-foot great room, a thirteen-by-thirty-foot kitchen/sitting/back-up sleeping area capped by a loft of the same dimensions, the six-by-thirteen-foot bath entry hall area on the west side, and the fifteen-and-a-half-foot long by almost eleven-foot-wide bedroom that ells behind the cabin on its east side. About 1460 square feet of living space all told, wringing wet. Quick and dirty. Easy in, easy out. And, with its covering of naturally weathering rough-sawn cedar lap-siding and trim that covers the places where the windows don't intrude (and that's intentionally not much), it's a most unprepossessing structure, nearly invisible among the popple and birch that cloak it. One frequently needs to look more than twice to see it some sixty feet from the little gravel spur of a road that crescents briefly around the point.

The land surrounding the cabin is overgrown with lupine, foxglove, and tiger lilies, old stands of pine and birch, a chaos of young maple and ash and popple saplings, and weeds a plenty. There's no refined and manicured lawn here—only the rough and patchy carpet of gnarled clover, weeds, lamb's ears, and buttercups thrusting up between the clay and brown stone-encrusted ruts of the drive, the depth of which marks the relative frequency of our visits. The remains of two lawn-mowers lay hidden in the shed when we took possession, but they're long gone now; there'll be no talk of lawn-mowing here. And that's the name of that tune. Simplicity.

Maybe so, but, in the twenty-nine years since my wife and I had the incalculable good fortune to buy it, and during the eight years since the remodel, Linda and I have taken the cabin light years away from the primitive state in which we found it. And, up here, it's wise to know, respect, and treasure the history you live in.

How we found it at all is another story. First, I should say that, before 1994, I'd never had anything but scant interest in the South Shore of Superior. It was Minnesota's North Shore that I lusted after and had something close to wet dreams about. Back in the summer of '84 the four of us made one short family trip up scenic route 13 to Bayfield, and, although I liked it, I was singularly unmoved. After becoming parboiled on a three-and-a-half-hour Apostle Island tour, locking my keys in the minivan on Madeleine Island, and being dragged into every gift and craft shop on both sides of Bayfield's single main street, I was grateful to leave with no thoughts of looking back.

Not so about the North Shore. Since accepting a university teaching job in Minnesota in 1981, and after taking a two-week family camping trip over "The Lake" down into Sault St. Marie, I was a man on a romantic mission. I wasn't so dumb not to realize that this love was doomed never to be consummated. Nonetheless, numberless camping trips up 61 above Duluth, visits to the newly-built cabin of mutual friends on Superior just south of the Canadian border in Tofte, and a week-long hiking trip on Isle Royale kept the hopeless flame smoldering. I knew there was no possible way; North Shore land prices had soared, not to mention my modest means and the imminent prospect of college for our two kids. Still, that didn't prevent me from fueling my fantasies by religiously pouring through the "vacation property" classified ads in the Sunday *Star Tribune* keeping a close look-out for that impossibly affordable piece of North Shore Superior or even a Tom Hanks' "money trap" with my name on it.

And, perhaps as proof that God looks out for fools and children, it happened. But not the way I'd fantasized. True to form, I was scouring the *Trib*'s Sunday real estate section when it stuck its tongue out insinuatingly at me. The ad read like a cheap seduction from the "personals" column. It invoked all the right adjectives—mature, dense, stately birch and aspen; pristine, lake-side Squaw Bay acreage, with breath-taking views of Sand and Eagle Islands; charming, rustic sided and paneled cabin. Simplicity—too good to be true. Probably just a cruel joke. There was more, but I was well beyond being able to read it. I was amazed that this listing, as stated, had ever reached the classifieds, never mind the Sunday paper.

It mattered not at all that this property was located on the South Shore—the exact location was not identified, and I didn't have a clue about the whereabouts of the two islands mentioned in the ad. An anxious call to the Bayfield realtor that had listed the property indicated that it was still available, but that three written offers had already been submitted. I convinced Linda that it wouldn't hurt to look, that we'd probably hate it anyway, that the ad was probably a gross misrepresentation of the unsalvageable wreck that it would surely prove to be, that we owed it to other vacation property suckers to unmask this agent and agency for the pirates they truly were, that there'd be no way in hell that we could ever afford it anyway, but that a quick overnight trip to see it would be the perfect excuse to steal a forbidden interlude away from the kids.

The rest, as they say, is history, but a somewhat convoluted one. After we arrived at the realtor's office, we piled into the agent's Grand Cherokee and traveled twenty miles west on route 13 to a rise overlooking the marina of the little village of Cornucopia. About a mile and three quarters further down a dusty dirt road past a little airstrip and a little hike through a driveway so densely overgrown that the light of a brilliant day could barely penetrate brought us to the small back deck of the cabin. And it became immediately clear that the realtor's description of the property was spot-on.

It was small, to be sure, but not as small as it had originally been when the owners had purchased the land and cleared a space to erect a twenty-by-thirteen-foot structure in 1951. The place reflected the original owners' dedication to keep the property "natural." Eventually, they would tack on the little deck we were now standing on, the little ell bedroom that attached to the cabin's east side, and a four-foot deck on the front, or lake-side, even though it soon became clear to us that at no time during their ownership had they cut enough brush through the thick growth of trees to have ever enjoyed the smallest views of "The Lake."

It took only a minute to realize that they'd done a hell of a job on what they had built. Mr. Dilts and his wife had cultivated a love affair with cedar. In addition to the rough-faced cedar boards that clad the exterior, the inside was covered with vertical tongue and groove cedar boards and trim.

Quarter-inch-thick four-by-eight sheets of stained plywood covered the ceiling. Single-pained sashed and primitive sliding windows admitted what little light there was, and an old Franklin stove was ensconced in the east corner on a rock-encrusted platform against a wall that had been lovingly covered

The lake-facing door and deck of the old cabin

The original 350 square foot cabin

Teaching Fools

Two views of the Dilts' cabin with improvements

with asymmetrical pieces of marble, slate, fieldstone, driftwood, and a bizarre collection of local art objects, some cleverly made by Mrs. Dilts.

Though the place was electrified, there was no well. The realtor regaled us with stories of the Dilts' determination to bring water from the well three miles away down in "Corny," rig up a primitive outside shower, and defiantly keep it simple. The outhouse was well-maintained, as were the other two storage sheds located toward the road. For nearly thirty-five years, this had been the Dilts' sanctuary from civilization—some three acres on the other side of the road and over an acre and a half on the lakeside, with about 145 feet of lake frontage that they could escape and disappear into before Mrs. Dilts contracted Lyme disease— maybe not here but surely on the farm in Hudson, Wisconsin, that they worked.

Two things became clear to us after viewing the careful workmanship inside the cabin and after stumbling down the nettled deer path that suddenly opened on the brownstone cliffs and a breathtaking panorama of Eagle Island and the North Shore: a keen awareness of why the Dilts had restricted their visits to short weekends, and an overpowering desire to buy it.

If we were overcome by the beauty of the property, we were nearly undone by the vicissitudes of the bidding battle that followed. Despite our limited means, we knew right away that we couldn't afford *not* to buy the cabin, and we were shocked at the actual affordability of the asking price. As near as we could wrap our minds around that $66,000 for four and a half acres of wooded land on 145 feet of Superior's cliffs, it boiled down to two factors. First, whatever land rush there might be in the Northland, it was concentrated in the North Shore and the mystique that area carried. The South Shore had been almost forgotten in that feeding frenzy even as late as 1994. By 2000 and with the improvements to the scenic ring route 13 around the Lake, that all changed. Secondly, the land and cabins that stood on them were owned by people who had held them for thirty to fifty years and had passed them down to successive generations.

At the time we were looking, long-time South Shore landowners were just starting to turn their properties over, a fact which within a couple of years impacted exponentially on the price of South Shore real estate and vacation property taxes.

The bidding process was anything but simple—more like Wisconsin's version of liar's poker. This was our introduction to blind bidding: as our agent explained with a wan smile, bidders (and there were three parties already involved in this sale) submitted a bid with absolutely no sense of what their fellow competitors were offering. The insane twist in all this was that the seller could, and often did, reject all bids or engage the most risk-taking parties in what amounted to an infinitely escalating number of bidding stages. We knew going in that, given our finances, we had only one bid to make. The good news was that the sellers settled for only one round of bidding. The bad news was that we failed to submit the highest bid and, thus, lost the property.

We grieved over that news as if one of our parents had died. And that grieving process lasted for almost three months—toward the end of August. At just the point when we were beginning to accept that loss and reenter reality, a call from Bayfield thrust us again into the bidding wars. As it turned out, the people who had successfully outbid us failed to secure bank financing, and once again the property was back on the market, this time with two contestants. Summoning literally all of our resources this time, we actually bid the asking price—we outbid the competition and finally realized our dream—at that time, a five-hour one-way drive for a weekend at our "hard pastoral" paradise.

For the next several months, flushed with our winnings while hyperventilating over paying a second house payment, we basked in the afterglow for the next nine months. Almost better than sex without consequences. After all, there was the brilliance of exploding fall colors of the sumacs, mountain ash, birch, aspen, and maple against the cream-capped sapphire blue and cloudless azure of Lake and sky, as sharp or sharper than I remember the autumn parti-color riot on Massachusetts' Mohawk Trail years earlier when we lived in western Massachusetts. And the bracing fall nights—well, if it wasn't the same as living by the ocean, it surely seemed like it. And the dizzying canopy of stars—so clear, so many, so close that it seemed possible to reach up and ladle out a personal pail-full.

But it didn't take Linda and me long to begin entertaining some serious changes to paradise. There'd been no satisfying Adam and Eve, either. When the weather snapped cold in November, the little stove clearly wasn't enough to keep us and two reluctant occasional visitors—Karen and Chris, our two nearly-adult children—warm. When the four of us were there, the place was awkwardly tiny; a trip to the refrigerator felt like a Vikings scrimmage without pads.

The primary reason for the financial risk we'd taken—the immediate proximity of Superior—made no sense since we couldn't see it. Oh, we could hear it, alright. Several sea caves extended far beneath the brownstone cliffs, and virtually any movement of the Lake would produce a deep, resonating boiling and burbling like a huge overfilled tub that sent its excess rushing back through the overflow. But, although the front windows were wide, they were frustratingly short. A huge, brown, windowless old door in the middle of the front wall of the cabin—when it could be made to open at all—opened upon a narrow deck from which one could stare into the impenetrable vegetation that threatened to overrun it. If this sounds a little like Conrad's *Heart of Darkness*, it looked like it, too.

But the biggest bone of contention—for some of us more than others—was the lack of a bathroom. To be sure, the outhouse—if an outhouse can be said to be good—was a good one. It was a mere fifty-foot walk from the cabin with what appeared to be a life-time supply of lime inside. But 1995 was an unusually cold winter. The Lake froze early, and, when the heavy snows came, a trip to the outhouse became a challenging adventure. I can recall, with no lasting sense of shame, a very early-morning trudge through a thick blanket of new snow with a shovel to rescue a family member who, at a particularly urgent moment, had fallen in a drift while trying to pull the door open through the heavy snow in front of it and could not get up. Enough said. Something had to be done.

With pencil and graph paper in hand, Linda and I toyed with lots of possibilities for making the cabin more user-friendly. At first, we only wanted to tack on a bathroom to the west side of the house. With allowances for a well-driller to be able to strike water through the brownstone at a reasonable depth—and on the first try—we understood this as our most affordable option. But, before long, we envisioned a more ambitious project. Why stop there, we rationalized? Why not build a great room out toward the Lake from the point at which our present front wall stopped? Oh, and what would be the chances of raising the roof and building a big lofted bedroom over the kitchen? And, while we were at it, why not add a three–car carriage house with living space above for the wait staff?

Jesus.

Upon closer examination, the chances for any of this were bleak. And money wasn't the only problem. Yes, we were financially strapped—Karen was still enrolled in a private college, but the sucking sound of our money being siphoned all the way to Philadelphia would cease in the spring.

There'd just be Chris, and he was still over a year away from re-priming the suction pump. And Linda had some uncashed bonds that would jump-start the project. But there weren't nearly enough to bring in a building contractor; if we weren't careful, we could be digging a large hole in the ground into which we'd be pouring money indefinitely.

Suddenly, we were looking down the barrel of "amateur night." I figured that I could apply blackmail to a few skilled friends to get things going—do the demolition, build the block foundation for the additional crawl space, frame the thing out. And, of course, I could always enlist the strong back of my son.

The biggest problem was that, when it came to carpentry, I would be operating with both headlights out. Sure, I'd taken some healthy low-risk bites out of some home improvement projects—I'd roofed my house and helped others do theirs; I'd replaced our clapboard siding; I'd helped a friend remove an old window and install a new one. I'd never framed anything, but I'd struggled nervously through a book that described the details of stick framing. In other words, I was stupid, dangerous, groundlessly optimistic, and an accident waiting to happen. And I was intent upon carrying the banner of my ignorance into battle with a construction project hip-deep in complexity. How does that saying go?—those that can, do; those that can't, teach? So much for keeping it simple.

Things were getting desperate. On top of the money squeeze, the personal talent vacuum, and my insistence upon employing a fool for a client, the window for lobotomizing the cabin and performing the rest of the remodel was rapidly shrinking. As summer approached, I surveyed the time I might have to work with. Given my usual habit of teaching the first five weeks of summer school, nothing but weekends (three-hundred miles away at that) remained before the session ended two weeks into July. But this was the summer (every even-numbered year) that I was scheduled to take thirty students for three-and-a-half weeks to England, Wales and Scotland. A great trip, but very bad timing. Under the most optimistic timetable, and barring any unforeseeable felonious disasters in Britain, I wouldn't be excavating for the new crawl space or demolishing any roofs until the end of the first week in August. That left just a short interval until September 10, when I'd begin my duty days for the new academic year.

That's when serendipity kicked in. Serendipity's name, in this case, was Dan Malsch, a young man who'd moved to Mankato with his wife and a couple of kids to pursue a divinity degree at Bethany Lutheran Seminary. As it happened, Dan came to town with some deficiencies in his academic background, and, while he took his language and theology courses at Bethany, he determined to fulfill those deficiencies by taking some evening and summer courses at Mankato State. It was my good fortune that Dan, somewhere in his thirties with long experience as a journeyman carpenter in Seattle working on large commercial projects for others and as his own boss, needed a Shakespeare course. I just happened to be teaching one in Shakespeare's tragedies that spring. Lay on, Macduff.

It took a while before I had any inkling of the talent I had sitting before me on the right side of that classroom. It seems almost callous and opportunistic to say that, but I intend exactly the opposite. I'll write a few illustrative words about this later—the assured confidence in his skills, his ability to size up the relative skills of others, and his adeptness at solving difficult problems that would have left others like me soiling their pants. During that while, Dan, I, and most of the rest of an enthusiastic class were having a high time with Hamlet, Lear, and some significant Shakespearean others. Dan loved the plays and the characters, making all kinds of connections between the complex and existential human problems those characters were puzzling through—just the ticket for an aspiring cleric who could see himself counseling members of a future congregation through similar crises about meaning and being. Just as Kent said in *Lear*, "Ripeness is all."

I was impressed. Dan was a dedicated learner. It was easy to see that. It was also easy to gauge his insecurity, his fear of failure as he wrapped his thick and calloused hands around the difficult material we were studying, reading, and role-playing. And he shared that insecurity after each class, pausing before my desk to set his chin in a broad and chiseled smile to test his small but real discoveries about the plays, to reveal the very different work life he'd come from, the religious epiphany that had galvanized a major shift of gears and relocation, and the difficulties he was experiencing in adjusting his rigorous study schedule to weekends leading crews in building decks and fences.

I learned much more about his vast building experience at such a young age a couple of weeks before the course ended, while helping Dan focus a topic and flesh it out for his oral presentation. He, in turn, became curious about the cabin on

Superior. Dan had been an avid bow hunter and fisherman while living in the northwest, and he thrilled at the prospect of plying an area so rich in deer as the South Shore. It didn't take him long to get me to describe the cabin for him, to relate my hopes and dreams for the place, and to hint about the manpower and time problems I'd soon face.

It was then that Dan's eyes grew bigger than his stomach. Dan volunteered his services. Well—not quite. After I told him that another faculty member with some practical carpentry experience and my son would be on site during the first week of August ready to pull their load, Dan jumped in with both feet. He said that he'd have about four weeks before seminary classes started up again in September, and, for twenty dollars an hour, would be delighted to direct the project. He detailed his background in construction—he'd done a great deal more than carpentry—and even indicated that an uncle of his, a master carpenter working in southern Wisconsin, might also be persuaded to join the crew. My mouth began to water.

As we talked more about the project, Spring Semester gave way to Summer Session I; this time, it was Shakespeare's Comedies and Histories, and Dan was still there, keeping pace with me, and making what for him were important metaphysical negotiations between Shakespeare and Lutheranism. But I was observing an interesting phenomenon. There were two Dans now. One of those Dans was the humble, respectful, and hesitant student, feeling his way carefully in the half-light of perception across the uneven terrain of unfamiliar linguistic phrasings, idioms, and partially-grasped conventions, looking to me for direction because, professionally-speaking, I was "the Man." That is, he expected no less than polished competence from someone who had, as a consequence of earning a terminal degree in my chosen field of study, created, in a manner of speaking, my own "masterpiece." I'd never put it that way—I still look at that unpublished four-hundred-page dust-covered dissertation on the Elizabethan plays of Christopher Marlowe languishing in my living room bookcase as flawed, the result of the most insane of hazing exercises on the way to being initiated into the fraternity of academics. But that's not the point. Dan saw himself in the role of apprentice-learner, setting his sights intently on knowing what I knew.

But as the summer session got underway and our after-class discussions on remodeling the cabin intensified, I saw a different Dan emerging. This Dan was confident, assertive, decisive in his articulation of the challenges, options, and pitfalls I'd soon be confronting in a professional vocabulary and series of building conventions that sounded like a foreign language to me. Suddenly, the roles had reversed. Now Dan was the master, speaking from a wealth of experience and a collection of similar construction problems whereas I was the novice, struggling desperately to keep up with him and to find the language adequate to convey what I wanted to do to the cabin.

The difference here, I think, is that Dan had me far more at a disadvantage than I him because what he was generously attempting to initiate me into was a particular kind of experiential learning—one could talk about it all one wanted, or even read about it in books, but the learning couldn't really start until the risk to *do* was taken, the tool belt donned, the hammer gripped, and the first nails crookedly pounded or sent careening into the ether.

These after-class sessions of earnest talking and pencil-sketching of what the cabin might be were fun but ultimately unfulfilling—somewhat like Philip Sidney's frustrated cry in Sonnet 71 of *Astrophel and Stella* for Desire to "give me some food." After consulting with Linda and getting grounded in her practical view of things, I decided to stop fooling around. I grabbed the sketches that Dan, Linda, and I had made and headed north in search of an architect. It would be expensive to have an architect design that cabin addition, but, Linda had reasoned, it might be more expensive *not* to. Although Dan knew what he was doing, we didn't; and, after Dan was done with his part of the construction, the rest of the job—certainly all of the inside finish work and any deck that was later added—inevitably would fall to Linda and me. Not only that, but, as Dan had wisely pointed out, any materials list for the project would come easily and directly from such a set of plans. If we were looking for a real bottom-line price for the cabin remodel (yes, I know now that that materials list probably must be multiplied by 150% to know the *real* deal!), and, if we wanted the bids we sought from competing lumber yards to be realistic, we'd be doing ourselves a favor by working from stable and clear blueprints.

I'd seen a shingle with the label "architect" mounted on a weathered post on a front lawn next to Oly's and Robbie's combination fish market and barber shop just above Bayfield center overlooking "The Lake" on 13, and on a long weekend I headed there first. After numerous front-door poundings and a battery of follow-up phone calls, I came up empty. It seemed that this person was either over-committed, on vacation, in jail, or working by a piquant schedule.

I discovered that it was the latter that Saturday morning when I drove into Cornucopia and sought out a highly-recommended self-employed carpenter for advice and a referral. As we sat across from each other at his kitchen table over coffee, Steve was immediately helpful in three ways. First, he aggressively steered me away from the architect I'd been pursuing. Secondly, while mild interest in the project I described registered on him, he said that a frantic building season on Madeleine Island would make it impossible for him to take a hand in it until fall. But the third point was the telling one.

Steve agreed that working with a reliable and efficient architect, one used to cooperating with building professionals and interested in bringing the job in on time with the willingness and flexibility to individualize and scale down projects to the needs and budget of the client, was crucial. He'd had occasion to work with an independent architect from Vadnais Heights, just north of the Metro, on several occasions and had found him extremely competent, fast, and personable. Steve was confident that this professional would design something that would enhance the rough, simple beauty of the building site.

When I got home, we contacted the Vadnais Heights architect, and he was enthusiastic about the project. He knew the character of the land on Superior's South Shore, and, after chatting about our spatial needs and wishes, he made a date to meet us at Emma Krumbees's, a coffee shop south of the Twin Cities, at which time he would seek our opinion on several design alternatives that he'd work up in the interim.

The meeting was a raging success. A couple of his side and frontal drawings of a window-walled great room and lofted rear portion with a reoriented roof transformed the old cabin into a whimsically stubbed little lake boat and deck house. After Linda recommended some changes to be built into a final design—a rather complex west-sided roof under the gabled dormer and over the side entry and bathroom as well as a balancing and slightly bumped-out east side and pair of windows—we signed the contract and the architect went away to construct the package of blueprints that we'd soon be working from.

I must note that this architect spent two days on a site visit to the cabin, walking the property and acquiring a "feel" for the kinds of design details and construction materials that would most effectively complement the predominantly birch and brownstone environment. That's probably why his final plans featured cedar— externally and internally—so heavily. Although his professional services were expensive—something around $2000—retaining him was the second best decision about the cabin we ever made. Besides grounding our dream in a three-dimensional image, the plans clearly indicated the means and materials by which we would marry the old cabin with the new into structural integrity. Also, the architect articulated a method—the thirty-five-foot set of bolted laminated beams—for demonstrating how the prowed window wall he'd designed would be safely stabilized, with no fear of collapse. The question of the structural soundness of the beam and window wall would come into serious question very soon after the actual construction began.

So, at this point, the end of June, the stage was set. Linda and I reconnoitered with Dan at his newly-purchased house—it was her first opportunity to meet him—with the blueprints. After giving them some focused and enthusiastic attention, we settled upon the following plan of action: I was charged with carrying copies of the prints to three South Shore lumber yards to obtain detailed materials lists and comparative cost estimates; securing a building permit; dismantling the front porch, railings, and stairs attached to the front of the existing cabin; and, because of time considerations and Dan's and my inability to free up enough of it to build a block-walled crawl space for the new construction, contracting with someone who would do that job just prior to our arrival on the job site a week into August. I ultimately decided to have the crawl space foundation poured, an unfortunate decision made in blind ignorance, and by a contractor whose faulty work nearly compromised the entire project—more on that later.

Dan and his pre-adolescent son would load a small open trailer with his chop saw, ladder, and tools and head for Superior at the beginning of August, just as soon as he had completed his Hebrew studies. My teaching colleague Ron would arrive around the 7th with his tool belt and a small hard-sided camping trailer to sleep in while he was working with us. It would be Linda's unpleasant assignment to deliver my seventeen-year-old son Chris and his girlfriend to the cabin to work; cook in a kitchen that would soon be open to the elements for this ravenous crew; arrange for some primitive shower facilities at Cornucopia's boat marina; be Dan's unofficial clerk and gopher for anything or anyone that needed to be brought to the site; call and negotiate with electrical or plumbing subs; and, when I arrived back in Minneapolis after leading the summer session in Britain, pick me up at the airport and ferry me immediately to the job site. In other words, Linda was the indispensable cog in the entire machine. Luckily for everyone concerned, she had the practical and directorial skills to pull it off.

That was the plan, but, in this, my baptism into building and contracting, something very different occurred. As we raced up 35 toward Duluth, Linda caught me up on the series of snafus that had piled up while I was gone. She assured me that everyone who had volunteered to come, including the lynch pin Dan, had, in fact, arrived and had begun work. However, contrary to my expectation that Dan would have arrived the Friday before I would and be making some progress, he'd only just appeared a couple of days before. It was of smaller concern that my friend Ron had shown up only the day before, although, as it turned out, there was precious little for him to do because of another screw-up.

Linda informed me that the crew hired from Bayfield to excavate the new crawl space on the front and west side of the building, build the forms, and then pour it, had been nearly a week late. They had come about three days before I did. And what they *had* done was almost catastrophic. In fact, Dan had come on the scene just in time to flag them on their inferior workmanship.

Here's what happened. After clearing and excavating the necessary ground, with no more than two to three feet of clay covering the rock where they had to dig, they formed and poured up to the existing crawl space. But, lucky for Linda and me, Dan, after doing some basic checking, determined that their new crawl space was out-of-plumb with the old one. When the two men who'd installed the foundation were confronted with their mistake, there was no denying it. They clearly understood that there would be problems linking the two pieces of the structure together, not to mention the difficulties of framing the new portion and equalizing the two floors. In fact, the senior person on the crew not only owned up to the mistake but offered to do whatever needed to be done in order to rectify it.

Dan applauded the gesture, but, when he contacted the owner of the construction company, he got a radically different reaction. There was nothing to rectify, the guy argued, no need to fix anything. When Dan confronted him with the evidence, he simply stone-walled and stated that his work was finished. I'd committed the cardinal sin here—in two installments over five weeks, I'd paid for the work in advance. I could have sued and, more likely than not, won, but at the tremendous cost of a job stopped dead in its tracks, additional expense, and all the available time I had set aside to do the job. Incompetence and unethical business practice had won out.

Thankfully, Dan came to the job as advertised—with a wealth of problem-solving skills. Linda told me that he had been able to use the jacks he'd brought along to bring the old building into plumb with the new foundation. Dan later informed me that the original crawl space was the culprit; however, as he noted, he would have been spared all of the jacking and shimming if those forming the new crawl space had taken a little time to look at the old one and orient their forms accordingly.

And that's pretty much where the job stood when Linda and I cruised into the driveway. Linda had already insulated the new foundation with Styrofoam, and Dan, Chris, and Ron had moved ahead on the installation of the floor joists. As I changed my clothes and looked out at the construction site, all three were gluing and nailing the three-quarter-inch sheets of plywood to the joists. And I quickly pitched in to help them.

Almost immediately, Dan directed us on how to begin the demolition of the roof. And, with a variety of bars, cat's paws, and hammers (the reciprocating saw came a little later), Chris, Dan's son, Ron, and I set about laying waste to it, with a beautiful vantage point of Superior before us. It took about a day for us to rip the roof away—perilous work, as I quickly found—and to fill a very large area to the west of the cabin with the resulting pile of refuse. Dan's son had gotten a fire going in a barrel and, with direction from his dad, was burning the stuff that was safe to dispose of. But there were huge pieces from the roof that couldn't be burned, lots of old insulation and wiring—even windows from the old front wall that had been torn away—and the pile grew. It would take another three years before the pile disappeared and the construction materials that hadn't been used went away. As we labored destructively, Dan installed a huge double curtain of clear plastic to keep most of the weather and the vicious biting flies and mosquitoes outside.

But things were about to change. Although we had expected Dan to stick with the job for about four weeks before school started and, in the process, to get the new addition closed in and roofed, that expectation shrunk to two. And, basically, after the first week, he knew that he'd have to leave after one more. It was school and his need to get a jump on the languages he needed to learn again. This time it was Greek. He apologized profusely for leaving us in what he termed "the lurch," and he quickly set about driving around the area with Linda as his chauffeur looking for a referral for a carpenter who could take on and direct the job to its completion. Our hearts sank. Looking for a carpenter on the South Shore in the middle of August during what turned out to be the first of several years of a burgeoning building boom—impossible. Locating someone available—not because of disability, drinking problems, or severe personality disorder who was competent and reliable and didn't object to having a small group of rank amateurs working alongside of him? Enter Howard Bowers. And re-enter simplicity.

CHAPTER 2

Matriculation At The University That Is Howard

"We have a situation up here..."
--Farscape

    By this point, things had proceeded a little bit further south than desperate, and, although the rest of my tattered little crew was rapidly packing up and preparing to head south, Linda and I couldn't. We were stuck. After standing at the end of the driveway at 8am on Wednesday and waving at the dusty cloud kicked up by Ron's tiny Scamp camper rocking crazily up the road toward highway 13, I turned toward the cabin to see what we had won.

    It wasn't pretty. The little cabin lay hatless and bald in the hot refuse-strewn clearing. As I walked closer, the lakeside deck appeared to extend out into the forest some eighteen feet, looking like a cheap dance floor. And, as I walked past the well pump on the west side of the cabin, I was brought down heavily by the mess that we'd made in little more than a week. First there was that teetering mountain of roof detritus that we'd ripped away with such destructive relish. This was a crew that knew how to do demolition well. And that pile was dangerous, its toothful smile an evil promise in the morning sun. A little lakeward were the more organized piles of building materials we'd presumably be using— as soon as we could find someone who knew what the hell to do with them: all manner of two-by-six lumber, from eight-foot lengths to twelves; sheets of hard Styrofoam insulation, leftovers from the blue stuff Linda had applied to the interior walls of the newly-poured crawl space before the joisted floor was constructed on top of it; four-by-eight slabs of ¾" plywood and ½" composition board; and an unidentified pile of dark, felted four-by-eight material that no one would own up to ordering, never found an application, and ultimately became a water-logged centipede factory; and a sea of fasteners of various configuration and size to be applied to I knew not what.

Facing those stacks of building materials was Dan's chop saw rig, all jigged out and bolted within its wooden frame to speed the job of measuring and cutting those two-by-sixes into the components for the exterior frame for the deck and, eventually, the knee-wall (what's *that?*—anyone?) to be attached to the yet-to-be constructed joisted floor of the loft. And, sitting rakishly askew ten feet farther toward the Lake under an enormous poplar tree was a rusted oil drum, still smoldering from the previous evening's offerings made to it by Dan's twelve-year old son.

This kid was starting to get on my nerves. He was getting way too much pleasure from pitching anything he could lift into the evening bonfires he'd been building and watching the sparks soar into the charred branches above. True, he was killing his share of bugs, but he'd denuded whole branches of the poplar and his dad didn't seem as concerned as I was about the imminent possibility of torching all of Squaw Point. He was a real hazard whose two talents—wholesale destruction and endless grazing in Linda's kitchen—had activated angry grumblings in my son about dumping him in his own fire. I could feel the esprit de corps of my little group beginning to unravel. The little bastard did have it coming, though. Maybe I'd help.

It was considerably after eight now. We were usually working by 7:30, but not today. Ron wasn't the only thing going south. Dan had been working at the job site for just a few days before I'd returned from the UK, and he'd done quite a lot. He'd supervised the crawl space fiasco, jacked up the cabin to correct the out-of-square botch of the job done by the criminally incompetent "Bayfield Boys," let Linda loose on the insulation of the crawl space while he, Chris, and Ron laid and blocked the joists for the floor over the crawl space and then glued and nailed the three-quarter-inch plywood over it. But, a week after I arrived, I was starting to receive glimmerings of Dan's imminent departure.

Things on the "home front" weren't going well for him—I wouldn't know just how badly until a few years later when a graduate student told me that Dan had suddenly dropped out of school, left his wife and family, and seemingly disappeared without a trace.

Dan had seemed so rock-solid, so supremely confident not only in his own professional abilities and accomplishments but in his enthusiastic commitment to this little job. He'd been the undisputed leader here, dividing the labor amongst us, barking out commands, keeping us on task, patiently taking time to educate us on the specifics of those tasks so that we wouldn't hurt ourselves or the integrity of the project. But we were approaching the point in the job when we'd need to graduate from tearing-down to building-up; we were moving toward that point unevenly, like several staggering drunks, but we were getting there. The moment of truth.

Enthusiasm. Those glimmerings I felt about an early defection by Dan were entangled with Dan's complex of enthusiasms. The previous evening, after we'd gotten through for the day, driven the three miles down to the marina to shower off the dirt and sweat of ten hours of work, and eaten a big camp dinner courtesy of the overworked and underappreciated Linda, Dan called Louise back in Mankato. After a couple of beers, he was waxing warm and nostalgic about her, his other two little ones, and some of the filmy hopes and dreams he'd built for them—a professional carpenter's version of Castles in the Air. They'd been through a lot together, from Washington state to

Mankato. They'd home-schooled their kids together—although, from what I'd seen of Dan's talents at people direction and motivation, I suspected that Dan had proudly carried the weight of the Christian lesson-planning and teaching on his own broad back—and moved to Mankato infused with Dan's mission to enter Bethany College's seminary and become a Lutheran pastor of his own congregation. Strong and heady stuff.

All that drove Dan was the tornadic energy of competing enthusiasms: an excruciating love for Louise, a desire to protect and provide for her and the kids, the weekend deck and fence-building jobs he took on to pay the mortgage payments of the little house he'd just bought near Bethany's campus, course work at MSU he was doing to erase program deficiencies, the rigorous studies in Hebrew and Greek he was wrestling with at Bethany that would be the brick and mortar of his seminary studies. I'd formed my own internal assessment of Dan's academic potential from the course work he'd done with me, and, despite his enthusiasm, I worried about his ability to do it all, about whether he was rolling a rock up a hill so steep that he might not be able to stop that rock from running over him on the way down. Regardless of his real and first-rate carpentry skills, he seemed a little like Wiley Coyote feverishly studying the plans from Acme to catch the Roadrunner that would always leave him grasping air while plummeting into oblivion.

Let me say at this point that, if it sounds like I'm calling Dan crazy, I am. And he was. But we're *all* crazy. Erasmus of Rotterdam made that irrefutably clear in his *In Praise of Folly*, published on the cusp of the Reformation. I'm not sure Dan would have appreciated the irony of this defender of moderation carrying on a continuing dialogue with his crazy contemporary Martin Luther on this and other related subjects. Personally, I lug around my own multiple insanities like an unwieldy box of baroque trophies. Nothing could be more nuts than buying a vacation property that I can't afford five hours away from where I live and work (in another *state,* for Christ's sake!), committing myself to an expensive expansion of that property before the goddamned ink had dried on our original purchase agreement, and blissfully imagining I could wear my ignorance and inexperience like a miner's helmet flickering in the dark toward the successful completion of that project. Sheer madness! And I couldn't even lay claim to the delusion of Don Quixote's *becoming* his madness after building a reading library solely devoted to the subject of it. I'd read both books on carpentry, and, as a professional "book guy," I was plenty old enough to know better. On the other hand, Dan had lived carpentry, but other all-too-human madnesses were pulling him away from it.

And that's how I found Dan a little after eight, sitting by himself on the edge of the deck, tool belt beside him, waiting for me. His mid-thirties compact frame—still mostly firm and broad—slouched as he began to disclose his contending dilemmas. He missed Louise, deeply, he said. He needed to finish up on his Hebrew course, which he'd left incomplete and, he feared, not nearly satisfactory. He felt surging guilt about the impending start of the fall term at seminary, how he ought to be there, counseling with his professors, strengthening his academically insecure position. In short, he needed to leave, and he felt overwhelming guilt about that as well. Ah, the contests raged between the attraction of the solid visible boards he'd be banging with (but, mostly for) me versus the compulsion toward the perfectly invisible source of his ministerial calling. How many angels can pound nails on the head of a pin—that's the point at which Dan was stuck.

And I understood the magnet that was pulling him. I should have been able to see the conflict that raged within him on several fronts—it was obvious; unblinking certitude usually is, no matter how attractive the package it comes in. But I didn't want to see it. That would have been way too inconvenient. I needed to believe that Dan would be there until the first week into September, on weekends thereafter until the new addition was fully closed in and buttoned down, now and forever, amen. He talked a great game, and if I may steal an image that Dan could fully wrap his mind around, he'd been preaching to the choir. In my naiveté, I'd considered no back-up plan. Suddenly, with the cabin opened up to the sky like a can of beans and protected from the weather on the deck side only by a floor-to-ceiling curtain of thick plastic stapled on the top and sides, things were looking expensive.

As Dan spelled out his newly-understood reality and inferred mine, he kept his head and resolutely expressed determination to do right by us. An un-Blues Brothers' "mission from Gawd." As much as he needed to go, he wouldn't until he'd managed to find a competent replacement that could carry the job to completion. We both knew how difficult a prospect that would be. Between big projects mushrooming on Madeleine Island and in and around Bayfield, most of the reputable carpenters were already committed until the end of the building season late in October. That left a ragged collection of crooks, liars, and sociopaths, Twin Cities runaways, the criminally incompetent "Bayfield Boys," and the raging alcoholics whose hands might shake so badly when they picked up their circular saws that they could complete a cut without ever plugging the damned things into an outlet.

Linda and I were no help here—we were simply too new to the area to have established even the beginnings of a "skill network." And folks who occupied cabins adjacent to ours had– wisely or otherwise—chosen to stay away during our two weeks of destructive pandemonium. But Dan was determined, and with or without Dan Ackroyd's hat and sunglasses, divinely inspired. The plan was simple and elegant—Dan would first call around to the names listed in the Yellow Pages and, when that tactic yielded the obvious, Linda and Dan would then set out into the Wilderness, with Linda driving, for a tour of the local lumber yards and sawmills for referrals.

While they were gone, the rest of us stayed busy—I on the depressing clean-up of the mess we'd been making in front of the deck, Chris on his attractive and nubile girlfriend off in the blueberry bushes somewhere, and Dan's son (just a little high and outside from *Deliverance*) on following Chris while trying to pick up a few pointers. In a matter of only a few hours, Linda was barreling down the driveway grinning that beautiful, broad Italian lantern smile I loved so much. It was starting to smell like team spirit again.

In their travels, from Bayfield to Washburn and Ashland back to Corny, Linda had thought to stop at a tiny lumber yard just inside the village line of Herbster on route 13, the village just east of Corny. We'd passed 'Cardinal Lumber' many times in our travels to and from the cabin, but we'd dismissed the place as too small and probably uncompetitive to do a materials list estimate. In fact, the place always looked faintly abandoned when we drove by it. But Linda was desperate, and it was one of the few places they hadn't tried.

As it turned out, Cardinal was open and doing a modest but regular and established local business. We'd find out later that the owner, Donnie Igo, was a prince of a man, a real pro with great generosity of spirit, a wealth of patience, and a gift for customer service. It was Donnie Sr. whom Linda and Dan asked whether he had a cork board where tradesmen and journeymen hung their business cards and advertised their skills and services.

Before Donnie directed them to it, Dan took great care in describing our problematic construction project, its location, the point at which it had reached, and the specific skills that would be needed from anyone who'd contract to do it. Dan was just the ticket to do this task. Would that everyone contemplating some sort of remodel could have a skilled professional versed in all aspects of the operations to be performed, the difficulties to be encountered, the probable length of time it might take to finish it, cost considerations for shopping for the people able enough to do it, and weighted with an anvil of guilt so heavy that lying was removed from the equation! Dan knew pros when he saw them, and he'd worked with plenty who said they were but weren't—he was ready and able to conduct a real job interview and, in the process, sniff out the charlatans.

Having heard that intentional preamble, Donnie took a card from the board and handed it to Dan. It read simply

"Howard Bowers—Master Carpenter." Donnie, in his unvarnished way, exuded a bit over the skills of Mr. Bowers. He owned a shop on 13 not even a mile west of the lumber yard, he said, and Bowers had been doing business there as a builder, remodeler, cabinet maker, furniture builder, and finish carpenter for about eight years. But Howard had gotten along in years, Donnie said, maybe sixty-five of them, and he'd reached the twilight zone of semi-retirement. He was working regularly alright, said Donnie, and as much as he wanted.

But, although highly skilled and respected for the quality of his work, Howard had been turning down more work than he accepted. He'd done it all, said Donnie, and he intimated to Dan that he'd done that "all" nearly everywhere across the length and breadth of what George W. Bush drawled "A-murk-ah"—he was, by local old-timers' estimates, relatively new to Herbster and the South Shore. He'd gotten particular about the big, outside jobs he took—he loved cabinetry and interior finish work, but the heights of roof work, climbing ladders, and lugging heavy materials around job sites had gotten older than he was. We could try his shop, Donnie suggested, but he wasn't sure whether Howard was currently in the middle of a big job. Donnie also voiced skepticism about Howard jumping in on someone else's project, and, as he scanned the architect's plans that Dan had unrolled on his counter, even greater reservations about Howard signing on to a project as "vertical" as ours promised to be.

Dan and Linda drove the short distance down 13 to the little hamlet of Herbster— all of two bars, a post office, a convenience store/laundry/gas station, a dead church, two gift shops, and a town highway department garage, with Lady Superior lurking moodily just one hundred yards from downtown Herbster's only intersection—and parked at Howard Bower's shop.

It was ample for a cabinet maker's needs; he'd kicked out the back and expanded it to accommodate his wife Sally's gift shop at the front and a larger shop area for himself. He was just as Donnie had indicated—very independent. But he was also, as

Linda described, soft-spoken, solicitous, gentlemanly in the old southern tradition (with the hint of the soft drawl of some as yet-to-be-identified southern state), welcoming and friendly, and, apparently, deeply interested in the job that Dan described to him. But, more importantly, he was interested in Dan.

That was the thing that struck me the most—the very thing that has endured from my hazy recollections of this initial pre-contractual engagement with Howard twenty-seven years ago to what would become our free-and-easy, friendly jokes and mock insults traded across a dirty table in the wintry draftiness of the Crossroads Café in Herbster. Howard had an eagle-eye for professionalism, competence, and respect for the craft. When I got to really know him, he was always quiet about it, like he was about most things—lying back in the weedy environs of an analytical mind and sizing things up. Howard determined on the basis of his first exchange with Dan that he possessed all of these qualities in spades. He'd given an audience to Dan, heard his story, and passed his blessing over Dan along with a promise to visit and evaluate the job site the next day, all on the basis of that one conversation.

And I'd grown skeptical—about Dan, about Howard, about my sanity, about lots of things. I'd gotten over my idealizations of Dan. This was no miracle man with a silver framing hammer. And his promises were beginning to drop like dominoes—lots of talk about staying the course and bringing in his heavy-hitting master carpenter-uncle from southern Wisconsin were turning out to be pretty much like him, here today and gone tomorrow.

And, on top of everything, this guy was lusting in his heart. It was a little sad watching this thirty-five-year-old loving husband, father, and aspiring Lutheran minister showboating and preening in hopes of attracting the attention of Chris' eighteen-year-old girlfriend. Don't get me wrong—she was definitely worth the attention, but displays of strength and agility that had him springing to mount a twelve-foot two-by-six framed wall only to trip and dive painfully to the deck below were more worthy of an adolescent-in-heat than a full-grown guy. But guys never lose that addiction for public self-humiliation, do they? I don't.

And Howard. Well. Dan had already shared with me his concerns about whether Howard was up to the task of outdoor construction anymore. He was sixty-five, for Christ's sake. Hell, I was fifty-two, and I knew how tired I was. I remember enjoying a brief waking hallucination of Howard stroking out on top of one of the twelve-foot two-by-six walls with a fully-loaded pneumatic framing hammer in his hand and pitching headfirst into the deck below with his gun blazing. What a law suit that would have made!

That's why Howard's appearance on the job-site was so mind-blowing. It was getting to be a very hot one when Howard drove down the driveway that August mid-morning—absolutely brilliant, bugless, and still. I got my first real look at him when he stepped up onto the eighteen-by-twenty-four-foot deck we hoped to see transformed into a great room. There was decidedly no grace in his step. He moved his blocky, thick frame with short and jerky steps, almost as if he were a bit hamstrung; I didn't know it then, but Howard was carrying himself this way in response to a balky, painful back condition. This was, I decided, a much-scarred veteran of the carpentry wars, but there was no mistaking the strength that his thick forearms and upper body still possessed when he reached out with equally thick and stubby fingers to shake my hand. The smile was gentle but guarded, his hard and crinkled and wide-set eyes firmly meeting mine, set above a broad nose that adorned a large sheep-like head. This guy wasn't going to win any local beauty contests. His neck was phone-pole thick, and there wasn't much of it that could distinguish where his shoulders began. His thinning and receding dark, wavy hair was swept directly back and cropped short. The skin on his face was heavily wrinkled and parchment thick from years of direct exposure to the sun and cigarette smoking, and that face, along with the light beard that mantled it, made the word "grizzled" sound like a euphemism.

And he was dressed in the "uniform" that I've come to associate with Howard when he wasn't "on the clock"—he was, as he was mostly, hatless; he wore a relatively nondescript plaid short-sleeved buttoned shirt—it was probably well-aged, but it was clean and neat; the pants were clean, heavy tan-cuffed khaki—not the kind of thing one might associate with casual summer wear. This was vintage "Howard," but, as I would come to find out, this was as good as it got for this no-frills man, the standard issue for job estimates as well as evenings out at restaurants; the shoes were of the heavy leather, low-cut work variety, and they, like Howard, had lots of miles on them. No false airs here. Take him as you find him, or the hell with you.

But Howard hadn't come alone. Another figure, considerably taller, much younger (maybe in his early or mid-forties), fit but for the beginnings of the softening muscles in the face, neck, and body that come with middle age. This guy carried himself with an attitude of studied ennui, a light touch of arrogance and aloofness that I'd felt at conferences from some professorial types who were full of the reputation they'd established.

As it turned out, the small-talk that followed confirmed my hunch that "Jerry" (that was his name) had recently been an academic in the art department at Iowa State. He'd been involved for some time in designing and constructing elaborate sets to display the work of important artists around the country—even London.

He'd fashioned some wood sculptures of his own, had become bored with teaching, and had become intrigued with the prospect of establishing himself as an independent building contractor while cultivating his artistic bent by designing, building, and installing one-of-a-kind wooden circular stairways. With his wife still holding a secure position in the Iowa State administration, Jerry had abandoned his own security, given up his tenured position, bought a piece of property on the cliffs above Herbster, and been splitting his time between local carpentry projects and the construction of his own small three-storied cabin overlooking even steeper cliffs above Superior.

Noting that the exposed ceiling joists would soon become a second-floor loft, Jerry casually handed me a professionally-made brochure that advertised a couple of Jerry's finished circular stair products—it was, indeed, beautiful craftsmanship, and I told him that we might be in the market for something just like it down the road.

As the chat over the building project became more intense between Dan and Howard, and as Howard began to scrutinize the details of the architect's plans, Jerry's interest and attention discernibly waned. It became pretty obvious even to someone as desperate for a bailout as I that Jerry disdained my little project—except for the views of the Lake it afforded. He was merely out for a Sunday drive. When he did hazard a comment, it was to gain confirmation for what he understood to be stuff out of Carpentry 101: the deceptively straight-ahead joisting and blocking of the old ceiling over the kitchen to create the loft; the four-foot knee walls on which would be mounted a plain six-twelve pitched roof complicated by a dormer on the west side; another slightly idiosyncratic little roof below that dormer that would sit atop the new bump-out for the bathroom and west-side entry. He seemed mildly amused about the problems of stabilizing that main roof whose weight would be borne solely by laminated beams to be situated—of all places—above a large window opening at the rear and over the two prowed front walls at their point of jointure. Piece of cake.

About as foppish as one could look in the middle of the woods, Jerry posed contrapposto with his arms akimbo in expensive print shirt, sailing shorts, and spotless boat shoes, his dark-tinted Ray Bans tilted jauntily toward the sun, his sun-bleached brown hair barely disturbed by the light breeze off the Lake. Within a week, he'd be brought to his knees by the hidden challenges of joisting over the kitchen and, after that, he'd lose his arrogance and become likable.

Meanwhile, Howard and Dan were bonding. The very best part of Dan showed through here; I think that the professional sympatico he felt with Howard was the key. Howard told me several times long after the fact that he felt those sympathetic vibes from Dan, too. A little like falling in love—maybe a lot.

But even though their discussion involved the expectable under the circumstances—a no-nonsense, jargon-driven explanation of what he'd done (the house-jacking; the careful interpretation of the architect's blueprints, along with commentary on the real engineering nightmares they posed)—there was no mistaking that this was a job interview. Weirdly, though, the roles were switched here! Whereas I would have expected that Dan would have been grilling Howard about his fitness and competencies for this job, it was clearly the other way around. There was nothing overt or aggressive about the role that Howard was playing. Quite to the contrary, he was quiet, respectful, very careful in the questions that he directed to Dan about what he'd been doing and how he'd been doing it. Quite naturally, he wanted to know everything about the project—including the building's history right from the beginning.

But the point of his questions had nothing to do with me or Linda. He was a perfect gentleman with us, and he never excluded us from the conversation, but his attention was riveted elsewhere—on Dan, on the plans, and on the structure. Howard needed to have two important issues confirmed—that Dan knew his stuff and could communicate it succinctly and precisely to Howard, and that Dan cared as much about the job and developing solutions to the problems it posed as Linda and I did. It was really quite Zen-like—I've found out since that one of Howard's favorite books was *Zen and the Art of Motorcycle Maintenance*.

And Dan, buoyed with the kind of guilt-driven, borne-again enthusiasm that drove him toward the ministry and an analytical competence now stripped of ego that had attracted me to him in the first place, did a hell of a lot more than walk the walk. Howard was impressed; he'd told me he was. It was almost Masonic, the two of them locked hermetically in their little cabala of carpentry.

The bottom line was that Howard saw precisely what Dan saw. Dan had zeroed in on weight-bearing wall problems, on the perils of spanning thirty-five feet with one beam, on the physics problems posed by the thin-prowed window wall—what would prevent those windows from breaking under the weight they would be bearing?

Howard unobtrusively solicited Dan's solutions to these difficulties, and Dan let it fly. Most of what he said was way over my head. Dan was convinced—where the dirty little felons from Bayfield were not—that the addition could be built, that the architect's recommendations, while somewhat short of realistic and relying on sky hook technology, were sound from an engineering standpoint, that the blueprints delivered some exotic and risky challenges in a very small package. Dan opined that, among those challenges, stabilizing the prowed window wall was the most crucial, and he discussed how he'd implement a variety of braces to get it done. In so many words, Dan was expressing his regrets at not being able to stick around long enough to wrap his arms and mind around those challenges. With all the construction he'd been involved in for such a young man, he saw my little remodel as drawing upon the sum of his accumulated skills.

As Dan spoke passionately about the project, Howard listened studiously, tilting his tree-stump neck to check Dan's comments against the details of the print, asking for points of clarification. As he made the outlines of a partial sketch of what he'd absorbed from Dan on a piece of two-by-six he'd picked up off the deck, he was, quietly and authoritatively, all over it. Dan had passed muster.

Much later, when I'd gotten to know Howard well, he explained his reasons for taking the job. I didn't believe him when, after Dan finished his presentation, he said he'd take it on because the problems posed by it were "very interesting." But he meant that. He told me that he had nothing further to prove other than how egregiously stupid he might be to put himself in harm's way by working beyond the point of his own safety. He had plenty to keep him busy, and the thirty-two-foot ladder, metal break, pneumatic framing hammers, and other tools of a young carpenter's outdoor trade held little fascination for him. In fact, he divested himself of all of these and much more for short or no money a few years later to signify that he was done with all that.

But the things that caused him to sign on to his last full-scale outdoor building project, I suspect, were the same things that still drove him to open his shop at 8:30 every morning, pretty much seven days a week, and keep the wood shavings flying until about 4:30 in the afternoon. He liked Dan. He liked the way that Dan respected his craft and him. He clearly enjoyed having a high-level technical discussion about some intricate problems related to physics and his craft. He knew he'd be inheriting problems, plunging in at mid-stream, but he knew from his discussions with Dan that he'd be picking up the baton from a fellow professional.

I suspect, too, that Howard took the job partly because he'd gleaned some degree of sympatico between us and him. It would never be prudent for a tradesman to contract only with people that he knows and likes—he'd likely starve to death. But Howard intimated later that he'd turned down and avoided lots of assignments with clients whose interests or personalities conflicted with his. And, after I'd gotten to know Howard, I found his explosive temper; this was a man who, when pushed to the limits of his patience with "fools not to be suffered gladly," could and would detonate in the offender's face with a mushroom cloud of the plain and graphically-epitheted truth that would set him free from that other's incompetence. He didn't balk at my request to work along with him as a helper on the job, but the understanding right from the start was that, if he saw my presence as a hindrance or danger, I'd be out of there. No, he took the job because it interested him, it set the gears in his mind to clanking and whirring, and it pressed him beyond the common and ordinary practice of his skills.

When all was said and done on that late Sunday morning, Howard stated that he'd be working for twenty dollars per hour—incredible—that Jerry, whom he'd worked with before on a couple of other jobs, would be working with him for the same rate, and that they'd be rolling down the driveway independently in their work vans before 7:30 on Monday morning. I shook the stubby fingers of Howard's lamb shank hand, and that was that. An odd combination of elfish Frodo and wizard Gandalf turned at his van, smiled broadly, and waved before following Jerry out of the driveway and up the spur toward thirteen. Howard was as solid and simple as the brownstone on which the cabin sat. And we were in business.

Looking toward Linda's gazebo

CHAPTER 3

Course Registration: Carpentry 101

"Gandalf struck a blue light on the end of his magic staff, and in the firework glare the poor little hobbit could be seen kneeling on the hearth-rug shaking like jelly that was melting. Then he fell flat on the floor, and kept on calling out 'struck by lightening, struck by lightening...' and that was all they could get out of him for a long time."
--Tolkien, *The Hobbit*

So that was that, and there we were. I was relieved that Howard and Jerry had agreed to take up the shards of our miserable little project while we still had a few dollars to throw at them and to work at what we felt were bargain-basement wages. Linda was relieved that her astronomical food bills and thankless Augean kitchen labors would be over now that Dan had dragged his bottomless pit of a son home to diet on what surely had to be more Spartan fare. And Chris was—well—just Chris. He'd be around a while to help me, but, besides his hormones crooning their siren tune, the school bell beckoned for his senior year, and he'd be deserting me soon.

At 7:30 the next morning, I found myself in a situation I'd not experienced since I'd begun to work as an unskilled laborer in the summers of my high school years. As I waited by the back deck in the dewy chill of that brilliant Monday, with the endlessly rocking waters of Superior laughing loudly behind me, I realized I was nervous. I'd had plenty of time during the previous two weeks to display my ineptitude in a wide array of tasks, but, up to now, I'd done it before friends and family. No problemo. Nothing new about that. No pressure, either.

But this Monday produced some churning in my bowels. I was nervous at the prospect of working with a couple of paid and hardened professionals, and Howard in particular. As I waited, I worried about being in the way, doing things wrong, misinterpreting orders and directions, slowing them down, being a distinct liability, and maybe even ultimately being forced into Capri pants and a halter top and getting banished to the covey of gift shops and antique emporia in Corny and neighboring South Shore towns that Linda had begun to ply. I was feeling the kind of pressure I remember oozing through my intestinal tract on the first day of those summer jobs at the Water Department in Braintree, Massachusetts, when wizened full-time "Townies" barked out orders to inexperienced teenagers with lousy work habits, terminal hangovers, and no common sense. I felt all of this as I heard the distant groaning of engines and grinding of gravel begin to swell as it rounded the bend just east of our place and then settled quietly into our rutted driveway.

It was the first of many mornings just like this over the next several weeks, and I had nothing to fear from any of them except fear itself. I helped them unload the tools from their trucks, and they set to the business of framing the exterior walls for the great room addition. Howard was good about getting Chris and me into the swing of framing. While Jerry began to study the layout of the joists of the old roof to determine whether they were salvageable, Howard proceeded methodically—I've always loved the fact that Howard talked to himself as he worked—in marking the placement of the studs, trimmers, and cripples on the deck and then on the bottom and top plates. Once he'd done that, he measured and made his cuts on the two-by-sixes, laid them on the deck, and instructed Chris and me how and where to nail them. As he watched Chris furiously attacking

Teaching Fools

Linda, me, and the window wall skeleton

the hammering task as if he were killing snakes on a plane, he carefully instructed the both of us on the correct way to hold and swing our hammers—with smooth and rhythmic arc shaped by the unstressed motion of wrist, forearm, and shoulder that soon enabled us to make more consistent contact with the sixteen-penny nails that we'd been destroying by the dozens.

Things went well that way for some time. For the most part, I was the spear-carrier. I was the guy who, without the physique to support it, helped the behemoth of a driver from the large lumber yard in Bayfield unload his truck laden with heavy building materials. The squares of shingles; the piles of ¾ and ½ inch plywood and OSB; the two-by-twelve rafter stock; the various lengths of two-by-sixes that would be used for framing. It was tough work. It had been a while since I'd done such sustained tough work. And, after a while, I could feel my body begin to accept it with gradually receding discomfort. When Jerry and Howard needed something, I was the guy, and, regardless of my being the one paying the bills, I felt the pressure of needing to produce what they requested immediately, yesterday.

Pretty soon Howard, who was clearly calling the shots on the job and daily determining the division of labor between him and Jerry, was shoving a sawzall in my hands and telling me where and how to clip the ends of ceiling joists in preparation for the construction of the floor over the kitchen. It wasn't long before Howard and Jerry had me cutting pieces of plywood and OSB with Jerry's circular saw—I was grateful for the lesson that Howard gave me in aligning the mark above the blade on the outside of the cutting line rather than hanging my face directly over the machine to check whether I was cutting straight. I was like a kid looking for approval, afraid of screwing up, devastated if I made the smallest mistake.

And Howard was great. Looking up with those large, crackling wide-set brown eyes, he generally smiled slightly and told me to take it easy on myself, slow down, back off, and laugh a little. It was the "wood is a living thing" thing repeatedly—he spent a career making mistakes, adjustments, and corrections, he said, and he expected that he'd keep right on doing it. If you get it wrong, he said, the wood is forgiving; you can always do it again.

I remember getting angry only once at Howard during the entire job. It was stupid, really, and a result of being physically overmatched by the materials that I was carrying. A load of four-by-eight sheets of plywood, the nasty three-quarter inch variety, had come, and I was left to unload all of it. Jesus Christ. It was brutal enough getting it off the bed of the truck and in a carrying position—my left hand cradled the top of each piece while my right hand held the weight of the unwieldy sheet. But it was a job made even more difficult by having to weave through piles of unstable building materials and waste and then lift each piece over the considerable step onto the deck and deposit it in a neat pile against the east wall. Man, that hurt. And I was getting madder with each piece I carried that no one was helping me. As I made each painful little crow-hop from the little wooden platform up onto the deck, there were Howard and Jerry talking to the driver—about the job, the weather, the nearly exponential increase in building starts, everything—ignoring me as if I weren't there.

Yeah, it was all about me. Stupid. It didn't take me long to get over that one. Howard didn't remember any of this, and whatever for? In a way, this was a test to see how much I really wanted to earn my way into a piece of this thing.

And, more importantly, it was a realization that I was doing the only job I was equipped to do. It was time to step up and grow up. I have never gotten over the feeling of dread when confronted with carrying a piece of ¾-inch plywood against a cross wind and suddenly turning into an unrigged sail, but I no longer take it personally.

But I did get to know Howard some during those weeks of my Sisyphean little trials, and the knowing was good and revealing. Of course, there were the coffee breaks occurring around 9:30. For a little while, these brief respites happened at the window wall, with Jerry and Howard grabbing their thermos jugs and reaching for a smoke. Sometimes I'd run in and make a quick cup in the microwave and join them, but, more often than not, Howard would pour me some out of his thermos and I'd steal a cigarette out of his pack of Merits—he'd quit cold turkey in a few years.

After they got the project into high gear, those breaks took place on the west side of the house, on the edge of the encroaching woods on top of a pallet of shingles that I recall the hell of off-loading and stacking. It was the easy affability that I remember, the identification of species of trees and berries on the property and Howard's disclosure, upon stepping into his private open-air washroom, of the location of a patch of blueberries on the cliff's edge that I didn't know was there, the discussion of local characters, the stories about the jobs Howard had held along the way toward finding himself here in "paradise," and his unqualified pronouncement that "you've really got something here, Bill."

And there were stories that spoke volumes about how Howard worked his way through to the completion of the skeleton of the structure. Howard, it seemed, knew everybody along the shore and was on solid terms with most of them. Those personal and professional associations ended up saving me lots of time, work, and money. When the four glue lams were delivered to the site, the question arose about how we were going to move these prohibitively heavy and unwieldy thirty-five-foot pieces into their bird's-mouthed niches on the window wall up front and the back wall above the window over the loft. There were some very pricey alternatives, but Howard indicated that he'd be stopping at Isaksson's sawmill just up the street from his house in Herbster after work to see if he couldn't arrange for one of the laborers to drive a pole truck out to do the job.

I was skeptical, but, sure enough, at the end of one of our working days, the pole truck arrived, and, not more than a pick-up truck-length behind it was Albert, the venerable and crotchety owner of the sawmill, who had come along partly because he wanted to make sure what his equipment and driver were going

Teaching Fools

Howard's Trojan Horse

to be used for, to partake in what surely would be an old-boy social occasion, and to satisfy his curiosity about what was going on in his neighborhood.

It was an incredibly efficient little operation. A capped, suspendered, and flannel-shirted Albert supervised while the driver set the ancient yard truck's stanchions, boarded the open metal seat at the back, and deftly tickled the controls on the boom which swung each of the glue lams like weightless twigs through the window opening, where we received and then guided them from a cat-walk that Dan and Howard had built into their resting place. Quick. Amazing. Howard had coached me to give Albert fifty bucks; as I did, we shook hands heartily. He said in his usual gruff manner to think nothing of it, that he was glad to help, and not to hesitate to call on him if I needed his truck again.

Howard immediately told him that we would, and, a couple of weeks down the road, Howard arranged with Albert to send Howard's friend Dickie Kuzol with the same truck. It took Dickie about thirty minutes to set the truck and then to swing up on the roof all of those bundles of shingles that we'd been drinking our coffee on. Dickie's response when I tried to pay him afterwards was dismissive—"We try to stick together and help each other out around here." But Howard knew how many perilous trips up that ladder to the peak of the roof with squares of shingles bowing our backs Dickie and Albert's generosity had saved us.

I might have learned more about Howard, though, the morning in mid-September when he came down the driveway at the usual time only to tell me that he wouldn't be coming down that driveway again for quite some time. Actually, Howard arrived a little earlier than usual on that chilly but sun-latticed Friday, catching me by surprise still at my coffee in the kitchen instead of at my usual post by the well head waiting to help unload the construction vans. As I burst out the screen door to greet them, I noticed that there was no "them." Only Howard's van had come today, and, as Howard emerged from it, I noticed, with my crack analytical skills, that he wasn't dressed for work.

as he walked toward me dressed in the standard "Howard" civilian uniform of khakis and short-sleeved plaid shirt, his upper body bent slightly with the promise of an impending apology.

And that's what it was. The sincerity was painful, quiet, even poignant. "I'm sorry, Bill, but I won't be working today," he began. Then he looked very intensely at me and said quietly but firmly that he wasn't really sure when he'd be back. I made a feeble stab at trying to fill an uncomfortable silence by asking him if he was ok, if anything else he might be able to talk about was wrong, or if Linda and I had done something to get in the way. Howard was all business here, and he'd clearly thought about and rehearsed what he was going to say to me that morning, but he didn't seem to have anticipated my concern about his situation, whatever it was.

Warmly, he intoned, "Oh no. Oh no, Bill. It's not you. You and Linda have been great. You've got a wonderful project here, and it's full of the challenges that make me get up in the morning. No. Oh no. It's me."

Very simply put. Very direct. And, with a little more leverage applied to open the closed container of Howard's business, I knew that what he had told me was true. He had hit the wall, he said. And it was a combination of things that formed the wall. Jerry wasn't there, and Howard said nothing more about him than to say that he'd told him what he'd decided and that Jerry would be coming to work as usual, probably by himself, on the following Monday. I wondered if they'd had a disagreement, a parting of the ways about the window wall or the roof, that made it impossible for them to work together. Their relationship would explode all over these peaceful woods in an acrimonious torrent of accusations about "sabotage" in a little more than five weeks, but Howard betrayed no hint that Jerry was driving him away.

No. At the heart of it were two reasons. His wife Sally the first, and probably the most important. He flat-out missed her. He hadn't seen her, he said, since last December. Sure, they talked at least once every day on the phone, burning the lines between

Herbster and Baltimore with conversations so long that they masked the fact that those "hi, honey, I'm home" chats weren't actually physical encounters. And Howard needed her physical presence. I'm not saying that it was rutting season on the South Shore and that Howard was doing his geriatric imitation of slamming his rack against the aspen and birch. Hell, we used to joke about that kind of stuff at lunch. But he needed to see her, and that was that. Howard expressed his resolve quietly and respectfully, but as an irreversible fact. Sally was down in Baltimore all alone, a diminutive but tough-as-nails woman running a warehousing business that was generally male territory, and she was doing it successfully. But she was getting close to selling out and retiring. Howard may have been physically talking to me, but he was already on the road heading for Maryland. Quite simply, nature was calling, and Howard was answering.

    The other factor driving Howard's departure was the building project. He didn't talk lengthily about this—hell, the whole exchange that morning didn't take any longer than fifteen minutes—but he had reached an impasse with the building. He'd listened to the wood, and he could no longer clearly discern what it was trying to tell him. The window wall—had he done enough, with the nail-gun blitzkrieg, the steel braces that he had made up over in Ashland, and his engineering know-how to anticipate and solve the racking problems that would occur with the first good wind off "Mother Superior?" The architect—was that guy and his plan to hold up that window wall with the single span of beam certifiable, or should he invest fully in the construction of reality that that architect had represented in his drawings? Howard needed distance— two-thousand miles seemed a bit much, I joked feebly, and we both laughed—to sort it out, to think it through, and to return with his ears pinned back having worked all of the possibilities into one cock-sure plan.

    In other words, this simple job was no longer simple, and Howard ached for a return to that simplicity and certitude. And that's Howard. In our discussions over the years, he'd told me that something perverse took over in him sometimes, when things got too settled, too secure, and people began to try to shape his life and work it into what they wanted rather than the free-form pattern that he needed and created daily for himself. Whenever that happened, Howard had a history of packing his car, saying his curt good-byes, and heading out toward the next uncertain destination with only his competence, his tools, and his desire to contract them out to keep him warm.

Whatever it truly was, it was amazing. As apologetic, respectful, and generous in his praise for the job and our patience in him as he was and as genuine as his regrets for throwing us into limbo, I knew there was no bending or blinking in Howard's decision. He was resolute. The van was pretty much all packed, he confirmed to me, only a few things remaining to grab at his house before heading out toward Ashland and then over through Ironwood and into Michigan's Upper Peninsula before hitting interstate 80/90 and pushing hard for Baltimore. He'd be driving straight through, as he always did. I first asked him tentatively if he thought he'd ever be back, working on my house, and he chuckled a "yes, if you'll have me, but I'll understand if you don't." I said "of course—you're the man," or something equally lame. But he didn't know when he'd be back—it might be a month or six weeks. It all depended on when things got simple and whole again.

It was getting a little awkward out there in the driveway, a couple of old kids trying to figure things out, determine who they were to each other, and find the appropriate signal for getting on and away. Laughing, and still a little stunned, I wrote out his check and told him that I was at his disposal. For his part, he said that he was as committed as he ever was about getting us closed in before the snow flew, and he'd make sure that happened. For my part, I had no doubts and told him not to call when he got back to Herbster but just show up for work. I reached out and grabbed Howard's meaty hand, shook it, and he was gone. And, as it turned out, for exactly four weeks. When he came back, he was refreshed and ready, more Gandalf than Frodo. Things were simple again.

So, what does this all say about Howard? Was this unprofessional conduct? The type of business purveyed by those highly prospering thieves from Bayfield? No. The type of grinding, peevish, irresponsible first-you-say-you-will-and-then-you-won't bullshit that lots more people than Linda and I have been victimized by whenever circumstances, weather, or flat-out petulance sent tradesmen running into smoke-darkened South Shore taverns, into the woods, or out on the Lake in their boats? Not a chance. Howard couldn't have cared less about hunting or fishing and he'd long since joined and lived the daily blessing of AA to the letter. This was the fierce independence that Howard valued so much in the South Shore old-timers and what had drawn him like a magnet to settle down here. And there was also some artistic license in it. It was a classic case of how business gets transacted differently up here than in the Twin Cities. The business relationship works more fluidly beside the Big Fluid Lady. The professional and the personal clearly carried almost equal levels of importance to Howard in his work. He'd since told me that he could have made lots of money if he had taken all of the jobs offered to him by people he didn't like. Better to contract with the ones you liked if you possibly could, to always shoot straight, and to spare yourself the inevitable parting of the ways when you'd have to bluntly tell those people what they didn't want to hear.

Besides, Howard would be back. He said he would. And he was a man of his word. That bitter blow-up between him and Jerry would, indeed, unfold like the raincoats of dueling flashers in an empty schoolyard, but Howard would suck it up, carry on, hire a rough carpenter when he needed to, and button things up way before winter. I've always said that everyone who works should receive a sabbatical. Christ, I'd been on one when the idea for this writing project first came to mind. And Howard, as I did, returned refreshed to finish what he'd started.

Some eight years passed since Howard had wrapped up the job at our place, sold any equipment that could ever tempt him outside to climb a roof or lift a framed wall, and dug in seriously to build kitchen cabinets and furniture at his shop in Herbster. Meanwhile, Howard and I became fast friends—the word "fast" must be taken arthritically. I'm not sure how all of that happened, really. A few incidental visits to the shop to see what he was working on. A chance encounter with Sally and Howard, after she had finally retired, sold her business in Baltimore, and moved back to the house that Howard and she had bought fifteen years before. At the closest thing that Corny had to a "boite", the Village Inn, well-known for their Friday night lake trout and fries and a very friendly place.

No. I know how it happened. It was Linda and Sally. Both competent and pragmatic women incapable of being daunted or pushed around by anyone. What a parlay. Sally's plans when she prepared to move back were to pour her knowledge of people and retailing into a new little venture—a gift and craft shop fronting highway 13 in Howard's building. "She who must be obeyed," as Howard wickedly labeled her, instructed him to partition the building, floor and panel with wood the "gift shop" section that she'd be occupying, and reorganize and compress his own shop, accordingly. But Howard was going pretty strong business-wise at that time, which required him to employ a more radical strategy—after building Sally's bailiwick, he kicked out the back of his shop and enlarged its size by about a third.

And so it came to pass that two people who had been living more than 2000 miles apart except for a couple of annual encounters were operating out of the same pair of pants. I won't comment now on whose pants they were. But a few years later, when Sally was careening around in her Dodge Caravan, beating the bushes for talented crafters who'd entrust Sally with exhibiting their creations in her shop, Linda and Sally became close. Linda spent as many weekends with me at the cabin as her work would allow, and, when she was there, part of her time was always spent obsessively visiting shops, pawing through junk at garage sales, rummaging through rummage sales, always with an eye for a bargain, always coyly negotiating. A woman after Sally's own heart.

It wasn't long before we were alternating the delicious chore of hosting the other pair for dinner, walking out to the gazebo and gazing at the Lake when they were at our place or ragging mercilessly on Sally when she hosted us for pouring us bad cheap white zinfandel out of a box. And soon it was a regular occurrence for the four of us to meet at the Village Inn, dine on fresh lake fish while getting our minimum daily requirement of grease, listen to the owners of the place wax poetic over the kitchen Howard had built for them, and, as we left, admire the wine rack and welcoming business counter that he had recently delivered.

But another motive drove my end of the friendship. In some infinitesimally small measure, I wanted some of what Howard knew. Mostly out of self-defense. I knew I'd never achieve any measure of competence at carpentry—I knew I'd be doing well if I was able to report to a relieved Linda that I hadn't seriously hurt myself. But, when Howard concluded our professional relationship in mid-November of 1996, there was much to do inside, almost no money to do it, but lots of time to read books that would provide me an entrée to tasks of widely-varying difficulty. And there was always Howard's willingness to listen to what I was doing and to offer advice, his challenging questions about the how and why of it, or, more importantly, warnings about what I was getting into.

I think that Howard must have reacted to my interest in learning some of the elements of what he'd been doing for fifty years with an admixture of amusement and flattery. And, consequently, over the next few years, through Howard's encouragement that I could do it and, if I screwed it up, "it's only wood," Linda and I created a memorably loud and obscene vaudeville routine for installing four-by-eight sheets of fir plywood on the eighteen-foot ceiling and boxing in the beam with cedar. I finished the inside in tongue-and-groove cedar, trimmed out the window wall and the other openings to great effect, built a rustic bathroom door, framed and fashioned a window seat running across the entire window wall, installed and finished a pine floor in the great room, and constructed a cedar deck and stairs that ran around the front of the cabin and extended in two levels out about twenty feet. I nearly had to be restrained from decking the entire woods. Man, was I full of myself.

All of this sandwiched around Howard's direct assistance in locating a set of pine circular stairs that had been installed in a cabin and been found unstable, his removing a window in order to transfer the stair assembly to his truck and then to my cabin, and then his disassembling, strengthening, installing, and then creating a supportive frame for those stairs into our loft that insured their safety. What a beautiful result. More on that one later.

In some small way, I had earned my stripe, not in competence, but in Howard's willingness to suffer at least one fool gladly. I think Howard liked the fact that I worried over the wood I worked and showed humility and respect for it, no matter how bizarre the result. No fucking around in church, as it were, but lots of license to bait and argue politics and swap lies outside of it. A solid base for a friendship.

A view of the cabin from the carriage house second floor

Street view of the cabin toward the Lake

The cabin in full natural regalia

CHAPTER 4

Building Howard University: The Curriculum Vitae

"What I'm going to tell you has something to do with how sometimes it's necessary to go a long distance out of the way in order to come back a short distance correctly."
--Albee, *The Zoo Story*

That small entitlement into Howard's confidence peaked my curiosity about where Howard had come from, where his southern drawl had originated, where his initiation into the working of wood had occurred, and how in the world he'd managed to land on the South Shore of Superior. Armed with tape recorder and legal pad, I showed up at the door of Howard's straight ranch, located a couple of blocks from Howard's and Sally's place of business, to find out. Howard had just gotten in from another one of his patented full workdays, and he hadn't had an opportunity to clean up or change out of his suspended work pants. But the broad and elfish smile was there, and so were the peanuts and soft drink that he set out on the table in the maple-cabineted kitchen that Howard had finally built for "she who must be obeyed" to escape the badgering. Sally was still at the shop, so we, the dog, and the cat had the place to ourselves.

"Balmorhea, Texas," Howard said. He had to spell the

name of that little west Texas town since I'd never heard of it, even though Linda and I had lived in Southern New Mexico for a couple of years and in spite of my having recently driven from Dallas to Lubbock for a Shakespeare conference near it. Balmorhea isn't far from Big Bend country, he told me, situated at the foot of the Davis Mountains, the southern beginnings of the Rockies. There wasn't much to the town. Howard recalled the four-foot canal, no more than an irrigation ditch, that ran right through the center of it. Flat as a pancake, he said.

I'm not certain whether Howard had thought about this stuff for a while, or even whether he cared to, but I could see eyes growing deep and focused as he gazed at the ceiling to summon back the details. Howard marked January 30, 1932, as his birthday, the same date, he noted, as Franklin Delano Roosevelt's, and the same year that FDR was elected to serve his first term. Mired in the depression. But, the ninth of nine kids, he was aware that the family was so poor that, when he was four or five, his mother took in washing—she did the laundry for the men employed by the CCC to build a recreation facility at Solomon Springs just outside of town. Howard remembered that she had an old Maytag sitting out in the yard driven by a gasoline engine. It was Howard's job to go out and gather cow chips to fuel the cast iron kettle for the washer's hot water since no wood was available. But his mom always had a penny to give him to go to Malden's store about a mile and a half across the highway and buy some candy.

Howard was hazy on his siblings' chronology; he had a sister, Betty, three years older than he; Paul was six years older, and Frank was the oldest. The only surviving Bowers besides himself was his sister Dorothy, who still lived in Texas and continued to think of Howard as both her brother and her son. He and the family lived in a detached house on a corner lot next to that irrigation ditch.

Besides listening to the west Texas wind constantly howling, Howard recalled always being a loner—great preparation for the existential snow-drifted winters he'd spend across the street from the Frozen Lady of the Lake—and he spent many afternoons just digging on the sides of the ditch banks, excavating pig nuts, eating them, and then walking out into the middle of the road and peeing on it. With a wan smile, he reflected that "I've spent most of my life pissing into the wind."

As I figured long before I asked, Howard's father's shadow loomed hugely in everything he learned and now was. Howard remembered him as always having some kind of "independent work" for himself. His dad was a building contractor by the time Howard was a teenager. Howard saw in his mind's eye his dad always working with his tools until his later, more successful years. And he was a character just like Howard, full of the Irish that he derived from—broad, chunky, feisty, and "effervescent and flamboyant" without being, as Howard framed it, a "manic depressive." But it was always all or nothing with his father, "either one way or the other...feast or famine," boom or bust. If Howard was never concerned about snagging and holding a steady job with a stable company, one need look only to his father for the source of that mind-set. Howard couldn't recall him working for anyone but himself; he was "bred on independence," and he clearly fed Howard from the same trough.

Howard's father had grown up in the hill country of Lyndon, Texas, the heart of Lyndon Johnson territory, tending goats on Howard's grandfather's ranch. Howard had never met his grandfather, but he must have been a taskmaster. He had kept two to three thousand Angora goats on that four-thousand-acre ranch and—Howard shook his head as he considered the craziness of it—designated Howard's father as his solitary goat herder. "Talk about working with independent critters," Howard laughed. Howard's understanding of what his dad had been up against came from owning his own pet goat at twelve—"an ornery, but smart and friendly and true pet," the best pet he'd ever had. Independent. It takes one, perhaps, to know one.

When I asked about the roots of the family tree, Howard came up empty, not because his memory was failing him but because no one truly knew. The research that his older brother

Frank had begun had ended in the proverbial dry hole. Some indeterminate number of generations expired between Howard's dad's Texas clan and the date when his forebears arrived in this country, probably from Ireland. Frank had succeeded in tracing the tree to Georgia.

After he'd retired as a master mechanic on the offshore oil rigs, Frank made extra money hauling assembled mobile homes all over the country. While he was waiting at the scales to be checked by a captain in the Georgia State Patrol, he noticed that the cop was intently studying the side of his truck. When the cop asked, "Which one of the Bowers are you?," Frank chipped back, "If you can read, you can see on the side of my truck that my name is Frank Bowers." The cop retorted, "Yeah, you're a damned Bowers alright." And so, uncannily, was the cop. They got to exchanging what they both knew about the name, and, as it turned out, the cop had been doing some of his own research. He'd reached a dead-end in the Tidewater area, where he surmised that the first Bowers probably came over in chains for stealing horses. Another whiff of the outsider and disestablishmentarian. Howard would revel in it if it were true.

Unsurprisingly, his dad was a taskmaster like his dad's dad. "He was almost a slave driver," Howard said. He lived, it seemed, by a simple, transparent, and uncompromising ethic. "He'd never slight you on what you were worth—he was always fair. He expected top quality, and lots of it. And he said the average woodworker wasn't worth a damn." Actually, his dad had shared this philosophy with Howard in much more colorful language. But why not? He had "a hell of a temper" that, like his financial status, blew hot and cold, off or on. He inhabited a world that was alternately black or white, one filled with faithful friends that fervently praised his character and talent as well as plenty of rabid enemies. "He'd call you an idiot," Howard said, "if he thought you were one." Howard's view of the world was both more complex and elegant than his dad's. Nonetheless, I saw him angry only once. On nothing more than that, I'd bet that Howard saw his father everyday in the mirror.

His dad moved the family to Pecos next, a larger town with maybe a thousand people around 1936 or 37. Howard remembered his dad paying his carpenters "about a buck an hour." That was followed, when Howard turned twelve, by a stint in Oklahoma, where his dad bought a farm because he'd grown tired of "eating out of a paper sack." But that enterprise failed brilliantly—"Dad was no farmer"—and, after another three or four years, when the west Texas oil boom began to gush, the family moved to Odessa.

As people poured into Odessa to work and live, Howard's dad's contracting business began to boom, too. Howard hung on there for another ten or twelve years, learning his craft, working for his dad after school and summers, and, eventually, dropping out. Besides carpentry, he'd begun to study girls and cars. In fact, both of his kids were born in Odessa. Howard was eighteen or so by then. He was a child-husband, and his wife was only 16. "Young and dumb," he murmured vacantly.

Howard's dad encouraged him to work with him early on in Odessa. When Howard was about fifteen, his dad was teaching him trim work, which, Howard explained, was the inside finish work on a house that his dad's crew had built. At first, he counseled Howard to go slow, take his time, and learn the job properly. However, after a couple of days, he'd come around to apply the pressure: "It's now time to really start producing. It's time to get your ass in gear."

Life became serious almost immediately after that. When he was sixteen, Howard had earned enough to set himself up with enough shop tools to equip a small wood shop, but, when he discovered girls, he traded those tools to his dad for the money to buy a '42 Ford. When he was seventeen he was contracting inside trim, often but not exclusively for his dad, and, by eighteen, he'd married and quit school, cock-sure that there wasn't "a way in the world that I could prevent myself from getting rich."

Howard pushed away from the kitchen table and chewed on his lower lip. It was 1949, he recalled. He fully believed then that he was boarding a "gravy train that wouldn't end." But, he admitted ruefully, he'd always read life this way—"if things are looking good, I think they'll always be good." Intellectually, he comprehended the craziness of that viewpoint, but knowing it hadn't prevented him from tripping and falling repeatedly over it.

So, when Howard broke away from his father at twenty and became a builder in his own right, he wasn't deterred by not being old enough to sign the necessary legal documents. He bought a lot, built a house on it, and, when he couldn't sell it, he moved into it. His father, observing the mess that Howard was making for himself, refused to intrude; he believed that kids should make and then climb out from under their own mistakes rather than running to dad for a bail-out every time something went wrong. His father told one of Howard's brothers, "what the hell's the matter with that boy, he doesn't know his own mind," expecting that Howard's maturity and survival depended upon resolving his mind into clear direction and purpose. Bootstraps. The independence ethic. Maybe that's one of the reasons behind Howard's dad's hatred for telephones—when the workday was over, Howard told me, the need to talk about work ceased, too.

But as tough as his father was, he and Howard were good friends. He was the kid that his father trusted the most, he said. That friendship continued through a long working life of seventy-eight years that included rediscovering and working again with his tools. He'd moved to Las Vegas, and, when the end came from a coronary, he was, typically, still embracing life more like the completion of a contract he'd penned his name to than a tragedy.

As Sally entered and began to prepare supper, Howard retraced the path of the successes that followed the failure of his first tract house built on "spec." The second one he built sold quickly, and he rolled the profits into several others over several years during the Odessa boom, which was driven as much by oil as it was by the end of the war and G.I. loans. Each new spec house improved on the previous one. The six-hundred-square-foot cracker box houses that he and others were quickly banging together sold "like hotcakes," and, before long, he'd developed a "hell of a reputation." But he knew even then that his good reputation flowed from his dad's. All of the kids had eaten, slept, and worked his dad's ethic of excellence. Howard recalled that, "if a house was listed in the paper and it was built by anyone in the Bowers family, people would say that it was a Bowers-built house. It would bring a premium on the market."

All of this framing, finishing, and contracting of houses prepared Howard incomparably for where he'd go after Odessa. When he turned twenty-three, he experienced a "rough patch" borne from doing what he'd do repeatedly in the future—spending it as quickly as he made it—and decided to try California. After moving there and passing a journeyman's test, he was sent to work on an office building site in Long Beach, and, within just a few days, he was made foreman in charge of about twelve carpenters, all many years older than he. Grinning like the kid he nearly was then, Howard said, "I think they were very patient with me." But the Long Beach job lasted only a few months, when a big concrete truck drivers' strike threw him out of work and drove him back temporarily to Odessa.

He would be making his last big play in Odessa, he said. As he'd done repeatedly, he threw up another spec house. But this one was different—much bigger and better, and built from all of the resources he'd been able to muster. And he'd also hired others to do the actual work. It failed to sell, and the bank foreclosure drove away any urge he might harbor for doing spec work again.

Howard's story reminded me of a similar one that my dad had told me of a former honey-wagon driver-come-contractor who'd extended himself with the local bank to build a large tract of upscale homes and, when they'd lain vacant for a fearfully long time, he drove his truck into one of their garages and lowered the door. And that was it for Mr. Swayze.

If Howard ultimately abandoned Odessa and his last failure in search of more secure, less dangerous work in a warmer clime, he got more than he bargained for. He chose Baton Rouge because he thought he'd get steady outdoor work, but, when the union hall sent him out to do an inside job where the thermometer registered 34 degrees, and after he'd been repeatedly rained out, he decided to hire out to do offshore drilling. "It was ten on and five off," Howard said. "We used up one of our days coming and going." It turned out that his brother Frank was a master heavy equipment mechanic on that rig, and he helped Howard get on. Howard worked as a floor hand on the drilling crew, doing twelve-hour shifts. He described himself as a "back-up man or chain man." Howard depreciated the serious danger attached to the job, but that danger bled through even in his understatement: "Not a lot of people got killed, but a lot of people got maimed doing it." The paycheck was "damned good," and, by now, he had a "couple of rug rats" to support.

Howard's description of his first trip out to the rig was harrowing. He boarded a boat at Morgan City and traveled twenty-two miles down the coast. Although Howard suffered from motion sickness, the "inland" portion of the trip had been "a piece of cake" until they hit open water. The seventy-foot boat he was on wallowed in fourteen-foot seas the entire one-hundred-and-two-mile trip to the platform, but that was merely the beginning. The water was so rough that, in order to transfer workers to the deck of the platform some fifty-five feet above the waves, a delicate dance between boat, deck crane, and a net had to work perfectly in synch. As the crane struggled to lower a hard-bottomed net onto the boat's fantail that would contain one man and his luggage at a time, Howard huddled on the floor of the boat's head, "tossing up my toenails," waiting for his turn.

Howard said that, due to the high seas, nearly an hour passed before the workers could be craned up to the platform. A nauseous initiation.

He liked the life and the work, even given the murderous wildness of the men he was working with: "the crew was called 'little Angola,' there were so many ex-cons out there." But he didn't get to do it for long—it was 1957, and Hurricane Audrey violently intervened. He had driven to Baton Rouge at the same time that Audrey had hit Cameron head-on. His boss had come around and told the crew that they'd all be put up until the storm blew over, but, when the storm stalled, they were all sent home. Just when Howard arrived home, the hurricane pounded in at the point where his boat had been set to depart, killing five-hundred people. The rig was damaged so badly by the storm that the crew was laid off, leaving Howard high and dry for over a month. He did a stint on another rig, this one inland, but, as he explained, "in southeast Louisiana you're still on the water," and he gave it and his motion sickness up after a month to return to carpentry.

The odyssey began to get a little sketchy here, like the fadings in and out of an all-night fifty-thousand-watt Mexican AM station. Actually, it was a blur, perhaps partially because we'd reached Howard's heavy drinking years. He moved to Iberia, very Cajun, he said, the oldest town settled by the Spanish in the United States, located about mid-state, only a few miles from the coast—near Avery Island, Bayou LaFouche, Bayou Teche. Howard savored the words as he listened to himself say them. There was a river there, a big one, Achapalaya. He subcontracted framing jobs with a couple of other guys there, but, when restlessness set in, the three of them traveled to a place in Alabama, Dofind, about a hundred miles from Panama City, to take on more framing.

He didn't remember much about his stay there except that his personal life was a wreck and that he had taken another framing job just after his wife had divorced him. Soon he was burning a jagged path, rambling up into Tennessee to work for a while. Lots of ups and downs. Working, partying, learning, forgetting, burning it at both ends. Living day-to-day. After a year, he found himself in Florida, framing lots of tract houses, attracting contracts for lots of finish work because he could do it so well.

It was late winter of 1963 in Dallas when he was seized by a perverse desire—to see upper New York state in the dead of winter and lake-effect snows, simply because he wanted to see it. On his way up through Missouri, it occurred to him that he may have left too early in the season to find work in New York, so he stopped in Springfield to hire out so that he could deepen his cash reserves. He found work in a church under construction and, for a couple of good weeks, did some substantial work there before he was suddenly struck by "my old nemesis"—commitment to a job, long-term, and working for somebody other than himself. One of the owners of the church—Howard hadn't a clue about the particular denomination—flew in from out of town, evaluated Howard's work favorably, and offered him a full-time, permanent job if he'd only agree to go to Tulsa and build another church. Things were about to turn serious again.

And that was that. He picked up his check, his tools, his great coat, and he was gone, headed northeast.

He encountered a hitchhiker in West Virginia and, departing from his usual practice, picked him up. This young man was headed for Fairfax, Virginia, and regaled Howard with stories about how much money there was to be made in the building boom that was underway. And, as serendipity would have it, Howard stopped there on the kid's recommendation. Just like that. Like the answer to an unspoken prayer. And he stayed for a good and eventful while. In fact, he'd be in the D.C. area for the next twenty-four years.

The kid was right about the "boom," and Howard went to work immediately as the carpentry foreman on a new elementary school project. The superintendent on the job was Bill Moore, a man of "unconventional methods" and a voracious appetite for women whom Howard would become fast and hell-raising roommates with.

Eventually, Bill's cavalier methods caused the Fairfax County school board to fire him. A few years later, in 1967, Bill wound up in Danang superintending the construction of a radar installation. Bill and Howard continued to correspond but lost touch. It was only through a chance meeting at a Krispy Kreme shop with a stranger who had a daughter who assembled a newsletter on people who worked abroad for the armed services that he learned that Bill was working in North Africa, "shacked up with a Eurasian girl."

During their working years together, Bill and Howard collaborated on a project to build some sixty-five two-story houses in Reston, employing twenty men, working like dervishes and partying every night. It got crazy. Both being, as it were, between wives, they shared a two-bedroom apartment where each carried on their own personal lives with "the ladies."

But Bill, Howard recalled, had a way of intruding into his. Bill concluded that Howard needed more women, at least a half a dozen at any given time. And, to get that ball rolling, he announced that he'd fixed him up with a blind date. He'd invited two women over for the evening; he'd be doing the cooking, and Howard would be consigned to washing dishes. There would be a phone call confirming the date from the woman. Howard remembered telling Bill that it was all over between them if he didn't like the sound of the person on the other end of the line. As luck would have it, the person whose voice he liked was Sally.

Neither Sally nor Howard could agree on precisely when this first fateful meeting transpired—a little friendly wrangling over the dinner table that Sally had been setting left Howard the temporary victor: 1966. The start of a forty-year relationship that had lurched along almost continuously. All relationships are strange, ineffable, often even to those on the inside of them. From my perspective, this "thing" between Howard and Sally was stranger still. I confronted Howard at the shop the next day about the apparent impossibility of it—Howard the loner versus Sally the obsessive joiner and organizer, Howard the craftsman not always practical about finance and business versus Sally the eagle-eyed accountant. Howard of the steel-trap memory who refused to write things down because it was "all up here" versus Sally who remembered the smallest business transactions over thirty-two years. If these differences weren't enough, each was capable of being territorial, independent, and explosive. Until recently, they'd thrived on living 2000 miles apart, while at the same time connected by the invisible tether of the telephone. They'd each logged hard miles on them with irreparable dings and scratches, but they started without fail, ran strong with some tender coaxing, and always got where they wanted to go.

Howard leaned back thoughtfully in his chair trying to identify when his history became hers. For about fifteen years, she'd been a partner in a warehouse and trucking operation in Baltimore, and for seventeen years before that she'd operated a business of the same type after beginning as a bookkeeper. She had three small kids when Howard met her. He discovered shortly that Sally had grown up on the South Shore, taken a job as an upstairs maid in Duluth when she was nineteen, and, not long after that, moved to Washington D.C. with a sister and several of her girlfriends to seek government work. She had decided upon Washington for her own reasons. When Howard and she met in 1966, they hit it off immediately and were off to the races.

What was there about Sally that could be labeled her calling card? Who was she? Howard viewed her as a practically-minded person, almost more than anyone else he'd ever known: "She couldn't tell you about the history of the Manchurian dynasty, or when and where paper was invented." However, should a social situation arise where Howard "would be completely baffled about how to proceed, Sally [knew] instinctively how to handle the situation." She knew people, he asserted admiringly.

She was also as tenacious as a dimpled rubber tub mat. He told of the time, three or four years after they'd met, when, because of a difference of just plain disaffection, "I had other fish to fry and I was gone from her life for ten years or so." When he showed up once again, her poker-faced comment was, simply, "I knew you'd be back, Howard."

That ten years would be a relatively large hole in anyone's life, and I would have loved for Howard to fill it in for me. But he never did. About six months later, when we were sharing some vein-coagulating bacon cheeseburgers and the biggest order of fries I'd ever seen at the Village Inn's bar, he opened up his very private window just a crack.

We were going over what he'd told me about those Virginia years, and, as he did, he dropped his guard. I'm not sure what caused that. We'd been bantering back and forth as we always did, cracking wise about nothing in particular, about his old nugget that the South Shore was the last area in the continental United States to be settled by European immigrants, and about the Scandinavians that made up a big portion of that mass—about how they'd found an environment very friendly and familiar to what they'd left, close to a huge body of water, rich in fishing, bountiful in farming land. For my part, I used my very limited knowledge of this emigration to note how hard it was for so many of the Scandinavians who'd landed in New York. They'd get bamboozled by con artists or thieves out of most of their stake, board trains that led to Chicago, and, once there, out into the great prairie lands of western Minnesota or South Dakota to face the alienation of settling in the middle of a very different and ominous ocean—this one of flat and grassy vastness that they'd never experienced before. Many of these people had banded together for self-protection, resisting the acculturation process, preserving their language, staving off the intrusion of other ethnic groups. Somehow Howard got on to the language thing, how his wife had been Scandinavian and how Howard had driven her and her mother, who'd been visiting from Sweden, around and was able to parse together some of the conversations that the two women were having.

Suddenly, I sensed that the wife Howard was referring to wasn't Sally. So I asked him, who *was* this woman? Howard drew back a moment, smiled distantly, and said, "Do you remember when I told you that Sally and I had a ten-year hiatus in our relationship? Well, this is where I was." That was it. He volunteered nothing more than to say that "to this day that woman's name is never mentioned in Sally's house." The other woman. The third wife before Howard returned to resume his relationship with Sally. It was his worst mistake, he said. He'd erased it from his living tape machine as if it had never happened. And then the crack in the window closed. Enough said.

Of the people who've been influential in Howard's life, Sally would be "right up there." She was the "anchor" in his life, not in Henny Youngman's tired sense of the "ball and chain" or "take my wife, please," but in the most positive way—the stabilizer, the stiller of his wanderlust, and every bit his match in a tug of wills. Everybody should be so lucky.

So, from the point that he went to Virginia, became gainfully employed there, and met Sally, Howard sank roots in the D.C. area. Surely, he took working vacations occasionally, but for the most part he was there. Part of the "comfort zone" that Howard came to feel with Sally may have resulted from Sally's understanding that she would not try to influence him directly in his work. Even when Howard and Sally reunited on the South Shore and worked out of two sides of the same shop, it was clear that their long-standing co-existence proceeded from a largely unspoken understanding. They were close, but they had "these territorial limits," silent and invisible, and both knew not to tread over those lines.

As Howard explained it, "we work in the same building, and even there there's a division, an unmarked line, and you're in her shop or you're in my shop, and we respect that. I do things for her, and she sells things for me, but that's the end of it."

When the time arrived for Sally to pull the trigger, buy the business she'd long been employed in, and locate a partner, she knew just where to turn. She and Carol had worked together in that business for many years and continued to be the closest of friends, and, when the company folded, they quickly decided to legally join forces and continue to operate the same kind of business in the same location. The warehousing and shipping business was a rough, risky, distinctly male enterprise, but Sally knew the business backwards and forwards, and, more importantly, she knew people. She thrived so successfully that, when she and Carol leased the last of the buildings they used, some 54,000 square feet, one of the biggest clients they had, McGough Labs, recognized Sally for operating the largest and most efficient warehouse of its kind in the country several years running.

Maybe her obsession with excellence accounts partly for their mutual attraction and support. Both possessed a wide compulsive streak. Both had been hard on themselves, and on those that worked for them if they weren't so inclined. Sally couldn't have survived as a slight five-foot-nothing woman among the hefty, sullen, and prophane tow-motor operators, warehousemen, and salesmen always looking for an edge over her. And, to hear Howard tell it, she always prevailed, the benevolent despot. Hers, too, was a career built on a foundation of not suffering fools or liars gladly. And, if nothing else would get Howard's attention through his years of wine and roses, that surely would.

Professionally, Howard was getting all the work he could handle, but the same old devils of self-destruction and claustrophobia conspired to overtake him a couple of more times. Actually, more times than twice, but two that can be spoken about without Howard's censure. He recalled a company, King Associates, that had both hired and fired him and, after all that, offered to set him up in business. Actually, he reflected, that company's entire organization had been "interesting," but he remembered one most exceptional person within it. That man, Chuck Kuhn, had worked as principal field supervisor for King, an effective motivator who could inspire trust and who became Howard's close friend for over twenty years. Howard had done some contract work through Chuck and, in later years, Howard would contract more work from Chuck's company. When the King organization began encountering bottlenecks among a variety of trades and stages in their several building projects, Chuck stepped in and suggested that Howard be hired to clear them. King had about five large projects going, but, although sales were good, production problems threatened to eat into the profits.

Howard knew all about such bottlenecks—they're a "normal" consequence of construction, he said. So Howard was brought on board with the mission to clear them, fire the offending sub-contractors, and then hire and train new people for whatever crafts that were interfering with production. He was given complete license to visit any of the five King projects, observe how the work was being done, and make decisions preemptively.

But that was precisely when his long experience and practical sense collided with his mission; he knew that each part of a building project was, as he termed it, "a private fiefdom." To follow his job description to the letter would be to upset the chemistry of the entire job. The more intense the internal noise of insubordination grew, the more stress he felt about the job. That internal melt-down was accelerated by the serious drinking Howard was then doing. Finally, after a year and a half, company officials confronted him with the earth-shattering conclusion that Howard "wasn't cut out to work for other people." Go figure.

But they were left with the conundrum of just what to do with him. They were going to let him go, but they applauded his enormous skills. In one wildly un-businesslike gesture, they offered to set him up in business when he was ready and to stake him as well. All Howard needed to do was acquiesce and, at the appropriate time, contact Mr. King, the head of the corporation, to set things in motion. But, being the stubborn person that he was, still relatively young and foolish, he never even had that conversation with Mr. King—"What the hell do I need them for?," he recalled sneering to himself at the time. Ultimately, he just walked away from it. Independence could be taken too far, he said. This walking away—it sounded vaguely familiar.

This last insistence upon snatching failure from the jaws of victory provoked still another story—the great Maryland Contractor's License Fiasco. Independent and bull-headed to a fault, Howard said he'd always balked at occasions when the government told him what to do, so he'd been contracting around Maryland for years without a contractor's license. Ultimately, he got caught, as he knew he eventually would. This was a huge deal. For one thing, a tremendous leap in reasoning needn't be required to guess that an unlicensed tradesman could get sued by disenchanted or opportunistic clients if they knew, and, without the license, one couldn't get bonded. Of course, Howard knew all that; when I asked him if it ever occurred to him to go and get one, he said, "Yeah, oh hell yeah"—and that had Howard written all over it. One could go to jail, he admitted.

After finally being found out and reported after contracting in Maryland without the proper credential for at least fifteen years, he was told by a state enforcement official, "you *will* get a license, or you *will* go to jail." And his respectful reply was, "I've always wanted one." He said that the contractor's test he took could have been passed by a smart monkey. On reconsideration, he asserted, "even a monkey that wasn't smart could have passed that test."

In the end, he said, it didn't really mean "a hell of a lot to the buying public" that the person they were hiring had a license, given Maryland's lax standards. And, of course, he had to get bonded, and that was a little more of a hassle, but he got it done. For the state itself, he had all kinds of regulative hoops to jump through, and finally, when he sent the last papers in to the appropriate state agency, he was told that he'd have to re-file them all because, as they explained, when they opened the envelope, they thoughtlessly cut those papers in two! Bureaucratic stupidity. Howard's dogged determination not to be party to it made more sense after I'd heard the whole story.

When Howard picked up the thread of his long and winding road over the bridges he'd sometimes built and torched, it was early the next morning, in the shop at break time in direct response to my query of when and why he first came to the South Shore. He labored over the answer as if he'd been here forever, then floated indefinitely between the early to mid-eighties. He was misremembering again, to borrow from our GWB's unfortunate parlance, something he often did with things immediately outside his focus on a woodworking job or the huge garden he was tending on a piece of land just outside Herbster. The right answer was probably rolling gently between 1988 and 1989.

In any event, his initial thought about relocating to the South Shore had burst upon him after some serious self-reflection. For people who weren't from here, he said, there came a point where having a lot of money or competing hard for more "stuff" didn't really amount to "a rat's ass." Just before turning sixty, he realized that "life is finite… it really is." Suddenly, looking back at the life-spans of his father and mother, and figuring for the x-factors of "bad weather and bad luck" and a toxic addiction that he'd beaten, he could probably count on living for another six to eight more years if his health held.

Looking back over the twenty-plus years in Virginia and Maryland, he knew that "I don't want to go in the city, in the concrete jungle, right up to that time." Howard smiled while remembering a "friendly conversation" with Sally. They'd been going back and forth on the appropriate timing for "pulling the plug" on full-time gainful employment. He declared to her that he didn't want to wait until seventy before going up north, finding and buying a place to live and start anew. He wanted all of those puzzle pieces chosen early, in place, and humming.

Whatever the exact date of this courtly exchange, Sally indicated no passion for returning to her childhood home, he said. However, they both could feel retirement looming just below the horizon. The loner inside him told her that he'd like to retire to a place like Herbster, working his craft in his own shop away from the big city rat race he'd been bucking. Sally liked the idea of moving to Florida, but Howard had lived and worked there and thought little of it. Unable to convince Howard to move south, she said that she'd agree to go back and give the South Shore another look, but only if he'd first commit to spending a winter there by himself. Sally would make the trip with him, and, if they liked it, they'd make arrangements to buy a house, but, when the cold weather arrived, she'd be leaving—it was up to Howard to reach an understanding of what winter up here truly meant. As she put it, he was perfectly welcome to accompany her as she made her annual trip at the end of December to Maryland; she had kids and grandkids there. But, if

Howard didn't want to come along, that was "fine;" she'd see him in the spring. For the Sultan of Stubborn, the gauntlet had been thrown. Bring it on.

During that trip, they did, in fact, purchase two pieces of property. The first was the straight ranch, located on a big lot only a few hundred feet off route 13 and away from the Lake, within view of the tiny crossroads of the town of Herbster. Not long after that, Howard noticed a commercial property for sale— the little steel-framed Butler building right on 13 no more than a block and a half away from their house and across the street from the post office; in typical fashion, Sally bargained hard to buy it, for peanuts.

And so Howard set about spending his first winter in Herbster. It was difficult work transforming that building from the refuse-filled wreck it was when they bought it to an open and usable wood shop. But, when he saw Sally again the following spring, he informed her that he hadn't changed his mind one bit. A shocking revelation. This was, he said, "the place." And he would never look back.

He understood Sally's predicament—the family roots that still grew strong in her birth place opposed by the thriving warehouse and distributing business she needed to tend back in the D.C. area. But, from this point, that business would be up for sale; it would be just a matter of time before a bonified buyer would put an end to Sally's long annual commute. Meanwhile, he'd be working in Herbster, happy and fulfilled.

From the very first, Howard's impressions of the South Shore had been positive, and there was never a doubt that, if he made the shift, he could make a go of it. When he had originally surveyed the area, there wasn't much building going on, and, with the winter coming, he knew there'd be a lot of laboring down-time. But he'd always meant to fill that winter period by making cabinetry of various types and descriptions. He'd operated his shop in the basement of their house in Maryland for some six years; he'd steadily been doing cabinet work there and, in addition, picking up contracts in building and remodeling on the outside. And, almost immediately, he did find plenty to occupy him.

That shop remained the focal point of what permitted him to stay in Herbster continuously after that and practice his craft. Howard recalled the possibilities he could see in it, but only if he was able to overcome some serious drawbacks. The building had a long and checkered history and had been employed for lots of purposes. It was honeycombed with partitions and had been left a mess by its previous owner, who was in serious jeopardy of losing it to unpaid taxes. After Sally bought it for a song plus taxes owed, Howard and Sally's brother Hank cleaned out the partitions and found a solid, well-constructed steel frame under the wood sheath.

But wait. Herbster. What kind of a name is Herbster, for Christ's sake? Beyond the fact that Sally originally hailed from here, this damned place seemed no more than an unattractive bump in the road that most people sped over without looking back. Where could the attraction, the esthetic, lie that could cater to that part of Howard that craved beauty? Howard, pointing toward the side door, replied, "Well, that body of water out there is number one—that great inland sea." He said that he loved the Brule River just down the street and being surrounded by forest, but he believed that, because he was an outsider, he brought a greater appreciation for what's in and around Herbster than those insiders who, by habit and custom, have become insensitive to what they saw.

Howard had shamelessly developed and refined a taste for nature's smaller and sweeter pleasures. The Lake is spectacular, but what surrounds it quietly complements it. Howard drew the beauty of the South Shore's rolling forested hills and alternately rocky and sandy shore into sharp relief when he compared the Appalachians to the Rockies: "the Rockies are spectacular; the Appalachian Mountains are beautiful but sedate. This area has that gentle sedate and laid-back beauty" that could suddenly, with Superior's intervention, become a maelstrom. In the midst of it, he could indulge his favorite pastime, woodworking, and, when custom orders slackened, he could build what he wanted.

And the people. By and large, he felt real kinship with them—strong and resilient upper mid-western people. He reminded me that, whether they knew it or not, they still had the remnants of the mid-western hard-working immigrant ethic: they looked after their neighbor, and there was still no need to be locking up after oneself. These people still had to go to work every day and grind out a living. And there's poetry in that.

After regaling me with the fiercely independent lifestyle of the people he dealt with daily, I related to him one of the first experiences I had encountered up here that taught me anew the meaning of independence and trust. A local electrician that I'd hired to do some rough wiring at the cabin and I had walked to the end of the driveway when we saw a "No Trespassing" sign posted at the edge of a piece of property intended, I assumed, to discourage hunters. The local electrician scowled, uttered an obscenity, and said, "This guy is no local." I walked away wondering about the person who had posted the sign, wondering whether he'd thought that decision through or considered that, by doing so, he'd loaded the heavy and disdainful chip on the shoulder of others like the electrician I'd been walking with. It seemed stupid to me— merely asking for trouble. Howard identified with my point and noted that he'd seen a couple of signs in the area that were worded, "Your land is posted. Stay the hell off of mine." We laughed heartily.

Howard told his own little story about the retired colonel that he'd done work for on occasion who'd visited the area, was pleased with his discovery, and bought an eighty-acre slice. After he'd been there for a little while and managed to rub his neighbors the wrong way by hanging "no trespassing" signs on his property, he approached one of them when a few of his hunting friends came to visit him and asked, "Hey, is it ok if we hunt on *your* land?" It hadn't taken Howard long to adopt the "insider" mentality. Perhaps he'd carried it into Herbster with him.

And Howard had encountered other "outsiders" who'd

carried that individualistic insider perspective with them. He drifted from his recollections of Freud's study of DaVinci— in which Freud had attributed DaVinci's genius to his asexual nature—to his friend Stewart, another "renaissance man" of sorts who had owned a large upscale bookstore on Michigan Avenue in Chicago. Stewart was a "real character" and author in his own right who wrote children's books. When Howard built Stewart's kitchen in his place out on Bark Point, Stewart had been on his way to Chicago to deliver a lecture. To Howard, Stewart, like other "people with talent and genius, never retire, but keep working at what most interests and energizes them." They may trade their interests in for new ones, but "they never lose their curiosity or their desire to learn or discover more," Howard said.

Stewart, nearly ninety then, had invited Howard to attend a memorial for the death of his wife, and he'd felt deeply honored. He recalled that a rabbi presided over Stewart's casting of his wife's ashes from a bridge over a small pond on his property. Always the character, Stewart informed Howard the last time he saw him that "this is the last time I'm coming up here without a woman."

Howard and I agreed that part of what made the South Shore intriguing were the oddballs, freaks, misfits, pirates, crazies, thieves, artists, and writers that disappear into and emerge from the woods without warning. But the South Shore will not be attractive to everyone. Certainly, there were those, like Sally, who'd grown up here, gone away for one reason or another, and found their way back because they liked and knew it and had people or land here. But there were others—strangers, aliens, outsiders, who sought the solitude, and came to settle in, or bury themselves deeply, or become invisible. Some were drifters, but some had come because they wanted to become someone else. Artists, crafts people.

CHAPTER 5

Howard University's Core Curriculum: Class Convenes At The Shop

"...you've got to ask yourself a question: Do I feel lucky? Well, do ya, Punk?"
--Dirty Harry

It was late afternoon on a warm and lazy late-August Thursday. The scrapers, water trucks, and front-end loaders were grinding robotically to the end of a day's nearly endless loops up and down route 13 in front of Howard's shop as they readied the newly widened surface for paving. We were in the shop, and we'd be staying late. My object was to learn more about the place where Howard did his work, how and why he'd set it up the way he had, and how he worked in it. Now was the perfect time. Howard was knocking off for the day, putting the shop and the chickens he'd bought and housed in the bi-level little pen to sleep. There'd be time later for me to spend days watching Howard and the shop cooperate, to listen to it whine, growl, and scream. But I wanted Howard to render an artist's interpretation of the still life that was the shop.

Necessarily, Howard took me over some old ground here. He'd mentioned before that the shop had undergone a number of transitions, before and during his ownership. When he'd begun to fashion it to his own purposes, he had about twelve-hundred square feet—a thirty by forty-foot space. This wood-clad steel Butler building had originally served as a restaurant, and, during that period, had survived a fire. It had been partitioned off and used for a number of purposes before Sally's brother Hank and Howard had removed the barriers. When Sally retired and moved back to the South Shore, he bowed to her plan to open a gift and craft shop at the front of the building; the only thing left for him to do was to expand his shop area outward.

Three years later, he added the space that now provides him a total of twenty-eight by thirty-six feet in his own shop, and, when he did, he expanded Sally's area as well. Howard directed my attention toward the front end of the shop, above the walkway that led out to the gift shop; the space he'd created would provide some storage for the inventory of rustic furniture that he was slowly building.

So far, he'd built up a backlog of finished and partly finished pieces, some of them occupying that space above the walkway and the others carefully filling the east and front portion of the shop. Those pieces ran the gamut from small end tables and bookcases to hefty dining room tables crafted from thick, cross-cut pine slabs with matching chairs, huge armoires, and entertainment centers.

The variety of the work done and in progress spoke clearly that Howard liked to have several jobs working concurrently. Howard explained that, besides the inventory of pieces he'd been building and the cabinet jobs he'd contracted to do, he'd always got a number of "pet jobs," the ones that artistically appealed to him, even though these didn't pay particularly well. Smiling slyly, he said that Sally urged him to work on the "money" jobs—he gently mimicked her practical advice to "take the money, take the money, Howard." But, he said, he hadn't given in to that quite yet.

Since Howard and I had just returned from his friend Wally Veitmeier's place with a contract to do a big kitchen job, I asked him how he'd manage the space for it. It was here that

Howard retraced the thinking behind his layout of the shop. There was no radial arm saw present, he said, since they had become outdated by the emergence of the compound slides—the chop saws. The work flow determined the layout, and he went on to describe the flow of the cabinet work he'd soon be doing.

First, Howard reminded me that virtually everything he did in the shop was custom work—except for the inventory of rustic pieces he'd been building a little backlog of, every job he did was unique. So he'd set the shop up to perform his work comfortably. No matter how much room he had, it would never be enough, he said. Therefore, the saws and machines that he employed the most dominated the space. Since he rarely had to use a lathe in the construction of his furniture jobs, he didn't have one usurping valuable shop space.

Several big machines discreetly shared the work area: the band saw, the smaller table saw, the heavy-duty table saw, the shaper. He had a lathe on wheels, because he used one so seldom; it's a piece of machinery, he noted, for hobbyists mostly. He'd located the compound slide saw on a platform and its six-foot cutting surface with mounted rule dead-center in the shop, immediately to the left of where he now stood over the business end of the large table saw.

Directly in front of him and to the rear of the shop was a large worktable used primarily for stock layouts and glue-ups. All the way up the shelved wall to the right of the layout table were housed a collection of routers, sanders, drills, a couple of biscuit machines, and a hand-held planer, along with countless clamps and containers full of fasteners.

Howard stopped in mid-description and moved to that shelved wall, where he lifted a wide variety of those power hand tools down to the table. "I've got most of these tools dedicated to specific jobs that perform particular functions for me," he said. He directed my attention to three heavy duty routers, each one dedicated to the construction of raised panel cabinet doors, each with a different cutter set and calibrated. He used these specific routers hundreds of times a year. It's all about efficiency, he emphasized. The seven electric drills he carried down to the table each were fitted with a particular bit, enabling him to "just reach for them when I need them."

Howard had fully considered efficiency on the side of the shop to the left of the compound slide. On the far side of the room, he'd set up his thickness planer, allowing about twenty feet of clear space on both the input and output side.

Parallel to the planer stood a twenty-four-inch-thickness sander for handling wide pieces of stock, next to which perched a band saw on wheels to enable Howard to move it in and out when he needed to cut rough scallops in the legs of the furniture he'd been making. Because much of his rustic furniture required a lot of dado cutting, he'd set up one particular small table saw to do it. Clearly, Howard had calculated the precise selection and arrangement of these machines.

And, of course, since he was a master carpenter and registered grown-up, he now owned all of the tools that he'd ever need, right? I couldn't believe I was hearing myself, a frustrated backyard mechanic, ask such a question! Howard generously responded, "There's no such thing." If one should ever reach that point, "then one just starts to upgrade."

This was, he reminded me, a "one-man shop." For a while, he employed a helper named Doug, who'd hired on with Howard specifically to learn finish carpentry. It took time to demonstrate and explain what he was doing and then to repair all of the screw-ups that would surely occur while an apprentice was learning. With Doug, it was a "break-even deal" over the period of a few months. At one time, earlier on, Jerry Tow had helped him with a cabinet job in the shop; there was a thirty-day delivery deadline on the job, so Jerry's help was enlisted, and they brought it in just under the wire, but that was a very special case. Normally Howard worked by himself.

Certainly, in his years contracting in Virginia and Maryland, he'd trained many people. In order to keep up with the huge jobs he was overseeing back then, he had to hire unskilled people and train them on the fly. But, as far as shop work was concerned, one "can't sue unskilled people;" he'd be on the hook. Besides, if he was going to impart some knowledge about his craft, he'd rather do it the way we were doing it—solitarily, talking out loud to himself and his chickens as he did customarily, and working without intrusion.

And let's not forget about the damned chickens, the other residents of the shop whose location Howard had planned with every bit as much calculation as the tools of his trade. Their presence had been all about the semi-solitude that Howard craved, and the birds contributed to it. The chickens had been reduced to one, the other killed by a goshawk that descended for a big lunch one early afternoon when they were pecking the ground inside the little pen Howard had built for them outside the shop. Howard was angry only for a moment. "Let it go," he said. 'It's nature's economy." But, originally, and for over a year, there had been only one. Biddy.

He'd never intended to bring a chicken into the shop. It all happened as a result of accumulating a huge pile of wood shavings and offering them to anyone who wanted them. His good friend Mike Iverson felt like most folks on the South Shore—that he should give Howard something in return for those shavings. That quid pro quo turned into a chicken. Mike came by and asked him if he wanted one, and, if so, if he minded that it still had its feathers. Howard expected something entirely different when Mike came by the next day with a live chick. After watching "the poor thing…shaking like a leaf," he realized that he could never kill it and decided to keep it until he could give it away to someone else.

Fat chance. But Howard had made an interesting point. It never occurred to him to turn the gift down or say he didn't want it. Howard observed that, "if someone is gracious enough to bring you a gift," you accept it and thank them before backing off to figure what to do with it. Sally didn't really care one way or another if he kept it, and, even if she did, that wouldn't have altered Howard's very independent outlook—"It's my territory."

What was he thinking? Almost nothing, probably. He'd

always liked small animals—he had a chicken as a pet when he was a kid and he liked the thing. He also stressed that chickens make very good pets. Biddy fully imprinted on him, followed him around like a dog, "stopped when I stopped, when I sat down it sat down," and, if Howard was ever talking to someone, it always made a point of situating itself between him and the other side of the conversation.

Once, to demonstrate how totally bonded to him Biddy was, Howard instructed a friend to watch closely when they walked away and left Biddy by herself. Howard promised that, in no time, Biddy would follow him across the shop and stay with him for the duration of their conversation. Sure enough. She needed to be a part of everything that he did, and "one grows attached to a creature like that."

Over the course of Biddy's life in the shop, lots of people became attached to her. Little children would sneak back from Sally's gift shop with their parents to see and carry on with Biddy, and many people from out of town would return repeatedly just to see how the chicken was doing. Howard gradually achieved, for Herbster, minor celebrity status. In fact, the bird got its picture in the local paper; Sally, always the canny promoter, arranged it and sent in the accompanying article. Howard had a little bench set up next to his chop saw, and, whenever he was working in that area, Biddy would follow, flying up to the bench to watch him when he used it. That's the picture that Sally took and sent in to the local rag.

But all good things must come to an end, and it came to pass that the bird was deathly ill. When she died, a physician acquaintance of Howard opined that she was morbidly obese—she'd ballooned to about sixteen pounds. She was a hybrid rock, known in the trade as a broiler, "hybridized to gain weight very fast and get to maturity so that they could be brought quickly to market—a designer breed." So, clearly, Biddy hadn't croaked because visitors were feeding her too much. She'd simply exceeded her life expectancy, zoomed past it to become a huge bird with a stratospheric cholesterol count ripe for a heart attack.

When she died, he thought he'd be happy not to have a big bird around the shop pecking at his shoe laces, occasionally offering her head to the chop saw, and sending Howard gliding one-footed through a minefield of chicken crap. However, when, after a couple of weeks, he realized that he missed having her around, that constant and unconditional company, Howard and Sally found two chickens to replace Biddy—Biddy II and Henny. But with a decided difference.

Whereas the first chicken had arrived serendipitously, dropped like an orphan at the door, Howard went after the next batch with zeal and intentionality. Suddenly, it wasn't just one chicken, and Howard did some careful research into getting the breeds and age-levels he wanted. He bought two because he wanted them to be company for each other, and he chose a gentle breed because lots of small city kids would be stopping specifically to see the chickens.

He told the lady he was purchasing them from that he wanted a Rhode Island Red and a Barred Rock. But, as he reminded me, "you don't order one chicken—the minimum order is twenty-five." Since the woman's father raised chickens, they agreed to simply tack on to his order the two that Howard would be buying. And he didn't want freshly hatched chickens because of the care that they would require. Besides, they needed to be at least a couple of weeks old so he could ascertain that they were female, because he couldn't risk having a big rooster in the shop flying low and terrorizing the kids.

By the time the chickens had arrived at two and a half weeks old, one of two things had occurred. Either Howard's local star had risen even higher, combined with his other eccentricities, or the chickens had become celebrities in their own right. Either way, the new chickens' presence impacted the volume of traffic herding into Sally's shop. Many returning customers, stopping by after winter to check on Biddy, were thrilled to find the new ones. Sally, hearing us talk about the chickens, sauntered into the shop to attest to their drawing power—people did, in fact, come to see "those damned chickens," she said.

Sally also found it "weird" that some people came by asking Howard about that "trained chicken that he had." He admitted freely that he'd never really done any of that; Biddy had been, as he said, like a dog who'd grown accustomed to his commands. It was true that he would frequently say in a conversational tone, "Say, Biddy, are you about ready for your supper?" And Biddy would come running. What a surprise. That's not training, we agreed, but a kind of vocal tonality that she was reacting to. An insinuating and coquettish "take a flying fuck at the moon" delivered both with the proper tonal emphasis and a handful of seeds might have worked just as effectively.

Sally had locked the doors and headed home to prepare supper for the three of us, still faking displeasure at Howard having called her "the bag lady" for again planning to serve the kind of wine that comes from a box with a spigot. While Howard fed the chickens a final time, the slab top of the rustic dining room table caught my eye. I asked him whether he'd gotten some confirmation that the lines of furniture he'd decided to build now—the mission and rustic—had found an enthusiastic audience. He responded that his customers were largely cabin people, and the kinds of furniture that filled their homes in the city simply didn't work in cabins. Certainly, he'd contracted to build the occasional solid oak raised panel entertainment center with disappearing doors—and one huge armoire in "blue pine" waiting to be delivered loomed up behind the chop saw— but only occasionally. Practically, he understood his trade was largely country and mission styles, most of which he built in knotty pine. When people came up here, Howard explained, they got into a "cabin mode," which translated into smaller, more rugged, and naturally fragrant pieces.

As we headed out to our ancient cars, Howard paused a moment to recall still another kind of shop tool that he'd neglected to show me. Frequently, he said, the creating modes associated with doing customized work required him to construct the tool he'd need to create the finished piece of work.

Some years ago, when he was building some Formica

counters and cabinets with some very weird angles for Andrews Air Force Base, he discovered that, to use a router on the substrate of the Formica, he had to make and mount several feet on the bottom of the router at various angles to be able to complete his pattern. He'd made lots of patterns and jigs to perform a specific woodworking operation. If he knew that in the future he'd be repeating the job he made it for, he'd try to remember to save it. Otherwise, he'd toss it.

As he crawled in behind the wheel, he laughed and recalled picking up one of the jigs he'd saved and forgetting completely what it was made to do. Once that specific job was done, he said, "you wipe it from your mind."

CHAPTER 6

The University Mission Statement: "Wood Is A Living Thing," And Other Related But Less Vital Speculations

> "In work thy rightful interest should be, nor even in its fruits, let not thy motive be the fruit of work, to no-work let not thine attachment be.
> --*Bhagavad Gita*

By the time we'd gotten to the house, Sally was in the process of bringing the kitchen to its knees. The house wept with the deep aromas of slowly braised chuck, onions, carrots, celery, and potatoes. Sally threw together the sliced mixture of freshly picked lettuce, tomatoes, and radishes Howard had reaped from his garden and drew a glass of red from the wine box—almost like fresh-squeezed, I wanted to whisper smartly. There was still some time before dinner for me to steer Howard from the tools he used on the wood to the wood itself and what it meant to him.

"Wood is a living thing" is an aphorism that I'd heard Howard utter so many times that it had become for me a Howardism, a Gregorian incantation within the liturgy that celebrates Howard's religion of carpentry. Why, when I hear Howard say it, I might as well be hearing that old Kung Fu master Cain, balancing motionless on one foot, the other leg raised and bent balletically above knee-level, his bowed head nearly touching the thumbs of both hands brought together in a namaste, surrounded by the broken wreckage of fallen adversaries and barroom furniture, intoning the measured syllables: "Wood is a living thing."

And I was quizzing Howard on it again, before supper. There's no joke here. Mine is the stupid response of the unbeliever struck to dumbness by the unfaltering strength of Howard's creed. When you think about it, it's a phrase that's filled with truth as well as wonder, the rational and the ineffable. And, besides, I loved to hear him say it. Don't get me wrong—I'm more than certain that Howard was not the only one who said it. The truth of the statement seems almost a Masonic mystery, a password into the fraternity of masters who see their relationship with the stuff they work as reciprocal. There's no question that Howard's full investment in the systole and diastole of the wood he cut, dried, shaped, and fastened into a new state of being gave him life as well. I remain sure that Howard wouldn't have lived long without the anticipation of the synergy between him and the fibrous, grainy, knotty, variously dense and hard wood he crafted.

So there. Take that. It seemed only appropriate, then, that Howard and I should sit for a while before and after supper to talk about what that statement meant to him. I'll admit now that (a) the idea for this topic was mine and that (b) I had great and feverish expectations about where this subject would take us.

And so it was also appropriate that the big-headed, neckless, bull-chested, and lame Hephaistos of an elf should disappoint me. It wasn't that nothing was there, or nobody was home. Hell, Howard was about as deep a practical philosopher as I was ever likely to find, graduate school-trained or not. It just turned out that—like the teachings of the Zen master—the statement was so transparent that it could bear no unpacking, no stupid intellectualizing, particularly from the uninitiated. Howard dismissed the question as if he knew he was talking to an apostate.

Howard deflected the question even before I could ask it. Very quickly we found ourselves embroiled in an active rehash of a portion of a previous night's Jay Leno show when my esteemed governor three years earlier, Jesse the Body Ventura, jack of all trades, master of none except hype and self-promotion, vamped like a painted tart over Jay's question of whether he aspired to "higher office." Howard was avoiding my interview of him by dragging in the subject of still another. One interviewee, my governor, had been mugging for the camera, with little to say but with a pathological need to say it anyway, while the other was Howard, knowledgeable, a man of few words who generally let his tools speak for him, who was performing his verbal rendition of "duck and cover." When Jay had asked Ventura how things were going with his job as Governor of Minneso-o-o-o-o-dah and whether he would ever consider running for president, Ventura did his cocky St. Vitus' Dance thing with his neck that made him look like the biggest bobble-headed Buddha doll ever. His voice dripping with testosterone, he confided, "Well, Jay, you ne-e-e-e-ever kno-o-o-ow."

And then Howard went off. What an overreaching, arrogant ass, Howard averred. He couldn't believe that the folks of Minnesota had elected that vain, stupid, loud-mouthed lout, except for the other "professional bull-shitting politicians" that were running against him who, by comparison, were making Ventura look good and honest, if stupid. We chatted about the fact that no one had really stepped out and distinguished himself in that governor's race; no one with any charisma had been running, he observed, and I noted that Ventura was fortunate to be running against two "Johnny One-Noted" guys who were almost clones of each other, saying pretty much the same thing, except that one was saying it more to business while the other courted union folks and teachers. There had been very little to choose, with Jesse responding to questions directly in ways that people weren't used to hearing.

For one reason or another, Howard made some connection between one of the candidates and the famous lawyer in the old Scopes "monkey" trial, Clarence Darrow. Quickly, Howard's mind had pole-vaulted beyond that and back to Tennessee where he had worked for a while. He remembered the little basket factory there and how they made them; he got onto the machine that cut the logs, those living things, out of which the baskets were made. He said he loved watching stuff like that.

Rather like my having watched Howard a couple of days before performing one in a series of glue-ups in the process of making the cabinets he'd taken on for Wally Veitmeier. As he'd prepared the seven-eighth-inch-thick boards for gluing, he patiently told me that "you've got to have an odd number of bar clamps." He could use either three or five— he'd chosen to use three this time. The bottom clamp—the one that you lay on the table with the wood—should be the same diameter and the same type of clamp, he said as if this dance he was doing with the wood absorbed him as much now as it did the first time. And the clamps should be attached so that the wood lies flat on the table. Never allow the glue to touch the clamp, he warned. After he'd cut the stock, he applied the glue to each piece with an even, unbroken, and steady bead, like a pastry chef squeezing icing artistically on chocolate ganache. He carefully tightened down opposing clamps to enable the glue to set.

As he moved fluidly through the process, Howard continued to talk to himself and then to me, chatting barely audibly about loving small towns. He also loved to lurk in the shadows of his small village, knowing that the big companies were catering to the needs of a generalized audience, whereas he could hang back in the weeds and fill up the cracks of what large companies couldn't and wouldn't make. The niche. I mentioned that in some places Howard couldn't afford to fill that niche; it would be too cost-prohibitive for him to rent the space and pay the utility bills. And then he'd be out of business.

Howard explained how he filled his own niche in such a cost-prohibitive market back in Maryland. For years, he did his remodels, projects, and cabinet jobs on that very basis. He purposely looked for and marketed himself to do jobs that other carpenters didn't want. Because he could always get his price. Besides, he always liked the prospect of doing those out-of-the-ordinary jobs. The odd stuff.

Like the CBS job, Sally chimed in, having entered the shop without our hearing her. It was the only job that he'd ever gotten a standing ovation for, Howard recalled. A contractor that he had often worked with many years before had been doing some remodeling for someone associated with the headquarters of the mid-Atlantic region of CBS Records; someone said that he needed a fifteen-foot-long cabinet with a bunch of cubby-holes for TV's and VCR's to be installed in their conference room.

When his friend referred CBS to Howard, CBS records quickly contracted for him to build it. Upon returning a couple of days after he'd installed it to make some final adjustments, he received his standing ovation. They then invited him to listen to some "history," their new release called "We Are the World." And that's the way Howard had gotten most of his work—through referrals. Good work. Good will. Associations. Knowing and respecting the wood.

After dinner that night at Sally's kitchen table, I confronted him again with the question: "What do you mean when you say 'Wood is a living thing?'" Looking at me as if he hadn't heard me before, or that he'd mistaken the drift of my question, he straightened and said, "It's all about water content." It seemed that the "living" issue revolved less around wood's intrinsic nobility, although I think Howard invested in that too, than around complex effects of water content. He wasn't sure when he'd learned this. However, he recalled reading many years back that, if you observed a piece of wood through an electron microscope at high power, it looks like "a handful of drinking straws." That's why, he explained, water enters a lot more quickly through the ends than it ever could through its sides. Once water is in the cells of the wood, it becomes "free water." The water in the walls of the cells is much more reluctant to come out: "Once wood is dried to a good moisture content, and it gets wet, that's only free water, and it won't take very long to dry it again."

A quick lesson, simply and patiently set forth. But there was more. At some point, Howard realized that, when he was approaching a particular kind of job, he had to be careful to select the wood according to its water content. When I asked whether anything beyond simple experience could guide a person on how long wood needed to be left to dry thoroughly, Howard shook his head while reluctantly allowing a little room for picking up such information from reading. Different woods, he said, give up their water at different rates. He preferred working with hardwoods that had a moisture content of about eight per cent. He paused to clarify that the relative percentage of moisture in wood referred to the percentage by weight of what a particular species of wood would weigh when dry.

When Howard built an expensive piece of furniture, he liked to know what kind of home it was entering and the nature of its "living' environment—heavily humid; dry; or somewhere in between; whether it would be exposed to a lot of heat or air-conditioning. He dealt mostly with cabin people whose cabins usually had no climate control, so he liked to use a lot of pine in the cabinets and furniture that he built for them. When he brought pine into his shop and allowed it to reach a state of equilibrium, he knew that corresponded similarly to conditions in the cabins that he'd be building furniture for. Taking one example, he said that white pine would reach equilibrium in the shop at about ten or twelve percent on an average day. When it reached that point, he felt comfortable working with it. Of course, "the average day will vary according to the ambient air, fluctuate, and one would have to watch that," he warned.

Thus, when one worked with solid wood, "you have to constantly be aware that it will expand and contract dependent upon the heat and the humidity in the environment, with the changes in moisture content." When he built something with solid wood, as opposed to plywood, he needed to "engineer" it to account for those potential changes: "When you make up your plan for that piece, you could get into a bad coefficiency problem if you had an end-grained section joined with a cross-grained section, because they'll expand and contract at different rates. Therefore, you need to anticipate that in advance."

But, I pressed, what kinds of water content problems

would he encounter if he were planning to work with an expensive piece of wood—walnut, say? How would he know when it was ready to work? Howard responded that he has always bought his wood from the sawmill. For walnut, he'd be looking for eight percent water content. If, just for the sake of argument, he bought it from a reputable hard wood dealer that was trading in kiln-dried stock, and if that facility was such that the wood would be kept protected, he'd expect to be able to work with that wood immediately.

Although he now bought his walnut from sawmills, he'd actually possessed his own kiln on two different occasions, in the basement of his own house, and, on both occasions, he'd built them, giving him complete control over that drying process. Having his own kiln permitted him a wide latitude in buying materials; instead of being dependent upon a local hardwood dealer and the relative quality of his materials, he could go directly to the source, the sawmill, select what he wanted, and then finish drying it to his specs. It gave him, he said, "a small amount of vertical integration." And that resulted in making him more competitive pricewise, too.

To show me what vertical integration could mean for even a small business-owner like him, Howard related a story about a friend of his who had cut maple from "Janklow's forty." Howard bought the logs, had them sawn on the spot, transported them to the shop, air-dried them, planed and processed them, built various pieces of furniture and cabinets from them, and then personally delivered those finished pieces to his customers in the trailer he'd constructed and pulled behind his old construction van.

Amazing efficiency and entrepreneurial independence that would be hard to match in the city.

I switched my line of questioning to the status of the wood that Howard bought at Albert's sawmill. I wanted to know how long that maple he last bought had been lying around—had it been cut three months earlier? four? Howard explained that the sawyers didn't want logs to lay for longer than two months. So, when Howard allowed that first batch of maple he bought from his friend to stand, he used his experience to factor how long it would take. When he really needed it, summer had arrived, and the atmospheric conditions of that season, at the latitude of the South Shore, impacted upon how well the wood had dried. The maple had come down to about fourteen percent in a well-ventilated area over a couple of months by mid-summer. They were then "stickered," outside, each layer of maple held apart from the one above and below it and given air by wood spacers.

At that point, the wood was ready for the kiln—certainly, he noted, its moisture content would fluctuate, from fourteen to sixteen percent and back again, but it wasn't going to fall much lower. Once in the kiln, it dried at moderate temperature, and in about a week he had it down to about eight percent. He directed me to a manual printed by the government that contained the numbers for moisture content for every species, as well as the relative temperatures at which they could be dried. But beyond that, he said, "you go by the seat of your pants, checking the moisture content in the wood that's being dried every day."

I was curious about the effects of moisture content of worked wood. What would and could the wood actually *do*? Had Howard, upon revisiting a job that he'd done, observed the effects of moisture on his "living thing?" Howard recalled a job that he and an associate had worked on a wood floor, and then returned at some later time to see that floor buckled, perhaps as much as a foot in some places. This had been an oak strip floor. There had been some mild flooding, and "you wouldn't have believed the expansion that had taken place from the wood having gotten wet."

One of the most common locations for water to cause contraction, he said, occurs at the inside trim of the house, where two pieces are joined at a right angle at a 45-angle cut. If they had been installed when they were wet, "they will separate from each other in the heel, not the point, of the cut." The following afternoon in the shop, Howard took me straight to the inside door for an example of this type of contraction.

Displaying my ignorance like a purple badge again, I observed that what he'd been telling me was sophisticated. I carefully ventured that people that I'd seen buying wood at a home improvement center might have considered the straightness and trueness of the two-by-fours they'd be buying without ever expressing any interest in their relative moisture content.

Even Socrates had never had it so easy as I'd just made it for Howard. Smiling far too knowingly, Howard said that a lot of what I may have observed related directly to where I and my over-achieving friends were buying our wood. This, in a way, was wood for dummies—wood that had been kiln-dried already or that had been sitting around for a long time, covered and wrapped, in box cars, in warehouses, on the flat-beds of Freightliners. But, he said, if this issue was important to professionals, it should be important to backyarders, too.

Important enough to educate ourselves—but, if so, how? Howard indicated that moisture content needn't induce paranoia for the average DYI-er. "If it's two-by-fours, the shrinkage is not that really important. If it's a piece of furniture, being an amateur, you're probably going to go to a retail dealer where they have kiln-dried stuff already. Once you'd become a hobbyist or a serious woodworker and were using a larger volume of wood, then you need to make this an important issue." Such a person, he said, needs to own a moisture meter, along with "engineering the pieces that you're going to build with the factors of contraction and expansion in mind."

I remarked that the South Shore seemed like a really dicey environment to build in, both outside and inside—a true four-season area, a long winter, high humidity, steep changes in the temperature gradient, the expectation of lots of snow and freezing and thawing, and hot stretches in the summer. And the Lady of the Lake changed the weather and fed the humidity content of the air momentarily. If, then, there was an esthetic reason for Howard to use pine up here, was there a practical reason for using it, too? Bingo. First, he said, most of the cabinets built for cabins in this region would be white pine, a wood much more stable than some others like popple, though popple works well as paneling. The bottom line, said Howard, was that, "unless you have an absolutely controlled atmosphere, wood is going to be affected by changes in that environment."

Howard yanked me back to the coefficency factor again. It can cause things to break apart and must be considered in general construction. Frost heaves can draw the coefficiency factor in. In addition, he warned, "you wanted to use the same type of foundation for your new addition as was used for the old because you wanted the two portions, once joined, to expand and contract at the same rate and in the same way. The house is going to move, and it would be good if the new portion moved at the same rate as the old part!" Ouch.

Nearly hyperventilating under the weight of what, for me, was new knowledge, I struggled to localize it to a particular situation. Could you, I asked, use moisture to get the wood to move the way you want, so you could shape it the way you want to shape it? I was thinking about Howard's application of a steamer to shape the base and banister of the bird cage that Howard had built at my place to stabilize the pine circular stairs he'd installed. Howard laughed and told me that I'd need to straighten out my terminology. "If you get the wood hot enough or wet enough," he explained, "you get the wood 'limber.'" 'If I wanted to bend some wood," he said, "first you need a form that you're going to wrap the wet and heated piece around. You're going to force the wood to a specific configuration; you need to move that piece immediately out of the steamer and into the form without any delay. The form must be there before anything else happens." So, then, this was an engineering problem. One that I planned for Howard to return to later and puzzle out for me.

As for the steamer, "It's extremely low-tech," he said. It doesn't have to hold pressure: "You make a box with a hole on the bottom on one end where you place a device—a container of water and a heat source—and at the other end of the box, another hole, a relief hole on the top, so that the heat can convect into the box, traveling the length of it, surrounding the piece that you have placed in there." Howard couldn't be specific about how long to leave the wood in the kiln; it's largely an educated guess, particularly if one hasn't accumulated a lot of everyday experience doing this sort of thing. As Howard put it in his acerbic way, "it feels awfully hot. Is it almost ready? Well, let's put it back in the box and leave it in here for another hour or so until it's done." Nothin' says lovin' like something in the oven.

Before I staggered out to my car, the cream between my ears completely curdled from the lesson he'd given me, I smartly asked Howard why he'd ever built himself a steamer. After all, unless I'd really missed the boat, Howard had never been into boatbuilding. Very quietly and matter-of-factly, he smiled and said, "That was for your stairs. After I got through with it, I dismantled it and used the boards for something else." It was always the same for Howard; he built it, in this case, because it served a specific purpose. But it was always about practicality. Just four boards held together with a couple of blocks on the end.

Maybe so. But, when he began to describe his construction of the kiln in more detail, it sounded much more like another engineering problem. He subscribed to *Woodworking Magazine*, the best periodical for professionals and advanced handymen, he said. He had all the back issues, extending all the way back to 1975. That's where he read about how to build a kiln. He knew that, when he was ready, he could go back and research it. The inside dimensions of this kiln were seven feet tall, five feet wide, and about 104 inches long. The stock to be dried, he said, usually "eight-foot rough stuff" (most of his were at 104 inches, so he didn't have to trim too many pieces) must be stacked and stickered so that the air could filter through and around it. On the "off" side, he built "about an eight-inch clear chamber from floor to ceiling." The "core side," the heat source side, "where you physically enter the chamber yourself, is a little bit wider, allowing you to get into it, and is where your heat source is located." He used a little two-burner stove to supply the heat.

The kiln must be thoroughly insulated, he said: "You build

your stack up to about shoulder height, and from that point to the ceiling you must have a curtain wall, and this curtain wall is where you have two fans, constantly pulling the hot air from the heat source side over to the eight-inch chamber on the other side of the stack, the far side, creating a pressure where it forces the hot air continuously through the stack, so it's constantly circulating, hot to the other side, back through, and bringing moisture, heating the wood and causing the moisture to percolate out." In order to expel this moisture, he opened two vents that he'd installed—a high and a low one. The air would convect out, bringing in cold air as it exhausted the hot wet air. After a limited amount of time, he'd close the vent again.

"Unless you get really technical, and you're drying something like oak," he said, "you don't have to get high-tech." In that case, sometimes steam is actually introduced at a given time to release the tension of the wood. Howard's second kiln was much more low-tech than the first one because he learned how to situate his ceiling vents in relation to the wood. He didn't need to have "a wet bulb, a dry bulb, and two different temperature gauges to measure the moisture of the air, which you'd need if you were working a commercial kiln, but it worked."

The thick stillness of dusk suddenly exploded into a downpour so heavy and dark that the community center across the street disappeared into it. The capricious Lake Lady again. Sally intruded sarcastically above the tattoo the rain was beating on the roof to comment about the effects environmental of having a kiln down in their basement in Maryland: "Whatever you do," she said, "make sure that it's lined, because it's hotter than hell, and it was in the house. And be sure as hell that you don't dry that damned oak, because it takes forever and smells like shit." Howard roared with laughter, and heartily agreed with her, except that, to his nose, the long, hot drying oak in the basement "smelled like piss." Oak takes about thirty days, even in a good commercial kiln, he said, because it gives up its water reluctantly. Thus, "you must go along with a certain temperature level at a particular moisture content, or you'll ruin the wood."

But it's the initial pressure, from outside to inside, that causes an unequal situation: "Sometimes that breakdown in the oak doesn't show up until you start to work it. When the outside is harder than the inside, you hear the term 'case hardened'; you'll get some severe checks in there. At your final stages with oak, you can go up to about 170 degrees, and it's hard to contain that kind of heat. Which is why Sally claims that she experienced what she did with that heat." Sally demurely retorted, "bullshit."

Howard assured me that it's illegal to run a kiln inside your house, but everyone in his neighborhood back in Baltimore knew he did it. All the neighbors were always asking him what the hell kind of wood he was drying that week. Sally and he had investigated how much money would be needed to set Howard up in a commercial location—about a half a million dollars for a shop in Prince George's County. "Forget it," he said. Sally was dead-right about the hellish environment he was creating by running it, particularly in the summer. As Howard confirmed, no amount of insulating was going to stave it off. But, nonetheless, Sally was "OK" with him putting it down there. Her eyes twinkled as he recited her pragmatic philosophy: it "has always been 'Take the money, Howard!'" Beautiful.

And there endeth the evening's lesson.

CHAPTER 7

An Independent Study With The Master: A Day In The Life

Benedict: A miracle! here's our own hands against our hearts. Come, I will have thee; but, by this light, I take thee for pity.
Beatrice: I would not deny you; but, by this good day, I yield upon great persuasion; and partly to save your life, for I was told you were in a consumption.
--Shakespeare, *Much Ado About Nothing*

The time had come for a tenderfoot's view of how Howard did his work and managed his day. The entire day, and a typical one. What the hell. A couple of days had passed since the sandwich of practical wisdom, politics, kiln-building, and the chemistry of wood stacked high like seasoned zucchini slices around Sally's wonderful dinner. I'd learned a little about the wood Howard worked, and it was time to watch him work it. What better way to understand what Howard did and how he did it than to be in the shop and watch as it unfolded.

And that's where I'd come that morning. As weather goes, it was not a particularly fine one for the south side of the Lake although, as Howard averred, any day on the South Shore is grand if you can open your eyes and get sufficiently vertical to see it. It was a mid-August Friday, but the freshening breeze off the

Lake on my bare arms carried the promise of fall. I exited my car at the west side of Howard's shop to muted sunshine, mottled by the crowds of bulky cumulus clouds scudding southeasterly above me. It again had rained hard and continuously all night, delaying the road crews that had been widening the winding stretch of route 13 that connects Herbster to Cornucopia eight miles away. That sun darted intermittently in and out all day, the breeze wringing tame rain squalls out of those clouds when the sun disappeared. But, except for that breeze, the most palpable quality of the environment was silence. The highway work shed across the road was still, occupied only by one construction worker refueling some of the heavy machinery that would rumble into action as soon as the road bed dried a bit.

Hardly a car passed the shop at a little after 8:30am. As Howard would say later, it was another day in paradise.

The double doors located on the side of the shop were spread wide as I entered, and Howard was in the midst of conducting a mealy communion for the chickens. After exchanging greetings—Howard's welcomes were large, loud, and open, befitting survivors of the Shackleton expedition—Howard and I moved to Sally's portion of the building. She was busy preparing to open up the gift shop, and, after we lugged a few pieces of Howard's rustic furniture outside to provide a little curb appeal, we returned to his territory to pour a couple of cups of coffee from his thermos and survey the work schedule. There was no rushing Howard.

As we sat in the corner at a large pine dining room table that awaited delivery, my eye was drawn as it had been for the previous few days to a huge double-doored oak armoire that occupied the middle of the shop at the end of the chop saw and table extension. It was gorgeous, besides being monumental.

As to why the piece still stood in the shop, Howard stated that he'd just concluded the labor-intensive job of finishing it. Some nine coats of finish had been applied to the armoire's surface, he said, each of them done carefully so as not to rupture the grain of the oak. His perfectionism really revealed itself here.

He explained that he had used two coats of sealer, but, when he'd applied the water-based poly, something happened to raise the grain. He admitted that no one else would have probably seen or felt those tiny surface disturbances, but he could.

The buyer had evidently come by a couple of days before, looked at it, and concluded that it was finished. However, Sally, who had just wandered into the shop, observed that Howard was always the "final arbiter." Howard concurred: "Nothing goes out of the shop until I'm satisfied enough to have my name on it. It doesn't matter if the owner is satisfied—I've got to be satisfied." In this case, the epic finishing journey involved nine coats—two of sealer; a water-based poly; two sanding sealer coats; two coats of shellac; and two final coats of water poly. He expressed a feeling of stupidity for having to re-apply some of these layers—he had "fucked up." When I felt the finished slab doors of the armoire, my fingers felt only silk. I couldn't even see or feel the joints of the five pieces of oak Howard had glued to minimize the "cooperation" of the wood from warping. Howard, Sally, and Sally's brother Hank would personally deliver this silken cabinet with equally silk-gliding drawers to Washburn, about twenty-five miles away, and he'd need to rig his pick-up truck, still another vehicle in his fleet of Leakin' Lenas, with a rough wooden frame to support it.

It was now a little after nine and time to "get after it." The agenda?—Howard had made the boxes for some of the cabinets he'd be building over the next several weeks for the Veitmeiers, who were equally unconcerned about deadlines since Mr. Veitmeier had considerable remodeling to do to prepare his kitchen space for what Howard would be building and installing. By the end of the day, Howard hoped to have constructed the face frames for the boxes, prepared the interior part of the boxes to receive drawers, and begun to fashion the drawers.

A very typical day, he assured me. What could be better?

The first step would involve planing down some stock for the face frames. In no time, the planer was whining like a low-flying Cessna. With my hands cupped tightly over my ears,

Teaching Fools

Howard set up a couple of short sawhorses to lay his long pieces of pine on. As he fed them into the planer, he kept checking the boards' thickness. The object was to bring the rough stock from one-and-$^1/_{16}$" to ¾", and that required sending the boards through four times. He noted, as the machine wound down, that, if he were gluing, he'd bring them down to 7/8" and then later glue them again.

Howard was interrupted briefly when Sally entered with a slab of pine with a design of pine trees cut into its face for Howard to take the roughness from. The synergy between the two was magnetizing. Sally responded to Howard's falsely gruff "I'm working" by calling him a "dirty old man." All of this transpired in barely a couple of minutes, but the quality of their interactive "work and play" showed through. To his puckish "in a minute, honey, I'm gluing up," Sally replied that Howard was never happier than when he was "pushing people's buttons." As Sally exited with her newly sanded carved slab, Howard, a little louder and more cavalierly than was necessary, called her his "apprentice."

As he resumed his work on the table saw, it was clearer than ever that he'd spent some time getting the set-up of the shop just the way he wanted it, for maximum efficiency. He was quick to point out that the chicken's cage, only a few feet behind the saw, had been built at the height of the saw table so that he could rest his stock on it, while the gluing-up table beyond stood just a little below the height of the saw table. That little extra height allowed him to run long pieces of stock through the saw and rest them on the table beyond it.

The birds were outside pecking away at the loose paint on the bottom of the passenger door of Howard's old Fairmont station-wagon as he worked. He stopped for a moment to remove a knot with his claw hammer from the board he was cutting. He then cut seven pieces, the last piece much narrower than the others, and then carried the remaining scrap to the chop saw before proceeding to the gluing-up table.

What a rough and ready picture Howard made as he

transferred his materials! The thick olive drab suspenders looped under his arms and clipped to the sides of his thick chino work pants, in addition to the black belt he wore; while the suspenders clearly kept his pants up underneath a fairly prosperous belly, they also served as a primitive back brace. Tucked into the pants was a well-worn pin-striped short-sleeved shirt with a collar. The work shoes appeared to have clocked about a hundred years. As he leaned to cut some of the waste at the chop saw, a patch of leathery skin showed on the crown of his head.

Every move was methodical—the arranging, cutting, discarding into the scrap box below. The shop was surprisingly quiet—no music, no contentious talk radio, no talking, except for Howard's soft running conversation with himself. Just the whirr of the tape retracting, the quiet hum of the fan in the east corner, and an occasional murmur from Howard as he measured.

It all seemed to work like a puzzle for Howard, one that he'd assembled and taken apart so many times before, one capable of reshuffling into lots of variations and permutations but still engaging and absorbing his attention. In a moment, he'd clearly made a mistake of some importance. That big sheep's head resting on nearly no neck turned to me, the eyes crinkling as his face bloomed into a toothy grin and softly uttered "shit." He'd slightly miscalculated and cut a board to the wrong length, turning it into instant scrap.

As the two chickens raced into the center of the shop and squared off under the chop saw, Howard was a study in concentration, the salt and pepper beard framing the slightly open mouth underneath the broad nose. He took a few minutes to clear from the gluing table a bunch of power tools spread across it since yesterday. I stepped to the outside door as he wrapped the cords around the assortment of routers, sanders, and pneumatic guns and put them away.

Outside the shop, one would never know it was a workday. At mid-morning, route 13 was empty. No voices. No movement.

The table now clear, Howard began the framing-up,

measuring meticulously and laying the pieces of framing stock on the table. He took great care in flipping the pieces of pine over and over, almost as if he were manipulating the controls on a foos ball table, to find just the right side to face up. That task done, he turned behind him to the well-shelved wall to look for the right tools to proceed. He reached for what he called a "dedicated drill," noting as if he were informing me for the first time that he was a strong believer in tools that he could calibrate for specific stages in the process. He stopped for a few minutes to talk again about how efficient it was for him to have a brigade of routers used only for one specific task each.

Just as Howard and I were stopping for a second cup of coffee, Bill Greene and his wife dropped by. They hailed from Chicago, were retired, and had come to the South Shore for "a spell." They were immediately drawn to the oak armoire and properly admired it.

Although Howard had confided to me more than once that he wasn't "a people person," he engaged the Greenes easily in a discussion about—what else?—the proper moisture content of wood. Bill and he spoke specifically about pine and when to work it, based on its relative dryness. The relaxed quality of their conversation underlined Howard's feeling that he had "the best of all possible worlds." Bill had been a sheet metal worker, a pipefitter. But his real love was clearly woodworking. He related how he'd been making birch plywood cabinets in Florida, and Howard and he compared loving notes about their mutual interests.

The chickens were roosting now in choric fashion on the low sawhorses beside the planer when, at about 10:40, Howard walked the Greenes out and moved back to the worktable. As he studied the pieces in front of him, he expelled the second of several "oh shits" to occur during the day. He'd forgotten to figure for the drawers, he said. From my amateur perspective, I was surprised when he said that he hadn't standardized any of these measurements. He'd think about that, he said. I'll bet.

Back from the table saw, where his hands gently moved

and caressed the pieces of stock close to and surrounding the saw blade as if he were tuning a cello, he'd begun to bring the separate pieces of the puzzle together. He applied his drill to the center piece, cutting angled holes top and bottom. It was a pocket hole jig that he was using to drill the holes. All of the boards received the same drilled treatment. He could use biscuits, he said, particularly for oak, but he'd have to wait for the glue to dry if he did.

This was the face frame that he was preparing. Using a little vice-grip clamp, he started to attach the pieces together with screws. Carefully—almost gently— he inserted the screws and secured them with his cordless screwdriver while managing the block. Nothing was hurried.

After assembling the face frame, he placed it like a template over the box to see if it fit. His realization that the bottom portion was too large elicited another "oh shit." Although he wasn't happy about disassembling the pieces, remeasuring, and recutting, he was under control, unflappable. "After all," he shrugged, "it's paradise." He noted with self-amusement that, when he cut his stock, he always cut extra, to allow for dumb mistakes" and "Murphy."

This time the face frame fit perfectly, and it was time for applying the brad gun and glue in order to securely fasten it. Howard gave me another chance to marvel at his wonderfully steady hand in applying the glue on the box front.

Howard then set about cutting a little sweep-corner angled into the end piece of the box. The purpose here was to give the cabinet a smooth and finished look. As he glued and nailed, Howard observed that he'd learned how to make cabinets this very way some fifty years ago. He noted that he rarely saw anyone performing the finished and angled operation on the end pieces anymore; he continued to do it simply because it added such a finished touch.

It was time to finish up after the nailing and gluing procedures. Howard puttied all of the little nail holes, carefully scraping and filling, working quickly and methodically across the entire face of the cabinet.

Stepping back for a moment, he said that all three cabinets, once completed, would have a piece of pine running over their bases to conceal the rough cuts. But, for now, he ran the orbital sander quickly over the areas where he had puttied. Actually, this step included an overall sanding of the face, with a quick compressed-air removal of the dust he had created. He employed another small sander to remove some roughness at the base of the frame. Afterwards, he moved that little sander over the entire face with a finer grit of paper. When I ran my hand over the cabinet, the pine pieces felt doe-skin smooth.

He gave all of the inside edges of the face the same sanding treatment. In typical perfectionist fashion, Howard continued with the orbital over the side of the box, even though he knew that side would face a wall. He simply couldn't keep his hands off any portion of his work.

In short, what he'd been doing consisted of a cavalcade of sanders, each dedicated to a particular piece of the frame and base— the orbital, the big vibrator, the small vibrator.

When we broke for lunch, he shared the usual understanding that he'd be taking a short nap before picking up where he left off. And, when I returned at 2:10, Howard was back and purposefully stalking. As I walked into the shop, he was cutting narrow pieces of plywood which would serve as fillers for the sides of the drawers for side-mounted drawer guides. They would all be cut the same in this case: a piece of pine would be laid up against the plywood piece so that it would run flush with the facing. He cut and screwed those pieces in, a total of four for each drawer.

Howard had now reached the draw-measuring stage. As he measured 4 7/8" down, he used what he called with studied incorrectness, a "little Mexican trick"—the use of a few finish nails to set the height of the drawer guides on the top level. As he speculated on the placement of a cutting board drawer and a sharp knife drawer on the top level, Sally interrupted momentarily to arrange with Howard for a time to deliver the armoire on the following Monday to Washburn; Howard wanted to allow enough time to get it there by eleven. Howard redirected his attention to the drawer layout. The two top drawers (one to accommodate a removable cutting board and big knives, along with another short draw) would sit over the middle tier of drawers that would roll out. Bigger bottom drawers would serve as bins for pots and pans.

The openings for the drawers were all 17 ½"; that being the case, Howard measured and cut them all an inch shorter. He would need to check the parallelism of those guides to each other. Howard decided to use a 22"-deep drawer; he'd go with a 10-inch-high drawer on the bottoms and 4 ½"s for the tops. That meant firing up the planer once again to mill down some stock to ½". To take these 1-and-1/16" boards down to ½" required much time and effort. However, as Howard noted, this was the most economical way of doing it.

And, true to form, Howard was still piloting the planer un-earplugged when I waved to him from the side door at 4:15. Romancing the wood proceeded without time clocks.

CHAPTER 8

Howard's Extended Campus: The Veitmeier Job

"This Doyce," said Mr. Meagles, "is a smith and engineer. He is not in a large way, but he is well known as a very ingenious man. A dozen years ago, he perfects an invention (involving a very curious secret process)...He is the most exasperating man in the world; he never complains."
--Dickens, *Little Dorrit*

It was time to hit the road. To put Howard's money where his mouth was. Or, to be more specific, it was time for me to move my insulated education about woodworking onto an actual job site. I'd been looking forward to this.

On this occasion, it was a trip into the Toolies. It required riding shotgun in Howard's far from road-worthy, headlight-less old Ford Escort (this heap had been on the business end of four deer collisions). We crept east on 13 for about a mile and a half and then veered south on Hungry Hollow Road, past the old cemetery on our right and out among the farmsteads scattered on various eighty and one-hundred-and-sixty-acre parcels. It was wide-open pastureland and hay country for a little while, until we turned right onto a rutted dirt road for about a half mile.

We could see the Veitmeier farmstead rising on the right. It was quite a spread. Wally Veitmeier, a retired aircraft mechanic with Northwest Airlines in Minneapolis, grew up here as a kid, learned all of the self-reliant skills of building, repairing, planting, and reaping that came with living on a farm, took all of those skills, along with his wife, to the cities to become an accomplished master mechanic on the big jets, and, when he retired, moved back to the outskirts of Herbster to take over the family farm once more. As we turned right into the long driveway of the Veitmeier farm, Howard was still waxing poetic about the virtues of hard work that Wally continued to exemplify during Howard's long friendship with him. This was a guy after Howard's heart, a rock-hard monument to self-sufficiency, a man's man minus chest pounding.

And there he was, ramrod straight in his middling height, emerging from the front door of the hundred-year-old farmhouse and moving quickly, smoothly, and unencumbered like the thirty-five-year-old that he hadn't been for nearly thirty years. This was a monument, alright—a salt and peppered grizzled one, equipped with all of his hair and the musculature that had enabled him to wield the heavy tools of his trade over long years. If this was retirement, Wally had clearly removed the "retiring" part of it.

As Wally strode toward the car, Howard directed my attention to the long stretch of cleared land behind the house and the barn-like shed at one end of it. This, Howard said, was Wally's landing strip, and that barn was where Wally kept his single-engine plane. Practically speaking, Howard noted, Wally had built that plane, and it was Wally who used his wealth of knowledge of aircraft engines to perform the required annual tear-down of its engine. He flew the plane regularly for relaxation and for taking aerial photographs of farmsteads, private homes, and points of interest for those who retained him.

I got out of the car and shook the vice of a hand that he thrust toward me. Howard made a little small talk about the root cellar on the side of the driveway that Wally had built and was now cultivating mushrooms in. He also pointed to other projects that Wally had underway—the improvements to the outside of the house, the apple tree plantings. It was an interesting ice-breaker for me, and Wally was cordial enough, but small talk was clearly not Wally's strong-suit. As I listened to what Wally had done, was currently involved in doing, and had on the drawing boards, I knew this was a guy, as nice as he was, who was far too busy to talk much. There were only new jobs, projects, and ideas filling his head and occupying his hands between his airplane jaunts and his twenty-mile roller-blade constitutionals.

As we ambled among the trees, up the front stoop, and through the entry of the house, I recalled what Howard had told me about Wally at the shop before we left and during the short ride to the farmstead. Wally, Howard had emphasized, was a German. That meant a couple of things to Howard proven out over their long association. Wally was a stickler for competence, craftsmanship, and detail. For Howard, that mania for precision, careful preparation, and a passion for excellence was a German trait.

Maybe. I didn't question Howard about that ethnic pigeon-holing. As Howard had unpacked Wally for me a bit, it meant that he had to know everything about a job, all of the subtle niceties, before he'd address himself to it. And his interests were far-flung; if he developed an interest in something, whether it was a problem of construction or invention or agriculture, he'd complete that task with every bit of technical accuracy that Howard indicated was a watchword in his long career in mechanics.

Another renaissance man—someone restless in his pursuit of new skills to learn and the methodology and theory for doing them. Howard smilingly pointed out to me that Wally was completely capable of building the cabinets and cupboards in the kitchen that he'd invited Howard out to do a site-visit on. But that's where things got interesting with Wally: he recognized excellence, bowed to the proven craftsmanship of others. He knew what he wanted, had so many irons in his own fire that he'd never be able to see his way to the end of them, had a plan he wanted executed, and wasn't insecure about bringing in that demonstrated craftsman to execute it. There was no discernible ego to damage in Wally—only confidence in his own intrepidity and problem-solving abilities. And Howard was the guy to do this job; Wally knew that, Howard intimated, because, in some indirect way, Wally had been interviewing Howard for this assignment for about five years now.

Howard had told me a little story weeks before that illustrated these "German" character traits in Wally. He said that Wally had broken the subject of the kitchen renovation with him five years earlier. They'd talked about it in some detail back then, and then Wally had brought it up several times over the intervening years. When I asked Howard if he ever doubted Wally's seriousness about re-doing the kitchen, Howard uttered a definitive "no." First of all, Wally, as nice as he was, didn't fool around about these things. Lots of folks kick tires, Howard said, browse over expensive equipment, or collect estimates on the cost of getting a house addition built but never follow through. Howard learned early in his dealings with Wally that, when he began to wrap his mind around an idea or project, he couldn't let go. But, in typically "German" fashion (in Howard's view again), he kept after it until finally ready to objectify it. Wally was a thinker and researcher, said Howard. He gave new meaning to the old pearl "no wine before its time" by refusing to address any job until every facet of it had been microscopically wrung out. In short, Howard liked Wally and Wally liked Howard because they were both uncompromising perfectionists.

Anyway, here we were at the Veitmeier's, ready to case the joint, listen to Wally's plan for remodeling the kitchen, locating new kitchen cabinets and a tall storage cupboard, and admire his progress with the old house. Mrs. Veitmeier greeted us graciously, offered us coffee, asked about her friend Sally, who, she was told, would be joining us later in the morning. Sally, Howard later told me, always acted as a "consultant" of sorts on these site visits. She was particularly valuable in kitchen jobs, providing practiced suggestions about where cabinets should be located, where to situate breakfast nooks, and how the insides of those cabinets should be fitted. She would provide an opinion on where appliances needed to be located. And she was rarely without a camera on these ride-alongs to take pictures of the workspace, given that Howard kept most of his figurings in his head.

It was a well lived-in place that we stepped into—rather ground under constant repair, I suspect. But it was lived in. We moved from the small entry around the corner to the right and through the doorless archway into the kitchen, which ran the length of the house on the eastern side. It was a shotgun affair, and somewhat dark despite its window at the farther end and above the sink. Opposite the sink looking out that window and located about midway into the room against the wall was the most wonderful old iron stove, which had served double duty for a couple of generations as both the engine of cookery and heat in the building. The face of one of its doors was decorated with the figure of a goddess—could it possibly have been Athena, the fosterer of arts and crafts and the creative heat of the community? The Norse goddess Frigga? This old light green and cream-colored main stove had two overhead warmers and could easily furnish the house's hot water.

Wally, his shock of undisciplined blondish-red hair falling across his forehead, gave us the true "cook's tour" of this rough but homey space. The room was about fifteen feet long and six and a half feet wide. In a space so constricted and currently devoid of storage space, this cabinet job would require careful engineering.

It was a delight to watch Howard work quietly and smoothly, absorbing Wally's information while soaking in the visual, spatial, and textural realities of the room. His rapport with Wally was easy, affable, and helpfully interactive. Wally pointed out a neat old cabinet that would have to come out— its folding front identified it as a Hoosier cabinet with a porcelain top, with neat chrome hardware similar to the latches on old refrigerators. And everything that then existed in the kitchen sat on an old, dark brick linoleum floor.

Howard and Wally gradually fleshed out the general layout

of the cabinet remodel, some of it based on personal preference but the rest dictated by what the space would allow. Wally wanted cabinets along the entire length of the outside wall, some thirty-five-and-a-half feet by Howard's nearly silently retracting tape. The height of these cabinets would reach all the way to the ceiling, and they'd each be equipped with roll-out shelves. Howard had no difficulty talking the practically minded Wally into installing heavy-duty, full-extension door and drawer guides in the cabinets. Wally knew what he wanted, but he also knew with certainty what Howard was doing, and, as one craftsman to another, there was no question about deferring to Howard on these matters of detail and precision. They agreed that there would be four doors seventeen or eighteen inches wide; Howard recommended two pairs of double doors because of the narrowness of the kitchen. Wally's wife Karen, who had made me comfortable with a cup of coffee, interjected a need of her own at this point—another drawer for her linens in addition to the other drawers and the one long shelf. Gradually, reflectively, and collaboratively, with Howard's tape snapping unobtrusively in the background, Karen and Wally settled on a three-door set-up, with all doors the same size, with two compartments, one of these to be half the size of the other.

By now, Howard's yellow legal pad had emerged, and he'd begun, as he moved slowly through the space, to sketch out his plan and to enter his dimensions. As usual, "Murphy" had accompanied us; Howard would be allowing an inch for "Murphy" on the dining room end. His rough sketch included three silverware drawers, too. That sketch would have to enfold Wally's intention to re-do the dropped ceiling and install sheet rock over the dry wall. The cabinets at the entry end of the kitchen would be installed flush with the ceiling. Howard and Wally agreed that the distance from floor to ceiling measured ninety-eight inches; the cabinets to be butted up against it would be thirty-seven-inches high and would extend from the wall inside the entry arch all the way to the end of the room.

Sally, who had arrived a few minutes earlier and had been

catching up with Karen, interrupted to talk Wally and Howard out of putting in cabinets at the end of the room to allow for the construction of a breakfast nook. She concurred, though, that the cabinet doors should have glass inserts.

The discussions now became more focused around the usability of the space, largely through the practical eye of Sally. Both Sally and Karen injected the valuable perspective of the "kitchen goddess." It would be Karen, a five-foot tall woman, who'd be doing the bulk of the cooking, managing, and organizing in it, and Wally, Red Baron-mustached and mantled in mechanic greens, gently deferred. Where Sally wanted the breakfast nook located, in the far corner against that wall's window, an interesting arch would frame it. Karen and Sally agreed that the table that Howard would build and install there would have cabinets underneath to maximize storage opportunities. The cabinets to be hung between the window and the nook would be symmetrical; Wally indicated that he'd soon be removing the current window and replacing it with a larger one, and Howard absorbed that expectation into his plan. The counter would be equipped with two sixteen-inch cutting boards situated right next to each other. Howard would use a deep drawer configuration on the cabinets on the left-hand side of the sink, but the layout in the upper cabinets would mirror the cabinets on the upper end of the kitchen. It was settled that glass fronts would be used on the left and right-side uppers. The cabinets would measure thirty inches high, eighteen inches above the counter.

But the figurings weren't done yet. Besides the good-natured badinage between Sally and Howard that her arrival had unleashed, Sally intruded the issue of a microwave and where it might be located. Then the question of Wally's huge wood box that lay next to the stove and extended down all the way to the basement emerged. For even greater and more efficient opportunities for storage, Howard introduced the possibility of incorporating a cabinet that he'd constructed for other kitchen spaces, a floor-to-ceiling cupboard, about one foot by two feet, with a two-foot depth that could be fitted and filled with forty-two hinged and layered shelves—an interesting option that the Veitmeiers would ultimately reject.

But the most intense discussions revolved around the breakfast nook. Howard noted that the normal height of the nook piece was forty-two inches. That became the starting point for lots of interactions about how it could be divided and set up in relation to the window. Howard's suggestion for continuing the upper cabinets into the nook sparked Wally's agreement that they should cut off the arches, a decision that would add three more inches to the nook.

Finally, all seemed to agree on an eighteen-inch pantry two feet deep. But wait!—Wally had second thoughts and opted for a sixteen-inch-deep cupboard; Howard assured him that the shelves to be built on its door would, in fact, work out. They determined to leave the space above the stove and fridge blank until later—this cabinet job, as Howard had predicted for me, would be a "continuing story" in a series of stages. The doors on the nook wall, continuing the line of the other cabinets, would be unbalanced, eight and six.

With that, we slowly ambled out of the kitchen into the warmth of the midday sun. It was nearly lunch time, and we'd be driving back to the shop to go our separate ways. But not before Wally shared one more pearl about the wonderful old farmhouse that he'd been attached to the hip of since he was a kid. He observed matter-of-factly that this was a "Sears House." Of course, Howard knew immediately what that meant, but I didn't. Sears was once in the business of making pre-cut houses. You'd order a catalog, read it carefully (presumably when you were tearing out sheets of it in a little building for another essential task), send in the dimensions of the house you were ordering to Chicago, and voila—some months later, your pre-cut house would be packaged and loaded on a flat car and shipped, in this case to Superior, Wisconsin, where Wally's father or grandfather had off-loaded it, carried it to the homestead, and assembled it. These were, as Howard observed, the days when a two-by-four

Teaching Fools

was a true two-by-four, not the one-and-a-half-inch-by-three-and-a half-inch shadow of a two-by-four it is now. Interesting.

Howard would be taking his lunch at home before his daily afternoon nap— partly out of self-defense at Sally's scoldings about the beating his veins would take if he had the greasy bacon cheeseburger and fries that he lusted for. Sally and Howard, the artiste and the raconteur, made quite a team. Not Martin and Lewis, to be sure, but sometimes the chemistry proved just as fragile and explosive.

A couple of additional points: when Howard and I left the Veitmeiers, there had been no talk, bargaining, or speculation about the cost of the job. Howard indicated that he'd be back in a week or so to figure a price estimate. The other thing was that any estimate Howard would submit for Wally's approval would be based on the final dimensions of a job yet to be determined. Wally intended to continue to do a lot of the inside and outside work on the house, and that work (the window job, the ceiling replacement, etc.) would continue at Wally's already mentioned deliberate and contemplative pace. Howard told me that, since it had taken Wally some ten years to actually pull the trigger on this job, it would be a decidedly leisurely pace that Wally would set toward its completion.

And he was right, as usual—Howard informed me much later that Wally had just recently contacted him about resuming the kitchen job—this, three and a half years after our visit to Wally's place. And, Howard assured me, this would not nearly be the last of the kitchen job!

Howard smiled understandingly at the bottom of Wally's driveway as he forced the recalcitrant gear shift from reverse up into first; this would be, indeed, a work in progress, one that Howard could address himself to with no deadline and could easily sandwich other jobs around. A pretty loose way of carrying on business, it seemed to me, but Howard quickly corrected me. The obligation to get to know who you were working for and the need to like them enough to take and keep working on a job was part of the work ethic here, and Howard was comfortable with it.

With the open-endedness of the contract, the dimensions of it, and the unsigned bottom line for completion and payment, we were clearly a long way from Minneapolis.

CHAPTER 9

Howard's Extended Campus: The Little House On The Prairie

Men who have lived in crowded, pent-up streets, through lives of toil, have been known to yearn at last for one short glimpse of Nature's face; and carried far from the scenes of their old pains and pleasures, have seemed to pass at once into a new state of being.
--Dickens, *Oliver Twist*

It was August 14th now. To quote Howard, another beautiful morning in Paradise. However, I felt that paradisiacal feeling blighted by the knot in my stomach and the tension building around my temples. I was starting to show all the tell-tale signs of incipient "duty days" at Mankato State. Within just a couple of days, I'd need to clean up my slovenly mess, scrape together my fragrant pile of dirty laundry, arrange my cadre of empty wine bottles on top of the refrigerator, and "bug out" for the Cities.

As I reflect on these kickings and screamings at returning to the work I continued to love with the gift of hindsight, I blush at how deaf and dumb we were to the September 11th looming before us. I know that, even after listening a few days earlier to intel expert Richard Clark discussing the imminence of terrorism on NPR and how the U.S. wasn't paying heed to the best available intelligence that warned something terrible was about to strike us, I was too intent upon staring wistfully across the Lake at the northern Minnesota shore and wondering how I could arrange to stop time and stay here forever to pay attention.

The primary reason for my "playing hookey" was to accompany Howard on another site visit. I'd loved my trip to the Veitmeier's homestead and the chance to observe not only Howard's manner of interacting with the site and his clientele but also Wally's array of personal gifts. But this visit was going to be different.

We'd be heading out Port Wing way, west and one town from Herbster, to deliver a table and benches to Janet Salyer.

But that wasn't all. As I helped Howard load the heavy primitive pieces of pine furniture into his ancient Dodge van, he told me what we'd be about for the balance of that crystalline morning. Janet would be occupying Howard's time through a good piece of the fall and the next spring. He'd contracted to build bookcases for her. And there was the matter of a bed that Janet wanted custom-built, done in the traditional Norwegian manner, big and ornate, along with a portable kitchen cart, food prep surface, and some cabinetry that Janet and Howard needed to agree on.

While Howard fired up the old V-8 and the blue cloud of smoke from leaking oil seals filled the cab, he told me Janet was a "Norwegeeo-phile," an engaging woman in love with all things Norwegian intent on fashioning her South Shore environment consistent with her obsession. Yet another South Shore obsessive personality. As we chugged slowly onto 13, he said I'd like her, and I surely did.

We rumbled over the Cranberry River and up the hill toward Port Wing in Howard's "B-17." Still running pretty strong, the quality of the ride spoiled only by a substantial exhaust leak, this had been his working truck in Maryland. "We never buy anything anywhere new." He'd had it maybe nine years. "Sounds like hell, runs like the wind."

He'd hauled cabinetry back and forth in it from Maryland. When he went there, people would give him orders for stuff, and, the next time he went down, he'd carry back a trailer-load of what he'd made. To accommodate those heavy finished pieces, he'd hung fittings on the inside to stabilize the load. The van, as well as his trailer, was rated for more than eight thousand pounds, and he'd run to Maryland with both maxed out. And it must have taken him quite a while to get there with a full van and trailer behind it, right? "Hell, no. I always drive straight through. You know, when you're running down a hill, this thing really picks up steam." He did, though, stay over a night in lower Michigan.

Superior peaked through the dense birch of the cabined cliff on the passenger's side as we cleared a second hill. Howard shouted above the noise that it was a glorious day, that this was surely the life. He'd been sorry to have missed out on Corny Days the week before, which had been nothing more than a big garage sale. We strained to converse a little about the auction that was going to occur on September 1st at the large storage shed next to the Raindrop Flower Shop just downwind from Cardinal Lumber and how I'd been looking forward to it. He wouldn't be going, he screamed, even though it would provide money for the next year's doings of the Herbster Community Club, of which Sally was president. Howard had made some pieces for the auction. They'd be the highlight of the event.

We roared down the last low hill into Port Wing. As we entered the local traffic zone and speed trap, we passed the two bars located next to each other just before the turn-off, and I observed how many of the bars and little restaurants up and down 13 were up for sale. Howard offered that "that's a high burn-out business," and a friend of his had told him that "unless you're a real pro, four or five years and you've about had it." Howard was astute about the work habits of restaurant and bar owners in these parts: "people buy 'em, keep 'em for a few years, reap some profit or not, and turn 'em over. That's a business in itself for a lot of people."

As we crept up loudly on the Cottage Café on the corner

of Highway H, he asked if I'd had breakfast. There was always time for fried food, especially away from the hawk-eye of Sally, who was always on a diet, whether she needed it or not, and always monitored Howard's predilection for greasy choices. I told him that I'd eaten, but, if he hadn't, he should be my guest. "I thought if you hadn't, we could just stop and pig out. Just for the sport of it." Vintage Howard.

After watching Howard eat way the hell too much pork fat way too fast, we piled back in for a four-mile ride up H that snaked south between the Cottage and Johnson's Store into real farm country just out of sight of the Lake—identical to the terrain I'd seen years earlier just over the Canadian border from Grand Portage up over the North Shore. As we passed a big apple orchard at the crest of the hill, I lamented that Linda and I wouldn't be picking any apples from our few trees this year—the damned army worms had ravaged them and all of the birch and aspen on our property, and, although the leaves returned to the birch and aspen, nothing doing with the apple trees. We'd seen the same evidence of their savage assault on large sections of forest coming down 13. The roads were green and alive with worms. A three-year cycle those worms were working through.

Beyond the orchard, beautifully and gently rolling hayfields and grazing land enveloped us on both sides of the road, and, only a mile and a half south, we could see the tiny house and outbuildings of Janet's place hunched low on the huge stretch of land off to the right.

We nosed into the dirt road that wound toward the entrance to her driveway. Howard pointed out one of what would be many individualizing features of the property. Along the right side of that dirt road and inside her property line were a series of ornately fixtured light posts. I would find out later from Janet that they provided light for her dawn and dusk cross-country skiing workouts—practical and, in two ways, illuminating.

We pulled into a clearing in a vast field—Howard guessed that we were entering an eighty-acre section of farmland. He recalled that Janet had intended to put a building up with a sod

Teaching Fools

roof to go "the whole Norwegian route," but it hadn't worked out. Howard speculated that she was a widow, but, even after knowing her for a good ten years, he couldn't say for certain. She did, though, have a couple of kids.

I was curious to know more details about Janet's story. Where did she come from? Howard wasn't sure. How long had she been up here? "Six or eight years ago, she'd bought the property she's now living on. Eight or ten years ago she lived her winters parked at Angelo Nicoletti's place, and the summers she spent at the public park across the street from the Lake in Herbster and looked after some of the property for campers there." Several years ago she'd purchased the logs and had them finished. Howard was sure that she'd be happy to give chapter and verse.

Now, a little sign—posted to the left of the new porch that would eventually have railings ornamented in the old-world tradition—proclaiming "I love Norway" told us everything we needed to know about how far she'd come toward realizing her dream. It caused us both to laugh at the incongruity of a sign that nearly no one would ever get to see except her. "Well, that's good. It adds a little interest, something that she's primarily interested in. When you lose interest in everything, that's when the trouble starts." How true. How wise.

In the distance toward the now-invisible Lake stood the outlines of an old farmstead situated close to the road on which we'd just driven. The barn was an old classic beauty, weathered to a grayish brown but, even from my distant vantage point, still solid and serviceable. Howard guessed again that she may have rented that portion to farmers who were still working it. Nonetheless, the still unmown hayfields that Janet had purchased not long ago spread out before us and back toward Superior, their gently waving green sea interrupted only occasionally by wire fencing.

Howard backed the truck toward the shallow deck fronting the little log cabin that Janet was still in the process of completing and that opened on the same clean and clear vista that had just left us breathless. Janet had kept things simple indeed. On our left was the somewhat smaller rectangular stick-framed cabin that Janet had lived in before the log cabin had begun to take shape. Out of my passenger's window I could see the area where Janet would soon erect her garage and storage shed. And, as we exited the van and moved to its rear to unload the furniture, Howard pointed out the area right at the front of the cabin where Janet would build the pen to hold the four sheep that she'd raised.

A tortie cat had already greeted Howard at the B-17's rear doors and made fast friends with him as we each grabbed an end of the heavy pine table. Janet emerged from the cabin with a middle-aged man in a flurry of energy and good spirits to greet us. It was impossible to guess how old Janet was, and even better not to try. She was still working—she did home and hospice care for the elderly, some of whom, like her current gentleman client, were grappling with terminal illnesses—but she was probably not far from the traditional retirement age. Whatever her age, she was as natural and independent as the building she directed to be built around her. A thick and short halo of grayish-black hair surrounded her face. She looked healthy and substantial, fit for her age, and quick to laugh. Her smile was wide and welcoming, and she cleared the way for us as we transported the heavy table across a bridge of hand-loomed colorful rag rugs laid across the threshold to protect a light pine-planked floor that had been recently installed.

We did what we could not to track in the red clay dust from the yard outside. Rubbing her hands across the table's smooth finish coat of outdoor spar varnish, Janet was pleased: "It's the perfect size for my small cabin. It's gorgeous. Wow." Howard warned that "the varnish would help the pieces retain their light natural color but that any clear finished wood would change color over time."

Once we'd found temporary locations for the new furniture amidst Janet's cluttered work-in-progress, we exchanged introductions all around. Janet's friend Andy cheerfully rejected her introduction of him to us as her electrician.

I apologized that I was just along for the ride. I was relieved that there appeared to be two of us there operating without proper credentials. And Howard further complicated my presence by indicating that my tape recorder had been brought along "for evidence." I scrambled to clarify my connection to Howard, and that nothing I might collect would be held against her. She was ok with the whole thing; she was as delightful as Howard said she'd be.

She was also grateful that Andy, who hailed from Philadelphia, had brought "all kinds of wonderful knowledge" as an all-purpose handyman to help make the cabin fully livable ("no I haven't," Andy grinned). Howard and Andy swapped stories about Philly and the Jersey and the Maryland shore. Andy had been a diver and had collected lobsters off the coast of New Jersey and Delaware. The talk drifted to the kinds of refuse that Andy knew by experience was being discarded off the coast. Howard noted that old cars were being dumped into the gulf coast of Mississippi, and Andy mentioned that in his diving experience he'd run into old ships with holes cut in their hulls that were being used as break waters. I chipped in that some four-hundred rusty cars from the New York Transit System had been deep-sixed to form a barrier against the sludge encroaching on Manhattan after years of garbage-dumping at sea.

Out on the porch, Howard, Andy, and I mused about the virtues of air conditioning up here and the effects of not having it, given the amount of moisture working on the wood. I shared my worries about the danger of having "forced" some of the pieces of cedar around the windows and doors in our cabin to fit too closely—not leaving enough room for the wood to breathe. My recollections of Linda warning me not to crowd those pieces and my determination not to listen came into play here, along with my admission that she'd been right.

All of this had arisen, I think, because we were all standing around admiring the newly built log cabin structure, but with Howard's experienced observation that, whatever work he'd be doing in there, he'd need to leave room for the logs to settle. All of that would directly impact the measurements he'd be taking and translating to his work.

The inside of this simple log cabin reflected, just as Howard had promised, precisely who Janet was and what she valued. The cabin was essentially a single room living space that was large enough to serve her several basic needs. With a small bathroom portioned off at the right rear of the cabin, the rest of the space would function as a cooking, sleeping, and living/sitting space. A brilliantly ornate stove graced the left rear wall—a Waterford, fit for both cooking and heating. Janet said that when you get them lit they heat up fast.

Janet talked about looking forward to moving in some of her Norwegian treasures, including a dark and intricately carved dresser. However, the arrival of those pieces would await the work that Howard had been commissioned to do.

She told Howard that she wanted to have a ladder built to the crawl space upstairs to help her better manage the smallness of her living space. It wouldn't be, as Howard initially thought, a pull-down ladder, because she had trouble managing and moving those, but a fixed one, a set of stairs built just to the left of and against the outer wall of the entry door. It would make the space look and feel bigger.

An unexpected and un-Norwegian challenge confronted us before Howard could take his measurements for a set of bookcases he'd be building to frame the bathroom door and "ell" up against the only interior wall in the cabin. It was Murphy time once again, and Howard alerted Janet to his presence. While we'd been moving the chairs from the truck into the cabin, Andy had been wrestling with a large, heavy cast iron claw-footed tub. It would have to be removed from the bathroom so that the rest of the plumbing and electrical work could be performed there. Janet poked her head in to explain that she'd mistakenly asked the men to put the bathtub in before putting the door on, not thinking about the plumbing. A little snapping and retracting of Howard's tape settled the indisputable—"Since the bathroom door is smaller than standard, the tub isn't going to fit through unless we remove the legs." The thing weighed a bloody ton. We spent some sweaty minutes removing the tub's feet and then scooting it along the pine floor on a thin protective cushion of woven scatter rugs and blankets. Janet's handiwork.

Once again, Howard stood to the left of the bathroom entry pondering how best to use the wall space for Janet's bookcase. She suggested that the trim could be taken off the bathroom door, but Howard said he was hoping to avoid that. It would be a floor-to-ceiling installation, and he'd have to allow for the problem of setting the bookcase upright after getting it into the cabin. "One solution might be to shorten the overall height of the bookcases and, after setting them upright, bring them up to their final height by setting them on a short platform." But Howard would think about the possibilities back in the shop and develop a plan. After checking the square and level of the wall, Howard figured that "I'll need to shim a half inch—not too bad."

Before he measured, Howard chatted with Janet, making a rough sketch of the bookcases on his legal pad as they talked. Given Janet's short supply of storage space, Howard planned to build the bookcases to the ceiling, with a thick sill over the door to join the bookcases on either side of the door as one unit. As he determined the measurement from the wall to the door at 37 ½ inches, Howard decided to allow for a little shrinkage in the logs—"I'll be working with an unpanelled two-by-six interior wall that will be faced eventually." He'd be going to the top of the outside bathroom wall, with the gap at the top of that wall showing.

The interactive rapport was delightful. Howard methodically snapped and retracted the tape, took some preliminary measurements, and entered them carefully on his rough legal pad drawing. Janet indicated she'd want the shelves to be fixed, with the big bookshelf on the bottom, about twelve-and-three-quarters-inches high. They agreed that the shelves would be framed in at the ends rather than left open.

Inadvertently, Howard uncovered one of the books that Janet had piled in her corner for storage in the bookcase. It was

Thoreau! All of us were thrilled, including Howard—"You're just going to have to let me borrow it one of these days." The title page read *A Little House Close to the Lake*—what could be more appropriate? It was the last manuscript to be discovered just after Thoreau's death and had just recently come out. Howard, his practical side taking over, took his measure to Thoreau's book, found it to be about nine and a half inches, and said, "what say we build all of your other shelves at twelve inches?"

It was settled. Whatever space would be left for the last shelf, maybe some six or seven inches, could be made into a little shelf at the top, a space for her trolls. She had plenty of them. Howard was delighted. He'd thought about getting them into Sally's shop. "There's more than one person in the area who's a troll-o-phile!"

During this chore, he queried Janet about the time factor—how long, given the rest of this work schedule, it would take to do the job, when it might be done, and when Janet might want them. We found ourselves talking about the Veitmeiers again, and we all shared a laugh that Wally had begun talking about the kitchen job with Howard ten years ago. "You can't rush into these things," joked Howard.

The issue of the odd corner the bookcase would snuggle into came up—this would be a custom job. Janet gave Howard full discretion here. As the cat strayed in again and found Howard's leg, they agreed once more on building a base for the bookcase and mounting it there. "I'm not concerned about the details, Howard, as long as I have a place to house my books."

Howard stopped for a minute, scratched his head, and recalled embarking on a job with one of his customers. He customarily presented them with a variation on the "twenty questions" routine in order to narrow the field of what they really wanted. "What kind of wood do you want to use? Light? Dark? How big? What will it be used for?" Is it bigger than a bread box? Is it Frank Sinatra? And etc.

Howard said that he hadn't gotten too far into the question routine when the fellow looked up, smiled, and declared,

"Howard, you have complete artistic license." Howard uttered that phrase with such relish, not with ego, but with good humor. He was grateful to be able to work through the checklist of his repertoire of experiences to reach a solution to this problem.

Near the end of the site-visit, Howard and Janet bantered about the cabinet that Howard was building for Janet's kitchen, the one that would hold her sink. But she hadn't actually bought a sink yet! She'd talk to her son about getting one, but, as yet, there was literally nothing solid for Howard to base his dimensions for the sink cut-out. "I think it best if I wait for you to get the sink that you want before I begin to craft the cabinet." She concurred. Howard allayed her concerns about engaging with a plumber to rough in the connections to the sink without the finished cabinet. "An approximation for that rough opening should be sufficient."

Then there was the business of the kitchen cart that she wanted Howard to design. "Do you actually have the finished dimensions worked out for it? I can't build it until you do." He'd be putting those two items on hold until she could furnish the height and width, and the location of an oven that she might be building over the cart.

And, finally, the bed. Howard wanted confirmation about whether he'd be putting doors on it in the strictest Norwegian tradition or leaving it open. "I've only been able to find the curtained doors so far, Howard, but I'm pretty sure I've seen examples of beds of this type with solid wood doors on them. I just need the time to track them down." To complicate matters, she admitted that she still had no definite plan or specs for the bed that she wanted him to build; if she couldn't find one soon, she might have to go with an early American design.

Howard was delicately fishing for details here, looking for some sort of direction, but Janet didn't have one. Both of them agreed that they were thinking of a design with shelves on one end of it. Janet asserted that she'd given Howard her own rough drawings of what she had in mind, at least for the drawers. Howard was less certain that he had those drawings than she was.

"Someplace you have it, Howard!" she laughed, as Howard did a quick survey of his often capricious mental file clerk's memory bank, and said tentatively, "Yeah, yeah."

Janet was certain, though, that they'd decided upon a double bed. She'd love a queen, but it would never fit in the cabin. With eye glinting, Howard asked her if she had a boyfriend, and, when she said she didn't, he suggested, "when you go shopping, you should check to see if one comes with the bed."

That sexual reference was sufficient to jump-start Howard's memory of their earliest discussions of the bed. "Didn't we talk about putting some storage underneath it?" Bingo. And he remembered that they'd discussed, for structural reasons, building a "roof" for it—bingo again. Howard begged her to be the tiniest bit more specific about the details. She promised that she'd be driving back to Decorah, Iowa, where she believed she'd located the layout and elevations that would stabilize what she'd been speculating about. The town maintained an historical library where she expected to be able to find the details about the cabinet.

So, the next thing on Howard's plate would be the bookcase. That's where we stood. And we were out the door. But not before I asked and was granted permission to come back when all the work was finished.

After we'd moved out to the truck and put away our tools, Howard rolled into his seat: "You know, this is another one of those benefits of working out in the boondocks. It's business, but it's not so serious that you can't take time to bullshit."

My feelings exactly: "That was part of the pleasure of the whole trip. Everybody's got stories. Everybody's tellin' them, and everybody wants to listen. They're all entertaining."

And isn't it good…Norwegian wood.

CHAPTER 10

The Alumni Association: Howard's Former Students Become "Friends of the University"

"When in April the sweet showers fall
And pierce the drought of March to the root, and all
The veins are bathed in liquor of such power
As brings about the engendering of the flower..."
--Chaucer, *The Canterbury Tales*

April 2003, Spring clean for the May Queen. But not quite. Those of us living on or visiting the South Shore had suffered into the seductive delights and disappointments of April tender and sweet. April means spring in a good portion of Amurk-ah. Azaleas exploding along the rolling, exclusive, mostly unplayed fairways of that monument to the rich and ancient, Augusta National. But not in northwest Wisconsin, usually. April delivers windshield-wiper-like extremes. It's the period during which we enjoy our deepest and wettest snow dumps; but it's also the time when warming temperatures and gradually thawing ground frost presage the whistling and booming of the Lake Lady's ice and a daily dance of fragmenting ice flows moving in and out of the Big Lake's bays—now you see them, now you don't.

April is different for those at Augusta, where the

plantation-style club house among the pines insinuates, "I've got mine, so go get yours." Where young Republicans practice knock-down fades into light cross breezes (no harsh, cold winds are permitted at Augusta) and laissez faire economics—whose Cadillac is *that*? Where white-belted old people watch old-thinking young men play for embarrassingly large purses at golf's most prestigious and shamelessly discriminatory event—the Masters.

And, of course, I'll watch the god-damned thing, like some destitute street kid rubbing his snotty nose on the outside of the showroom window of F.A.O. Schwartz. As a golfer of some seventy-one years now (and a decent one for a short time), there is no escape.

But on this Saturday in April 2003 when the third round of that year's Masters would be played, I'd deferred usurping the big screen from the heavy-drinking hockey fans at Corny's Fishlipps until mid-afternoon. First, though, I'd need to seize an opportunity to experience some aspects of Howard's world—aspects indispensable not just because I can't account for them in other sections of this manuscript, but because they truly define Howard, Sally, and what it means to live and work up here. Some of these aspects are unavoidably "historical." Howard was a devotee of history—not just his own or his family's, but of important people; he loved biography, from the life of the exquisite worker of wood Sam Maloof to John and Abigail Adams as well as the development of political trends and things that grow.

But the real history that I wanted to track on this day was the little slice of Herbster that came to belong to Sally's family—that connection with the area that ultimately drew Howard back with her. There exists a wonderful little history of Herbster written by a life-long resident, but, though I looked through it to find out if the "Touve's"—Sally's family—were represented in it, how far it went back, when they settled in this area, what kind of immigrant stock they were, who built the house and bought the land and when, and what part the family played in the development of this little community, I found nothing.

And I didn't get any further with Sally on it. Probably because, when a lot of this was unfolding around her, she was too busy outside a cold dark house full of kids at 4:30 in the morning feeding the chickens, helping in the kitchen, and getting ready to walk to school to care much about it. When I interviewed her a bit on what she remembered, what it was like to grow up around the South Shore, and how that road I traveled off 13 with Howard to her family's old place came to have the name of her family on it, she wasn't helpful, unintentionally or otherwise. I still wanted to know why that road had her name on it, although I think I know. But, although I also wanted to know what family member, and during what time, graced the road with the name, I doubt I ever will.

When I climbed into the cab of Howard's rusty B-17 early that Saturday morning with my little tape recorder, I'd envisioned beginning this chapter with a recreation of an historical vignette. One that Howard could relate that would, indeed, have come directly from Sally's own experience—something that particularly stuck with her over the years. Maybe something related to that road we would travel shortly after lunch on our way back to the shop. It might be her recollection of travelling down that steep hill near her parents' farm on her toboggan with family and friends, somewhere in the depths of a real, deep north woods winter before or during the war, what it was like to travel at what must have been break-neck speed down that precipitous incline and to let that sled release on the ice at the bottom and glide noiselessly out another quarter mile to the point where the road turned sharply to the left toward the family farm. It might be some other personal reminiscence, about her family, maybe a story nearly transformed into myth about an ancestor a couple of generations back, something Jack London-ish and related to fires and matches perhaps, but maybe, still, something about one or another of the many other characters people still tell stories about. Maybe an Albert Isaksson story. Maybe an Angelo Nicolletti story.

But, whatever I might have been able to glean from Howard, and as much as my questions might have led to a combination of things, a thrusting-back into time, in the early morning of April 11th of 2003, it would have to share equal time with a Saturday morning and early afternoon chase across the countryside with Howard on a couple of retrospective site-visits. And maybe it would require me to environmentalize a little, like saying what the town and its surroundings looked like back seventy-five years or so, how there was a little boom-town going on, how there was actually a Billy Herbster serving as paymaster and chief mail person at the town's new sawmill, how the roads, such as they were, were dirt and that highway 13 was merely a strip of gravel threading up and down through the woods, the current 13 only an unintentional glint in the eye of the engineers who would ultimately design it.

Yes, it was another perilous bombing mission in the B-17. Unlimited ceiling and visibility. Engine smoking and oozing oil like an overcooked pig on a spit, but roaring smoothly as Howard and I taxied away from the shop for take-off. We'd be delivering some bar stools and a little step stool that Howard had just finished to the Davies' place, south of Port Wing on old County Road H again and over to the edge of Iron River. This, in itself, would be a history lesson, partly a history of the relationship between Howard and Sally and the Davies which had flourished subsequent to Howard having contracted to build their kitchen a few years back. It was another of those results of a job done well where Howard smiled and said, in semi-wonderment, "It happens so often that I end up liking the people I take jobs from. Or is it that I take those jobs because I like those people?" Something like that.

The ride was typically raucous on this bright, clean, clear, and brisk spring morning. The backfires. Howard's attempts to blow the damned muffler system off. My pleas that he never get the gaping exhaust leak fixed, ever. Stupid. Childish. Child-like. Free. Forget about the tape recorder.

I could never have found my way to the Davies' on my

own. Somewhere about a mile after the incredibly sharp hairpin to the right that astonishes even during the daytime, we left H and drove toward Oulu, another Finnish enclave, until we came upon the dirt road that bent right past the nearly melted snow around the trees at the edge of the road that bore buds ready to burst. And then we were there—the incredible opening-up of the trees to the house. Howard had pictures. We knew how long it took for the Davies to build it.

Amazing.

My words are insufficient to retrace the process of the incredible beams they'd framed their house with—the old 1850-vintage barn that they'd seen in a little town snuggling in Door County; how they'd agonized over how they were going to have to find a way to own what they'd immediately fallen in love with; the purchase of the building and the dismantling of it; the loading and the transport of those timbers in a semi that this retired over-the-road trucker had borrowed from a friend back to the thirty acres of land they'd recently purchased outside of Iron River.

And the difficult and painstaking process of hiring the skilled people to help him shape those beams into the house that he and his wife had dreamt about. The sandblasting of the timbers, the alignment of them, the chinking, the hiring of the iron railing artisan who worked his own magic on the balcony overlooking the entry way, while including some of the antique pieces the Davies had collected over the years into his design that framed the periphery of the loft. The stairs and railings they'd fashioned. The high-ceilinged bathroom they'd built toward the rear of the main floor, all of it framed and set off with a wall of glass blocks that admitted so much light into a shower that needed no door and that widened into a space nearly big enough to accommodate the Minnesota Twins. The solarium on the south side of the first floor that admitted so much light that it required very little heat on the coldest of days to warm it. The first-floor bedroom, stick-built and added on like the solarium and nearly as sunny, that was brightened even more by a beautiful wide-planked pine floor. An expansive entry way and living room whose antique furnishings were highlighted by an earthy gray tile floor composed of rectangular pieces of irregular sizes. A lofted ceiling of wide-board tongue-and-groove pine whose ends of random length were beautifully finished with a chamfer. A large full basement under the main building housing an efficient hot water heating system and the wires for heating the floor threading up to fulfill their purpose.

And, of course, there was the kitchen, to the left of the wide entryway, most of which Howard had built: the cabinets, the counters, the island, and, around that island now, the stools that we'd just delivered.

There's a lot to mention here, about the house to be sure, but much more. These people were doers. Clearly, Cal Davies appreciated people who did excellent work, craftsmen. But I was impressed that Cal had participated in every operation of the assembly of that "cabin," not just pitching in, but performing some very sophisticated operations and working right beside the experts.

And, then, there was the snowmobiling. I cared little about it myself, but Cal did. He started and kept vibrant a snowmobiling club on the South Shore. This sixty-four-year-old guy and his wife took annual trips of prodigious distance with their clubbers—the cross-country trip to Manitoba in well-below-zero temperatures that took about ten days back and forth really struck me.

Their mutual passion for antiques—that curved-glass fronted and topped seven-foot piece sitting next to the stairs holding all of Cal's wife's Christmas stuff; Cal's Soap Box Derby car, one of several that he'd built when he was a kid, one that he'd ridden to the semi-finals in Madison, one race away from the magical trip to Akron for the championships. It looked pretty much race-ready, and Cal talked about preparing to mount it on the wall in the basement. And they recalled how their snowmobiling interest had caused them to make their way up to this area, to fall in love with it sufficiently to buy this parcel and another one they still own on a lake outside Iron River in 1964.

And, of course, they talked, as we all did, about the impossible rise in the price of land and property just since the nineties. We all had stories to tell here.

But, then, there was the trip back, to see the three Adank brothers that Howard had worked for maybe ten years before, one after the other, from the smallest project that he nearly turned down, the assembly of a shed that one of the brothers had purchased and wanted to employ someone who'd let him work with him and learn through the building process. It seemed too small to bother with. But it led to two other projects—the addition on one of the brothers' cabin, and then to the full-scale construction of a cabin for another brother. What was noteworthy here were two things—first, Howard permitted, even welcomed, the brothers to work along with him in all three projects, and, secondly, he had a hell of a time doing so. As a consequence, Howard had become fast friends of long standing with the three of them, another instance of what Howard's history revealed about the profits other than money that accrued from his work up here.

And that's where we were headed on our way back from Iron River. After a quick external application of saturated fat at a little greasy spoon downtown ("Someplace Else", indeed), we blew up "H" again, Howard fiendishly accelerating and backing off the gas to produce a deafening explosion. One of the brothers—the one who'd participated in Howard's construction of his cabin—was Howard's object here. He'd called him the day before to tell him that we'd be dropping by.

It was early afternoon now, the outside temperature hovering right around a balmy 50 degrees when I suddenly noticed that the tape recorder I'd been resting on the consul over the engine had suddenly come back to life. It had absolutely let me down on the trip over to Cal's, had retreated into full abandonment during Cal's tour of his wonderful place, and I'd just about given it up for lost when I noticed that its little spools were slowly whirring again. But the machine was useless now due to the combined din of the unmuffled engine and wind flapping against half rolled-down windows. Howard screamed from the cab's driver's side that he'd just remembered that he'd found a bunch of tongue-and-groove maple that he didn't think he had. Cal, I believe, had asked him if he had some in his shop and Howard had scratched his head and replied that he didn't have it, that it was gone, that he'd used it. Now the forty-watt bulb had suddenly flashed on like my tape machine.

Howard's response?—"You know, the mind is a funny thing. We take information and throw it into the hopper, and what happens? It comes out sometimes not necessarily in the same order that it went in."

My riposte: "Well, it might have actually bypassed the conduit of the mouth and traveled further south and come out the other end, you know." Howard guardedly agreed.

We were busily trying to blow the exhaust system off the B-17 again when suddenly my own light bulb illuminated. Memory. Brain cells succumbing en masse to a Tsunami of Inver House half-gallon bottles. Ray Milland's lost weekends. The somewhat blurred days of wine and roses. For some reason, Howard and I got on the "AA" issue. Howard had always been open about this, among many of his obsessions. I had to nearly sit on top of the console to follow what he was shouting at me, and, as I tilted my good ear toward him, I began to get a little closer to the bottom of his bottle. There was stuff in those shouts that I'd seen among too many of my own family members—and just a bit in myself. His story about coming home one evening after work and opening up the Vat 69 or the Inver House or other dirt-cheap scotches in convenient unbreakable plastic bottles. While Howard was drinking the stuff, he decided to chase a bottle full of pills with it as well. He was pretty much cashing in his chips, he said.

This would have been 1988. Sally remembered as if it were yesterday, even though she was in the drinking game with him for a time and was evasive about admitting how immersed she was in it. Howard murdered a lot of brain cells that evening, but Sally remembered with clarity rushing Howard to the hospital, where he de-toxed and had his stomach pumped. Sometime later, he'd check himself out of the hospital, walk along a busy highway in the mud in his bathrobe with one shoe, and arrive home with his other sock chewed up. He was a disaster, but this was the beginning of something. An awakening. The cocking of one half-opened and bloodshot eye, at least. He'd soon be deeply invested in AA for support, and he'd soon be talking to Sally about getting out of the toxic soup and finding less traveled ways. He probably wouldn't like reading my retelling of this at all if he were still alive.

And, quickly, we bellowed our way out of one reverie into another. About half of the twenty-mile distance between Iron River and Port Wing, I asked Howard to walk me through his association with the Adanks as he'd begun to do at dinner the evening before. Richard had stopped by the house probably seven or eight years ago to inquire if Howard would consider assembling a storage shed, maybe eight by ten, and let him help. That helping-out had nothing to do with economy, it turned out; Richard's "main thrust" was to become involved and learn.

They completed the shed and, in Howard's humble way of expressing it, "it had turned out okay." Richard's brother Don, who owned the cabin next door and had observed the happy little collaborative venture, then asked Howard if he'd be interested in working with him to add a couple of bedrooms to his place on the same basis. And, sure enough, Howard would direct that project and be the carpenter while Don and his two brothers (Richard and Dallas) would crew for him.

So they completed the job, did it well, managed to have a lot of fun ("you can never forget to have fun" had become one of Howard's most common refrains). Then, somewhere on down the line when Richard was ready to build his cabin, Howard and Richard collaborated once more. And, Howard observed nostalgically, "we had a good time. Richard always paid his bills on time, which is always good, and there was no question about the pay. He had a good time because he was working on his own cabin. Richard is that kind of guy—well maybe that's natural with an educator, a professional educator. He really enjoyed learning, and he had a ball learning about construction."

Just then, as Howard accelerated again and backed off to create more loud explosions ("twenty-thousand feet and plummeting"), a pick-up truck passed us going the other way. It was Richard's, Howard said, and the driver was his brother Don. This was likely to blow our plans for visiting Richard all to hell. We had been dragging our feet that morning. Cal, who we'd spent so much time with earlier, had walked in on us at the greasy spoon to pick up a paper and then spent more time gabbing with us. Howard knew that he'd probably missed his chance with Richard. That's the way it went up here, where the pace of things was determined less by the time clock and more by the quality of unscheduled human interactions. I figured we'd catch him at another time, but Howard was disappointed. Don and Richard must have traveled up together, he figured. But we'd drive by the cabin anyway, just on the off-chance that Richard was there.

We passed the next few moments speculating when Howard would be getting the stuff for his garden into the ground. It wouldn't be until late May or early June, the way things had been going. He would, however, be doing something different in the garden this year. His two varieties of melons had done famously last year, but they'd become favorites with the raccoons as well, who just about cleaned out the two crops. He wouldn't be making that mistake again this year. No more cantaloupe, no more corn.

Strawberries, of course, because he'd spent considerable energy getting those plants going over the last couple of years. Certainly tomatoes. He'd have a couple of hills of yellow squash, a couple of zucchini mounds, maybe a dozen cabbage, but that was about it, and he'd have a yard full of roses growing at the house for the first time since he'd left Maryland for Wisconsin.

And, he said, he'd expected the roses to survive because he wouldn't be planting "the carefree type. I'm planting the long, thin beauties. Modern roses are like a beautiful spoiled woman. If you really give them everything they want, and carry them around on pillows, and take care of all of their needs, they will reward you greatly. But, if you don't, you just get some skimpy-assed returns." Really! If you want the real beauties, he said, you have to get into the real thing, like hybrid teas, floribunda, Granda floras, polyanthas, some of the shrub roses. Howard characterized his discovery and experience with roses as "an interesting journey," reading about them, their history, breeding, and cultivation. He did roses for over twenty years. Even during his "liquid diet" period, he was still tending them. It may have been the thing that kept him from going completely off the rails. Even then, he hadn't let his roses lapse. He'd be out there working on them, just he and his cat Socks, with his scotch and water not far away.

We'd passed Janet's cozy little sheep spread, coasted over the hill and into the astonishing mural of Lake Superior as the view from Duluth up the North Shore coast opened up before us, and nosed past the stop sign at the Cottage Cafe onto 13 toward Herbster. Just after clearing the second of the two bars outside of town and just before the first of the low long hills began to rise and snake toward Herbster, Howard veered abruptly right onto a dirt road, up past the old Johnson spread with the covey of wooden butterflies mounted on the side of the house. I'd remembered the little Johnson farm from the time that Linda and I had seen the garage sale sign, driven back up that dirt road, and then right into the stately trees surrounding the neatest, cleanest set of outbuildings I'd ever encountered along with a quiet, beatific old woman working on her knitting. We'd even bought a couple of things from her.

And, as it turned out, she and her husband were contributors to the stock in Sally's shop, members of Sally's stable of crafters. She was, as Howard remembered, an intrepid maker of the sugary confection, krumkaka. And her husband made little wooden humorous pieces, the kind of thing that swells the stock of any self-respecting country gift shop, except his stuff had some charm. Howard remembered one of the little pieces, a box that said on its lid, "a three-course chicken dinner," only to reveal when the cover was lifted three little kernels of corn. Not bad.

It was in fact a beautiful spread set back from the woods. Both of them were unfailingly "nice, a little shy, reserved, the salt of the earth, they worked their asses off for many, many years." And they had also resisted, Howard later told me, installing a hot water heater in the house—attribute that militant act of self-denial and masochism to the otherwise silent and pacific Mr. Johnson. As I thought of the quiet and deferential little Mrs. Johnson sitting in her absolutely impeccable barn the day we visited, a little wave of terror washed quickly over me. Life was still hard and isolated up here.

Then Howard announced what I hadn't noticed on my other trip not nearly as far into this road. This was, he said, Touve Road. It was named after Sally's grandfather. On her mother's side—her mother was a Touve. Sally's grandparents had come over from Sweden. Their name was Touveson, but, as was frequently the custom among European immigrants back then, they shortened it to Touve when they got to the U.S.

The old homestead was, Howard announced, just up the road, and we'd be driving by it. Traditionally, he said, the roads up here were named after the first family who occupied a place where the road was built.

Just then, we crossed old 13 in mid-woods, and Howard alerted me to it. Amazing. More buried history. This brought us back to the early primitive state of the road system in this country, the fact that it had only been recently that roads like the graveled old 13 had been abandoned for wider, paved, and more convenient versions, that the interstate highway system was barely past its infancy, even though it had reached a point of corrosion and dilapidation from the wear and tear of truck and car traffic since the fifties. Old 13 is still usable.

And on we lugged up the incline of Touve Road, seeing the occasional house set back deep into the thick birch on the left. The truck was laboring as we passed the unexpectedly modern dwelling of architect Jim Held. Another of the many members of Cal's snowmobile club, Howard said. In the last few years he'd moved up here full-time and continued to carry on his business out of the woods, thanks to the miracles of electronics. As we drove by, what looked like a pool built into his wide deck became visible. Howard had never noticed that before. Most uncharacteristic for a climate where the earth never stops heaving.

As the Held house swept away from us on the left and evaporated into the woods, brush, and blueberries, in a mile or so and just below the crest of the hill on our right we came upon the Touve or Touveson manse—Grandpa Touve's farm—the ramshackle old farmstead, with the house still on it. A little dirt road peaked through further to the right of the house. Howard said that if you took that little road, followed that tree line in between the first and second batches of hay and over to the right, you'd find the original old homestead of Grandpa's farm. It was a big stretch of land—Howard speculated that originally this tract was a one-sixty, the normal size of the pieces that people bought, carved out, and farmed up here.

We were at the top of the hill now, and the whole valley opened up for us like a magnificent blooming floribunda. A little haze obscured the horizon, but it was breathtaking. I'd never seen the land of the South Shore just a little inland from the Lake from this perspective before. Over to the left was the orchard of Mike, another Isaksson, pretty much abandoned now. It turned out not to be economically feasible so he let it go some time back. Mike wasn't the kind of guy, Howard observed, who would stay with something if it proved unprofitable. My exuding over the environmental beauty of the place was momentarily lost on Howard, whose attention became fixed on a new radio tower that had just been erected over to the left and the large sand pile left beside it. Over to the right of the tower was Paul Isaksson's cabin. He didn't live there anymore, Howard said; now that Albert had died, he'd moved into the house that he'd inherited from his father.

Howard directed my attention to the incredible view from my window off to the east over multiple eighties and one-sixties and lots of woods that, as Howard had reminded me, had been clear-cut not all that long ago. But then he juiced the gas pedal just a bit, and we fell from that view as if from a trap door down the unexpectedly steep hill that Howard told me used to be the place where Sally and her friends did their tobogganing and sledding so many years ago. As we fell away from the crest, Howard directed my eyes forward to a corner some quarter mile from the bottom out into the distance where the road turned left. He said that the kids had to station one of their friends at that corner to make sure a truck didn't come around it and run them over. And, recalling my own exploits on little sleds that I'd directed off little cliffs and rode over clear ice for hundreds of yards, I felt from the cab of the free-wheeling B-17 some of that empty-lunged exhilaration of just falling to the bottom and then gradually coasting as the road opened out into the distance. Pure.

We were coming up on Richard Adank's place now, up and around that left hand turn and sloping down again. Small groups of early-afternoon feeding deer cluttered the road—road rodents—and delayed our progress even in broad daylight. We'd just crossed the imaginary line from Port Wing township into Clover township, Howard told me. And he pointed out a thick blackberry patch on the left as we moved down the shallow grade to the Adank cabins. Don's came first; Howard noted the two structures projecting from the building as the rooms that he had built with the owner. Richard's gate to the driveway was open, and Howard was momentarily buoyed by the prospect of finding him at home. As we pulled in, Howard drew my attention to what looked like a log cabin construction, but I knew better. "You faced it," I said. Howard had installed log cabin siding because Richard had wanted to make it look like the real thing.

Howard was being incorrigible with the engine's exhaust leak as we sat in the driveway next to the side door of the cabin. When he finally killed it and got out to show me the neat little storage shed that had been the entree to his relationship with the Adanks, he was still hopeful that Richard was in the house, but I was skeptical. What with the drapes pulled and the din that had announced our arrival, I said that, if he was actually in there, we'd need either to resuscitate him or get ready to breathe through our mouths. That sort of thing happened a lot up here, particularly in winter.

Well, he wasn't there, and we headed out. I observed the wood foundation that surrounded the crawl space under Richard's place as we moved on into a stretch of road once called Carmichael Road, taking over at the township line for Touve, but now the whole thing, said Howard, had been named Touve Road. On the right was a little cottage that Howard said was once inhabited for years by two old guys from Czechoslovakia. Howard hadn't ever known them, but every body knew about them.

Tony and Jim were their names. One of them was blind and they made their own wine in that little house. In their "geezerage," Howard said, they went back to Czechoslovakia to end their days. But how, I asked, had people from Czechoslovakia ever found this place? What would have made them come here? Howard responded with "who knows? A lot of the Scandinavians found it," with some amusement. About the same latitude as Czechoslovakia. Lots of free land. And not too long ago, that land was almost free. I expressed my amazement at the paltry $225 an acre that Cal and his wife had paid for their thirty acres of paradise.

We were chewing up the gravel that skirted the Cranberry River on our right now, raging and roiling brown with the recent melt-off of the two feet of snow that was disappearing fast. The snow was all but gone. It wouldn't be long now. The Cranberry would run all the way into town behind Howard and Sally's house a few miles north and into Superior. When we turned left sharply from Touve Road onto Cranberry River Road and headed up another rise, Howard said that we'd be going by the place that Sally grew up, just on our right. And there was the old farmhouse, part of the old farm. We saw Sally's sister's "significant other" moseying across the front of it. As we drove by the east pasture of the farm, Howard expressed some surprise at the density of the trees growing on it—it had only been ten or fifteen years since this area too had been clear-cut. But, he said, it's amazing how quickly the land will recover its growth if it's given the opportunity.

Before Howard could point it out to me, I identified the acre of cleared ground on the right perched at the top of the rise that Howard called his little "north forty." It was the little hunk of acreage that Howard gardened every year, nearly bare of snow now, the water wagon he used to transport the liquid to irrigate it sunken down a bit in the middle of it. And off we went to the left, heading down now to downtown Herbster and its sleepy boulevard of broken hearts.

The few miles we traveled looked like a rustic country painting—the hard ground thawing into spring mud, the rusted farm machinery and implements, the well-built if faded arched barns scattered across the landscape as if they'd been dropped negligently from the sky, the silence of the still life before us, disturbed only by the B-17. One of those barns to the right belonged to Sally's brother Hank, Howard noted. Howard observed that it was so wide open out here that Hank could step out and piss off his porch, which "I do occasionally."

Howard waved at the strawberry farm over to the left. Strawberries used to be one of the major sources of income in Bayfield County, but, the modern transportation system being what it is, people aren't likely to ship such a crop from this area anymore. I observed that one of the top ten pleasures of being up here was the openness, the spaces between places.

And then we were back, having driven by the Isaksson sawmill, past Howard and Sally's house, the regrettable oil slick that was Tracy's-by-the-Lake, and into Herbster. I told him how lucky he was to be able step out, unthreatened, in the middle of a street used only by the occasional logging truck, rusty pick-ups, and a few dirt bikes to view things uninterrupted—past his never-to-be-finished house, the cancered examples of state-of-the-art transportation that littered his driveway, and over between the recreation center to the shop. It had been a beautiful day, despite the arbitrary and capricious tape machine I'd been using. An

Teaching Fools

informative interaction with some of Howard University's alumni, not all present and accounted for but there nonetheless. Sally met us as we pulled into the little lot next to the shop and reminded Howard that they had a funeral to go to later in the afternoon. Typically, Howard had forgotten all about it.

As I climbed into my hardly less-rusted CRX just before 2pm, the breeze had freshened, and I really needed the sweater I'd been sweating through only a few minutes before. The contrary Lady of the Lake again. But, after all, this winter and early spring were all part of what Howard would call "the Wisconsin surprise"—the six inches of snow that would fall on April 21. Crazy. The entire meteorological gamut was run—the lining up of six planets, two days around 91 degrees followed by three days in the low forties. And, when it was 91 down in Minneapolis, I could muster only 39 of those degrees up at the cabin. Incredible.

And then it was up the street to suck down several Bloody Mary's and watch the Masters at Fishlipps—more history of a sort, if a little racist, sexist, and downright elitist. There you go.

The bi-level cedar back deck with flower boxes, seating, and old person

Lake view from the deck

CHAPTER 11

Externship I: The Sorcerer's Apprentice: From Skill-less Bankruptcy to Marginal Competence

Clown 1: Who builds stronger than a mason, a shipwright, or a carpenter.
Clown 2: Mass, I cannot tell.
Clown 1: Cudgel thy brains no more about it, for your dull ass will not mend his pace with beating. And when you are asked this question next, say a "gravemaker." The houses he makes last till doomsday.
--Shakespeare, *Hamlet*

To be or not to be a carpenter—that was the question that this brain cell-fried mind and old bones had long been laboring over. Whether it would be nobler in the mind to suffer the slings and arrows of capricious craftsmen, or, by opposing, fire them. Ah, there's the rub—would I, in fact, have the courage to act on my desire to take on a building project, under Howard's encouragement and guidance, and bring it to closure without depreciating the property's value or my life span? And would I be able to turn a purposeful and tense project into an act of creative and exuberant play?

Those questions flowed dreamily back to me at about half past midnight on a warm July 2003 evening. Sitting on the steps of the side deck of my cabin, I stared through the moonless dark toward the carriage house and the state at which it had now reached.

Suddenly, that second glass of primitivo I'd cradled between my knees brought it all into perspective—I was looking at a straightforward, humdrum box which was mutating as I drank. Off the north side facing the Lake an eighteen-foot-long shed roof running from the edge of the building all the way to the ridge had muscled through. I could barely make out the corner of the deck at the back of the building riding nearly ten feet off the ground. That deck extended another six feet toward the Lake, turned for a six-foot run along the north wall before dropping a step for another six feet, and then descended elegantly into—nothing. A run of about fifteen feet of stairs four feet wide would have to wait until I installed the two monstrous double-cranking casement windows on the second floor with the help of Dainus Symchka, a twenty-one-year-old med student from Estonia visiting Russian relatives in Corny. The seven-by-six-foot openings centered in both the front and back yawned ominously at me, anticipating the slider I'd soon be installing in the rear opening and the inward-opening French doors—again with an hour's assist from Dainus, along with the raised bucket of Doug's front-end loader from Birch Street Excavating Service in downtown Corny.

That decision to put in the French doors committed me—and perhaps commitment could actually have happened when this thing was all said and done—to dreaming up a little seven-by-three-and-a-half-foot deck above the garage doors to guarantee that Linda and any future visitors wouldn't open those doors and take an airy walk into the gloaming—a little tough on the old house insurance. Oh yeah, and then, of course, there was that big cupola that I'd decided I'd need to build and install at the mid-point of the roof where the 6-12 south side met the 3-12 shed. Maybe it was the alcohol, but what I saw looming darkly before me was no longer just a garage but the Incredible Hulk. This project was slipping out of any prudent control.

So what was going on here? Had I lost my mind? I'm pretty clear on it now—what I was looking at was my own little

Teaching Fools

jungle gym for Old People, Pee Wee's playhouse. To put a more forgiving spin on it, I was now in the process of creating my own little Academy for the Experientially Challenged. Without realizing it, I'd taken a middling amount of information that I'd soaked up from Howard and started practicing on a project that had morphed into several instrumental but integral carpentry tasks. Work was going along fairly smoothly on the Hulk and at the pace I always seem to work at—slug speed. As I sat with the sediment of that second glass of wine, what scared me was that most of what I'd done and would be doing soon would be my first dance. Scary. Foolhardy. Hubris. So how had it reached this pass?

To answer my question, I'd need to flash back two years before this Wednesday evening of July 30, 2003, to my decision to build the garage, the kind of structure I'd originally envisioned, how I decided its configuration, where I determined to site the damned thing, and what Howard thought about it all. Obviously certain other questions need to be factored into the mix, like who the hell did I think I was and what the hell did I think I was doing. Most important was the tutorial relationship I'd felt developing between Howard and me, between mentor and student, and the need I felt to move out of his little classroom and build a piece that expressed what I'd been learning. A lot of this seemed uncannily reminiscent of the medieval guild notion of "master" and "masterpiece."

"Masterpiece"—as I mentioned earlier, it's a wonderfully storied word, with all sorts of associations. A dubious connection to a run-of-the-mill steak sauce notwithstanding, the word possesses connotations that we're all familiar with—a complete game, one-hit shut-out by that right-handed little dealer of heat, formerly of the Boston Red Sox, Pedro Martinez, Senor Smoke, who called into question the most basic postulates of physics every time he flung his arm toward the plate; the name of a program on PBS period pieces of great literature seen by miniscule audiences; a stunning rendition of Rimsky-Korsakov's *Scheherazade* whose orchestra magically recreates the movements of a ship breasting billowing waves and makes its audience feel them; a painting of an English sky and country vista by Constable whose rendering of its subject, its use of color, perspective, light, and space commands even the unschooled museum visitor to lean toward and then into it.

But, from my earliest teaching experiences, I became aware of the origins of the word's literal meaning. It relates to the craft I'd been watching Howard practice. It's important, though, that I don't limit "masterpiece" to merely carpentry. The term grew up during the high Middle Ages on the worn heels of feudalism, a system in which the nobles owned the land, the serfs were tethered to it, and precious little existed in between. That set of social relationships became complicated with the populating of towns, the development of a money-driven economy, and the need for a wide variety of skilled craftsmen to wield the tools that would erect these towns and actuate the businesses and services that would drive them.

The vacuum that would need to be filled by stone carvers, masons, carpenters, and lead-pouring and slate-laying roofers, among many other trades, required a set of standardized rules and procedures for the training of workers in these crafts. A pattern for educating those entering the trades had to be created, a means for differentiating the responsibilities of apprentices, journeymen, and masters, a method by which the developing skills of an apprentice could be evaluated as sufficient to be awarded the rank of journeyman. But an overarching hierarchy of "masters" of the trade held the system together. They settled upon and monitored the curriculum of those entering and proceeding upward through the trade and sat in review of the work of those skilled enough to attain the designation of master themselves.

And that's where the word "masterpiece" comes in. In the life of any guild of artisans, an aspiring master would be required to create his own "masterpiece" to showcase those nuanced expressions of his craft and eventually enable others to associate his name with his work. I love that process. I've been a part of it, both in the painstaking development of a "doctoral" endeavor of original design that required the submission of my work, and myself as its crafter, to a committee of recognized experts, "magisters" in the medieval sense as the universities began to operate within the same guild framework.

Howard was such a master. A master carpenter. In his nomadic career, he'd created many masterpieces. One of these, built for a D.C. lawyer, Howard spoke of several times with a pride of accomplishment that caused him to smile faintly and lose eye contact.

Howard no longer needed to prove his status as master. He'd earned it through many years of craftsmanship, satisfied customers, and a list of referrals that stretched far enough beyond the horizon to enable anyone so inclined to visit a number of residences or business establishments around the country and view for themselves the quality and variety of his work.

So what does all of this "master" stuff have to do with me? Literally, nothing at all. I could watch Howard till the cows came home and I'd never develop a fraction of the knowledge, skill, or experience necessary to begin to shadow what Howard has done. And, while Howard dissolutely framed his way through the southern portion of the country and built numberless houses and commercial structures, he'd always been a finish carpenter first, a builder of fine cabinetry and, more recently, furniture for cabins, homes, and businesses. I didn't want any part of that action. I knew that I couldn't pretend to anything more than the competency of a rough carpenter, and that suits me. And watching, listening, and asking questions of Howard toward that end—house framing, stick building, and the skills and tasks that correlate to it—had become a mission with me.

That's where my "masterpiece" of sorts spins into play. Nothing terribly ambitious, particularly for the likes of Howard. But, for me, the Taj Mahal, the Breakers, Monticello, bigger than big, apocalyptic, and, perhaps, impossible. What I had in mind was a garage. Well, not just a garage. For the past year and a half, I'd been envisioning a two-and-a-half-car affair. Perhaps a knock-off of the one-story eighteen-foot-deep two-stall, nearly flat-roofed shed that my neighbor Dixie and her husband had been using to store their garden tools. It was simple, functional, and, as garages go these days, probably cheap to throw together. I'm using the phrase "throw together" cavalierly here to suggest that I, as the "thrower," had sufficient experience to do that throwing in an intentional and progressive way when in fact nothing could have been further from the truth. But I *wanted* to build one.

My concept, though, began to mushroom far beyond Dixie's humble structure. I wanted storage—lots of it. I needed a place to store my and Linda's expanding collection of tools beyond the old outhouse and the "shed." Yanking open the doors of either building could get one killed from the cascade of building materials and other stuff trying to force their way out. That meant something considerably wider than Dixie's cramped space—maybe a standard twenty-four feet to accommodate a couple of full-size vehicles as well as my '74 MG Midget and the '64 Morris Mini Minor collecting spiders and mice beside the driveway. If I were to do it right, I should make the space deep enough for some work benches and cabinets against the back wall, a spot for my table saw currently monopolizing most of the space in my little shed and its extension table languishing in the deep grass behind the outhouse. That might take twenty-six feet, and, just maybe, that space would be sufficient to house a small un-masted sailboat, too.

But, as I thought about it, perhaps one story wasn't enough for my masterpiece. Maybe, if I was successful in building something to a second story, I could really design some serious storage areas, and, while I was up there, perhaps carve out that substantial craft space that Linda had always yearned for as well as a large guest room—maybe even a little bathroom, too, so that guests wouldn't need to run down the outside stairs I'd need to build and into the house to answer nature's call or, much worse, piss in Dixie's general direction. And, unless I intended for my guests to perform their excretory functions on their knees, that meant vaulting the ceiling.

As I continued to wind the actuating key to the toys in my mental attic, I knew I'd need sources of light for any imagined second story and visual access to the Lake and the low Sawtooth Mountains thirty-five miles on the other side of it, more than likely double casements of the sort that we had in the main cabin, one for both the guest room and Linda's toy box. Just to ensure ample light and ventilation, perhaps a couple of screened skylights, and, certainly, a large slider at the back of that second story and—what the heck!—double French doors overlooking the yard from the front of the structure. And, of course, if I intended a slider in the rear, I'd have to make provisions to build an elevated deck, and why not make that deck run the width of the rear of the building, as well as several feet around the north side leading to the outside stairs? And, if I was serious about the French doors that would open inward, I'd be insane not to build a short but usable balcony for those doors to open onto.

Yikes! Why the hell not, while I was at it, build a double helix stairway to heaven, attach a couple of stone parapets, scrap the garage doors for a chain-driven draw bridge, and, when I was done, float the entire thing over to Scotland! The chances of my building what I had in mind were about as high as Macbeth's castle being assaulted by the forest of Dunsinane. I was making the kind of wish-list that one delivers to an architect and that depends for its successful execution on the skills of a highly recommended builder. And I hadn't yet even built any free-standing, fully enclosed structure as big as a damned bird house. What was called for here was either the administration of large doses of elavil, a lobotomy—move over, McMurphy—or commitment.

But that was the vision of my masterpiece. I began to air it out with Linda, test the waters gingerly with those who ought to know better like Little Donny who inherited Cardinal Lumber from "Big Donny" down the street, Sean of Kahuna Electric who owned a cabin at the end of the little dirt spur Dyer Straits sits on, and, of course, most of all, Howard. As I heard myself whispering like a mantra the vocabulary that expressed the conjoining of plates, studs, joists, gable ends, rafters, ridges, fascias, returns, flitch plates—ah, more on that one later !—barges, and shed dormers (on Donder and Blitzen!), the more I felt I was describing reality, a fait accompli. Kind of like a religious fanatic speaking feverishly about "the promised land," how some will be chosen and others rejected, how those who truly believe will be born again while the rest—mostly rationalists and secular humanists—will go directly to hell without collecting two hundred dollars. And, how the fanatic had come to know with unshakable certainty that the promised land existed, that he knew where it was and how to get there, and that, when it was time to go, he wouldn't need to pack his asbestos suit. Yeah, right. I'll be down to get you in a taxi, honey—better be ready 'bout half past eight.

The funny thing about all of this nonsense was that Howard didn't discourage me. And I think I was expecting, maybe even hoping, that he would. Go ahead, Howard, punch a hole in my dream. Drive your rusty Dodge van through my plan. I dare you. Quite to the contrary, Howard listened quietly and respectfully to my recitation while he ran some stock through his table saw in preparation for still another kitchen cabinet job. I brought my roughly drawn plans, laid them out on his glue-up table while Howard poured us both a cup of coffee from his bottomless thermos. He looked them over, riffled through the several pages of elevations and cut-away drawings I'd assembled as close to a one-inch-to-one-foot scale as I could, and stayed quiet as he proceeded.

There was none of the convulsive laughter I might have anticipated. This was Howard in full concentration, looking for logic, struggling to transfer my rhetoric and flat drawings into the three-dimensional mental picture he needed before he could embark on any of his own jobs. He asked the kinds of analytical questions I'd hoped he would.

"Where will the load-bearing supports occur within the first floor of the garage, and how will you incorporate them into the plan of the entire structure? Which way will you be running your joists for the second floor, and why? Have you considered what mechanisms you'll be using to vault the second floor and to negotiate the twenty-six-foot free span of the ridge beam? What's the pitch of the main roof, and what will the pitch of the shed dormer be? Since you'll be vaulting the roof, what provisions will you make to adequately ventilate that second story?"

Never once did he check to determine if I had my pants on backwards, nor did he stage a test to see if, like the hapless student in my favorite "Far Side" cartoon, I'd try to open his shop door from the wrong direction. I think he'd concluded I was crazy. But, except for his signature ocular gleam and a thin smile of the type that Richard Nixon wore when he delivered his "I am not a crook" speech, he betrayed no hint that he was mocking me.

I took Howard to lunch that late fall day, at Tracy's-on-the-Lake, the latest reincarnation of the infamous Crossroads Café where the grease used to be so thick that one could skate to a table from the front door. Over a couple of California burgers and curly fries, I was waiting for Howard to demonstrate the impossibility of what I'd just described. But he didn't. He was more interested in *why* I wanted to build it. I was hoping he wouldn't. I gave him all of the reasons I'd been able to identify—a desire to really own my property by fully investing myself in it; a need to test my ability to start and follow through on a very difficult and complex project with minimal intervention; a commitment to learn the skills that make a journeyman carpenter; and, perhaps the biggest motivator of all, pride.

There's no denying it—the whole thing could crash and burn, and I could encounter any number of problems along the way that would send me pleading for a paid professional to bail me out, but, if, no matter how long it took, I was able to pull it off, my chest that had slowly sunk south of Kansas would harden and lift, my flaccid stomach soon needing a porch of its own would achieve six-pack definition. Hey, I'd be the man, mon. I mocked myself thoroughly as I told Howard what I was thinking. I may have been kidding myself about whether I could do the job, but I knew myself pretty well, had no illusions about the pride factor, and intended to address myself to the task with humility.

Howard talked soothingly about how he'd broken into building, how his taskmaster father had showed him how to perform a particular carpenter's task and then expected Howard to carry it through with speed and correctness. In no time, he was building his own houses, and, through all the jobs he'd supervised and the hundreds of workers he'd trained to implement the staged systems of his building strategy, he'd understood that working alone was best and that trying to carry an apprentice to the point of holding his own and contributing to an enterprise was the abysmal worst. "Doing one's own thing is the real deal." That's what had drawn him to the Northland. That's why he was working by himself out of a shop that he fully owned next to a Lake famous for brewing up her own weather systems, regardless of what was happening in the rest of the region.

And that's why he loved to go on and on about the small battalion of individualists buried in our midst. Like the ancient and ornery author, painter, and ex-Chicago book store owner Stewart Brent; former TV anchorman and insurance agent Gary Perkins of the long Arizona-to-northern Wisconsin commute and his wife Lorie the restaurateur; the airplane mechanic, jack of all trades and long distance rollerblader Wally Veitmeier; that displaced computer programmer from the Cities "Dr. Mac" now plying the area for Macintosh computer repair jobs while wearing shorts so brief that they more than stretched the boundaries of indecent advertising; the deceased lumberyard owner Albert Isaksson who's said to have buried the first and every subsequent dollar he ever made in coffee cans on his rocky, stumpy properties.

Howard's final word? "Do it if you really want it." This wasn't advice he was offering me, nor was he irresponsibly turning his eyes away from what could be some serious safety issues.

"Bill, from what I've seen of the work you've done

recently, you've got the basic skills to get this new task done." Really?

"You're a big boy with enough intelligence to bring you out of the rain and to do the necessary prep work and self-educating to ensure your own safety and a decent result." A lot he knew! He could tell I'd been preparing, but he cautioned me to strive never to get ahead of myself.

"Break the job down into learnable and doable operations—little systems—and fully understand before you start the *logical sequence* required to bring together parts of the building up from the ground." He asserted that he would make himself available as my consultant through the duration of the project, and he made a standing offer to loan me any tools that he hadn't yet sold and that I didn't own.

That was very big to me, even though he was making a big mistake because I'm notorious for never bringing things back. But also getting bigger was my growing impression that Howard thought I could do it, that it was wood I'd be working with, that I'd be measuring twice but cutting once—I continue to be seriously confused about this one—except when I made unfortunate mistakes, which could be corrected by simply doing it all again. Comforting.

It was then that I began to softly croon for Howard and other patrons challenging their health in Tracy's the first lines of the old standard, "Fools rush in where angels fear to tread." Howard would be using that opening phrase on me regularly when I dropped by the shop to give him an update on my progress.

So, alrighty then. Let's have a bit of a go at it. And I did. And it was good.

But, as with most things I do, it was good only eventually. To be good, this was a show that first had to bomb humiliatingly in New Haven before it was ready for Broadway.

Don't get me wrong. I'd rehearsed hugely before I began to bomb. I'd spent a lot of time on the preliminaries through the fall and winter of 2001 and 2002. I knew this one well. It was a great Hamletian delaying tactic as well as a manifestation of craven cowardice, but, in this case, my terror stood me in good stead. It was just the ticket for making me really think out all of the angles of the job that I shouldn't have been doing but was bound and determined to do anyway. I acted out my terror severally: my anxious "elevation" drawings from every view; my attempts to measure everything in scale well in advance; my development of a materials list, or lists, depending upon what day it was and what version of the building I happened to be pondering; trips to various lumber yards pestering estimators for price quotes, and—my absolute favorite—endless tool shopping. This is a great one, a rationalization for loading up on lots of things one might like the looks of but never in a million years use.

Except these hunting expeditions were complicated by a little wild card. When, as a teenaged hot-rodder, I used to visit the speed shops and the tool department at Sears, I pretty much knew what I wanted, knew what the tools were for, had watched other mechanics use them, and, in many cases, had used them myself—valve grinders, ring and valve compressors, torque wrenches, various and sundry gear pullers, taps, dies, micrometers—you name it. I was no past master at auto mechanics, but I was young, insatiably curious, loaded with tools and not afraid to use them. And that adventurousness, now somewhat tempered by years of expensive mistakes and more complicated cars driven by computer chips, still persists. It hasn't been that long ago when, during a total breakdown of my 1974 Olds Cutlass Supreme in the wilderness of British Columbia just below Banff during a family summer vacation, I tore one of the heads off a sizable V-8, sent it to a machine shop for milling, replaced its seals and valves, reassembled it, and drove an anxious car full of people eighteen-hundred miles home uneventfully. I was, then, the man. Or, with a lot of dumb luck and shameless bluff, I was able to get away with pretending to be.

But shopping for carpentry tools in early spring of 2002, although every bit as thrilling as filling up the cart with auto hand tools, was fraught with mystery. Christ, I'd never used many of

Teaching Fools

the tools I was on a mission to buy, and I had no clue how many of them worked.

The danger light should have been blinking in my thalamus, but I'm certain that it had burned out. Think about it— here I was, with little experience with levels or chalk lines or squares, aggressively plying the tool department of Home Depot looking for some really sophisticated stuff. Yet I knew that what I would be investing in would make my solitary job easier if I could just manage to develop enough working knowledge to maintain possession of my hands and toes. It had only been a couple of years since I'd invested in my first professional circular saw—a 7 1/4" Bosch—and had never overcome my feeling of discomfort with the machine, an expectation— borne from my experience with the big deck facing the Lake—of big kick-backs, a blizzard of stinging chips, and a blade that I half expected to spin wildly loose from its centering bolt and take my arm off. I'm not good with saws. I've got a dubious history with them. Part of my problem may be seated in my willful neglect of the operating manual. Directions take time to read and absorb—why not learn while cutting an unintentional swath through a stand of both human and tree limbs?

I've had two recent and unfortunate encounters with chain saws. The first one occurred about two months before I actually began to build the garage. I'd located the best possible site for the carriage house, but it was a fairly rough patch, directly west of the main house and into the woods a bit. I liked this spot—it was surrounded by lots of birch, aspen, fir, and maple of various ages, whereas the area I wanted to clear had mostly scrub and dead trees in the middle of it, with the exception of one towering dead paper birch. When we'd built the main cabin, we'd used this area to deposit most of the building scrap—there were two huge roughly-framed boxes overflowing with refuse from the old cabin. It took several days to pick it all up and dispose of along with the endless network of brambles and blackberry runners.

The big dead one, a rusty axe, and Bill's act of contrition

But, when all was said and done, there was the tree. I'd bought a chain saw just for this purpose, one appropriately labeled "the Wild Thing." There wasn't much to it, really, beyond a sheath of Kelly-green plastic covered with multi-colored logos. After I'd given the manual a cursory scan—the information related to fueling and starting it up attracted most of my attention—I assembled the bar, mounted the chain, oiled the machine, and fired it up. No problem so far. Overwhelmed with my success and "the Wild Thing's" throaty roar, I waded into the underbrush toward the huge birch and a number of small standing or already-fallen dead ones. Prudence required that I take a hack at some of the smaller stuff, so I set to the remaining high stump of a tree that had been felled a year earlier. No problemo. Ditto for the assortment of dead ones spread on the forest floor. Linda stood behind the screen of the sliding door and watched nervously as I gained confidence from the successful cuts I'd been making.

It took me thirty minutes of indiscriminate slicing through downed logs and into the ground before I reached the big dead one. As I held the idling saw, I harbored second thoughts. I knew the way I wanted to make the tree fall—away from the house and somewhat west through a little slough that opened toward the water. And then I looked back at the house—uncomfortably close, perhaps seventy-five feet away, a distance maybe ten feet short of the height of the missile I might be launching at it in Monty Python fashion.

As Linda opened the slider and stepped on the deck to get a closer look, I approached the tree and applied the bar against the side where I wanted to cut my first notch. No sooner had I revved up the saw and touched the chain to the tree when the entire bar collapsed and fell in painfully slow motion to the base of the tree. The engine of the saw continued to idle—the saw barless and its operator brainless—as Linda leapt off the deck and plunged toward me into the brush to determine that I hadn't eviscerated myself. But really stupid people, I've come to find out, rarely get hurt; it's the innocent and unsuspecting who are caught up in the collateral damage.

In this case, the idiot walked away unscathed. But this was too beautiful. I'd neglected to perform the most basic maintenance function on a new saw—re-tighten the two main bar bolts after the first twenty minutes of the saw's operation. The most just result would have had me sliced and diced in the truest Ed Popeil tradition. Instead, after unloading a full measure of scorn upon me, Linda made me gather the shards of the saw together into a little basket and transport them to the saw repair service in Herbster, where I was forced to repeat the story of my "Wild Thing" mishap to the wild amusement of the laborers and locals in the shop. I'd created a new House of Mirth. And the technician was able to tell in an instant that I'd ruined the chain by repeatedly grounding it on the forest floor.

Thrilling public exposure of ignorance and humiliation. I'd fully earned it. And this, all in the first twenty-four hours of having owned "the Wild Thing." One would think that that, and the two hours it took me to cut the big dead birch down with a dull axe, would have been enough to convince me that I should put the power tools away for good and hire a carpenter before putting myself at risk again.

But there was more damage to be done, more petard to be hoisted. After I'd given my hands a chance to heal from the axe-flailing two days previous, it was time to reclaim "the Wild Thing." When Linda refused all my bribes to pick it up for me, there was nothing left to do but suck it up and make another personal appearance at the House of Mirth. Dismissed by the technicians with a stern warning not to use the chain saw bar as a garden weasel along with a chorus of laughter, I sped back toward the cabin knowing that there was one more large piece of tree surgery to perform. Linda had requested that I get rid of a large birch tree that had emerged from the middle of a topped fir only thirty feet from our back door and now hovered some ninety feet over the new roof of the cabin in some unknown state of decay. She'd made it clear that I could call a local tree surgeon we'd used before if I didn't feel capable of performing the task myself. But, armed with a new chain, a fresh read of the owner's manual, and chastened by my experience with the big dead one, I was ready to have a go at it.

To my credit, I took plenty of prep time. I considered the wind, where and how I wanted the trunk to fall—westward, away from the house and toward the road, away from the poled electrical wires halfway up the driveway. I noted where I'd need to make my first cut, and where the second one would need to go to initiate the trunk's descent in the intended direction. I considered the difficulty of having to wade into the thick lower limbs of the fir tree to get at the birch, the width of whose trunk was beginning to look more imposing with every passing moment.

I'd taken sufficient time to have grasped that this was a dangerous job, potentially expensive if the tree fell in the wrong direction, particularly since my insurance carrier would have shown no empathy in finding me liable for the damages. Oh, I fully understood all of those things, but, even with a boatload of sweaty foreboding, I, in the words of Paul McCartney, "just had to look, having read the book." What could I have been thinking? The headlights were out, the plug to the commonsense terminal yanked. And, to add insult to injury, I even scraped a line in the driveway's sand at Linda's feet to signal the direction in which I intended to drop the tree—the very spot previously occupied by the big dead one.

As I recall, "the Wild Thing" made the first angled cut perfectly—not too shallow, not too deep, but just right. For just an unfortunate moment, "the Wild Thing" and I were one, an engine of perfect competence.

But all of that changed when I made the second cut. It was the perfect location for it, but, when I set the bar a bit higher to remove the wedge of wood that would set the tree a-falling, I cut too deeply. Even from thirty feet away, with my body obscured by pine branches, Linda knew it too. And, even if she didn't, with the resounding crack emanating from the cut, she could see it all swaying toward her. In a frozen moment, as I stood like Oedipus asking the shepherd that last fateful and doom-driven question that he already knew the answer to, the huge tree trunk started ever so slowly to waver toward me. Linda screamed for me to run. I believe "the Wild Thing" was still running, but I could think of nothing but Wily Coyote about to be crushed along with his latest gizmo from the Acme Company as I pushed my laughably insufficient weight against the birch's twelve-inch trunk. There was something wrong with this physics problem.

Luckily, I stepped back—maybe a full eight feet—there was no telling what kind of a dance that tree could have done off the cut I'd made, and there were, for just a second, all sorts of ways for a stupid person to get killed. But, suddenly, the trunk half-pirouetted, jumped from the cut to the ground, and began ever so slowly to teeter toward the house.

I remember doing all sorts of weird mathematical problems in my head with Linda's voice screaming faintly in the background—what's the angle of the tree falling in reference to that big four-by-five-foot window situated directly below the free-spanned thirty-five-foot glue lams that hold up the house, and will the force of the tree falling on them be enough to collapse the roof? If two trains were heading toward each other, one beginning in Chicago and the other in New York, how long would it take me to be on one of them? How many angels can fit on the head of a pin? Where are the Snowdens of Yesteryear? Ho ho beriberi, and balls.

Well, I firmly believe that it took that tree about an hour and a half to complete the curve of its descent. At least that, as the dossier of my insupportable incompetencies passed in full-dress attention before me. But, again, if there's a god, even the god of small things, that god may look out for fools and children. When the tree hit the house, it did so in perfect execution of an eleventh-grade physics class demonstration of a fulcrum and lever experiment. For the trunk made contact, not with the big roof of the cabin, but with the ascending rake of the much shorter "ell-ed" addition that protruded from the main cabin some

A comedy of errors

thirteen feet closer to the tree, at an oblique angle. Because the tree struck the house as it did, it hadn't time to build up sufficient speed or kinetic force. And so, on contact, the falling trunk stopped, kicked up to the west side of the house, and tilted up and over the ridge of the little roof. I might add *way* over, since that little roof supported about fifty feet of the tree's weight, with another forty extending over the other side of the roof into the next property. The tree contacted the ridge with a heavy, dull slam. I was fearful for the little roof's ridge beam and rafters, but no damage was visually apparent, no slumping or obvious breakage.

But there was still more. The huge birch trunk still needed to be removed from the little roof. There was still a golden opportunity to snatch defeat from the jaws of victory. And "the Wild Thing" had barely been warmed up. Mounting the roof and surveying the scene, I could feel the roof still held its solidity. I made two cuts, both of them ill-conceived. But I deserved much more than their cumulative results. The first cut sent a large section of birch rolling off the east side of the roof on top of an old but serviceable birch-strip canoe I'd set up on a pair of sawhorses. Still another justification for a garage. It would have served me right if the canoe had been turned into splinters. But the birch delivered only a glancing blow, succeeding only in barely cracking the canoe's bottom.

After I made the second cut, I attempted to push the trunk from the roof with my feet. It would have been better for the building if I'd not succeeded, for, when the enormous weight of tilted trunk went over the side, it kicked back toward the house, striking the gable end just above a large window. No damage though. The huge trunk still lies in the underbrush at the base of the "ell." I have had no heart, and no skill, to finish the job of cutting, splitting, and removing it. And that's been pretty much it for "the Wild Thing." Brilliantly remembering to shut it off first, I latched it immediately into its handy carrying case and consigned it to the darkest corner of the tool shed.

So… some tools I have known well and used intelligently,

but my track record with power tools, particularly saws, shocks and awes. Still, there were important choices to be made of power tools that would, should I learn to respect and use them with care, save me time and labor. Of all the choices I could have made, along with the thousands of dollars I could have squandered, I settled upon three main ones. The most important was the twelve-inch compound slide chop saw I found at Home Depot. I'd learned from the construction of the remodeled cabin that a set-up chop saw could save time and make repetitive cutting of studs and decking a dream. It was a sizable investment for me, almost three hundred dollars—Howard had since shown me his catalogue of Korean power tools through which I could have gotten one for less than a hundred. The carriage house was still just a gleam in my eye and some nine months away from getting started, but I justified the expense with the need for a tool that would make my reconstruction of a basement bathroom in our Bloomington place go more smoothly. It did in spades, and, when I told Howard what I'd bought, what I'd paid for it, and the name of the maker, he praised the versatility of my choice. With Howard's official imprimatur to support me, I knew I was on the right track.

The other two pieces of power equipment were no-brainers, although I wish I'd had better luck in the brands I chose. I knew I'd need a power nailer, both for the shingles I'd eventually be installing and the roof sheathing. And that meant, since no cordless nailers exist for roofing projects, I'd need to buy a compressor. There was no question about buying as opposed to renting. The cost of purchasing these two tools would be quickly recovered given the extended time I'd be using them to complete the roofing job. As I looked out toward the fall of 2002 when I mistakenly expected to get to roofing, I knew I'd be doing the job myself and that I'd probably be able to devote only a day per weekend to the job. I'd be slow. I'd be working on a rather steep six-twelve pitch on a second story. My progress would be tied to the weather. And I'd be tethering myself to a tree to retard my probable plummet to the ground.

Unquestionably, renting would be more expensive, inefficient, and inconvenient. But the nailer that I bought has been troublesome and balky. I'll demonstrate how in the next chapter.

My project would never progress beyond pretty dreams until I'd fully bought into Howard's first principle—"there shall be sequence." In terms of my own profession, I recalled those old teacher evaluations and the item I always got the lowest numbers on— sequential development. I'd actually become scrupulous about including an assessment question that asked students to comment on how well I did in this area. Sequence was a very humorous part of my building experience, and it was an issue that Howard continually harped on. In fact, when he found himself losing his own sequential bearings in the summer of 2004, it disturbed him enough to take a short sabbatical tour of the paper mills up on the Canadian border to get his mind back on track. I'm overestimating his difficulties here. However, before he left, he'd turned his table saw into a ham-slicer and took off the end of his left thumb down to the base of his nail. A digit of absolutely pivotal—pun intended—importance to a cabinet maker.

I'd gotten better, but I was still handicapped by an inability to locate my own ass at any point in the job, or to know where I'd dropped my tools, my tape, the nails I needed, or to think beyond the end of my nose when I addressed a small but essential segment of a job. Loser.

The farther I progressed into the project and the more I proceeded with sequence as my guiding principle toward its appointed end, the more frenetic things became. I attribute much of that implosion of semi-professionalism to having rarely finished anything I'd ever started beyond the ecstatic conjoinings with Linda—and even those, I fear, should I have consulted about their details with her, were far too quick. By the last two weeks of summer 2003, for instance, I'd gotten the little jobs down to a precious few but found I was struggling to address them in some semblance of a rational sequence. Process began to collapse into what a writing teacher or literary analyst might label as a "huddled conclusion."

Along the way toward that huddle and muddle was the installation of the two eight-foot-wide garage doors. I recall my encounter with "the Big Kahuna", Sean, at the recyclable shed next to the air strip one Saturday morning and what he said about how garage door installation is one of those "hand-off" jobs you give to the experts—actually, I got the distinct impression from Sean that any amateur guilty of installing his own garage doors was giving *himself* a hand job.

"It doesn't pay to do them yourself," he said, indirectly but clearly mocking me; "too many opportunities to get tangled up in the cables," which he said had happened to him; "too many prime chances to get a launched spring embedded in your skull," which I quickly granted.

"Give it to an expert," he opined. He said he had a guy who did all of his doors for $80 to $150, and that, he bragged, was the rate charged for the sixteen-footers that he dealt with. Why, "I've got a guy who comes in and does the whole job in about three hours. Time is money. It's stupid to let anyone but the professionals do this job."

OK, Sean. Thank you very much for making me feel like a grade B jerk-off.

Another confirmation that Sisyphus lived and worked on my carriage house. Rolling rocks or ricocheting two-and-a-half-foot torsion springs off every corner in the garage, doors falling from un-square and unstable tracks to shatter on the concrete floor—what's the difference? The versatility of this Sisyphus was limitless—he could do it all. He is the man. And, four hours later, after switching some hardware around that he'd bolted to the wrong locations, Sisyphus lifted the doors of the garage and emerged smilingly to the brilliant afternoon sun and the adoring applause of the universe. Albert Camus would have been proud had he not already careened off a French road and killed himself.

To gain respite from Sisyphus' and Sean's ridicule, I sought the consolation of a short conversation the day after the garage door installation on August 3rd when I left Linda at the shop with Sally to get Howard's truck for the work I'd be doing the following week. Sally had said that Howard had gone home to vent his bladder, which I'd thought strange, given the constant availability and airy freshness of the executive washroom behind the shop. I found him in his darkened living room regaling with stories a man named Gary, who was partners with his wife in the Village Inn Restaurant in Cornucopia.

Gary was an interesting set of stories himself. A successful insurance salesman for years in Wisconsin, he received a promotion that required that he move to Phoenix, and so he'd been commuting back and forth for the past few years to their remodeled home down the road in Port Wing until recently, when he opened up his own office a short hop away in Superior, Wisconsin. Gary looked a bit like a stock Dickens character. He was tall, his hair darkly tinted Reagan-style and brushed straight back with a wave in the front, making him look like he'd just emerged from a wind tunnel or a wing-walking exhibition or an audition for a TV anchor position, which he once held. He was an aggressively confident, impatient, and endlessly optimistic grocery bag that had been too generously overstuffed.

Gary was there to schmooze with Howard a bit but also to ask if he'd build three identical corner hutches for the newly finished barn next to his house in Port Wing. "There's no such thing as identical hutches," Howard said. The wood, the circumstances, the mere fact of human measurement, humidity and atmospheric conditions made "identical" impossible for pieces crafted from wood.

Howard told Gary that I was engaged in "an imposing building project, a carriage house with a full two stories, one that [I'd] been doing by [myself]." I was uncomfortable with Howard talking up my project to anyone else. It felt kind of like somebody blabbing to an outsider about a writing project I'd covertly been developing and didn't want to acknowledge until it was done. It felt a little like bad luck. I was glad, though, about the way that Howard characterized my relationship to the job—I was, as he put it, "not a carpenter." He talked about my project to Gary partly as if I had no business doing it, but also in admiration of someone without the requisite skills who'd managed to put together a solid structure not about to fall down. That felt good, coming from the master.

How far I'd come from my first day of work on the carriage house and the first of many purposeful interventions by the master. Only a year before that chat with Howard and Gary, I'd finally pulled the trigger on the project after making excuses for nearly a year that I was too busy with other things and needed more time to properly site the structure.

After contracting with a young man named Billy from Herbster, on Howard's glowing recommendation about his reliability and the quality of his work, to pour and finish the slab and set anchor bolts for my building, I'd waited for a couple of months for Billy to show up. When he did, it was the middle of July, the summer was half gone, and I would have a mere three weeks to get the project literally off the ground before I'd have to return to the classroom. Billy's little three man crew did a competent job, but, again, in "South Shore time," meaning that, from start to finish, there were some open and unworked days in between.

I waited the necessary two days for the slab to sufficiently harden and cure, on Howard's recommendation again, which brought me to a brilliant, if hot, humid, and still Saturday morning. I was out in the yard as nervous as a cat, anxiously collecting all of the tools I'd purchased in the middle of the night at a Home Depot on my last trip up to the cabin. Chief among them were an eight-foot straight-edge and clamps to ensure true cuts with my circular saw; a grade A, first-class four-foot wooden level, complete with its own plastic house; a killer twenty-ounce Kevlar-handled framing hammer that has been priceless even as it has unhinged most of my muscles and joints from my fingers to my shoulders and made it almost impossible for me to sleep; a nylon tool belt attached to my waist with both buckle and Velcro with so many hangers, hooks, and pockets that I could have lived out of it and that, no matter how tightly I attached it to my waist, would usually slide down around my knees; a small rafter square, which confused the hell out of me when I first saw one and on which I consorted with Howard for a short working lesson; and a large carpenter's square for stepping off rafters with all of the necessary computations stamped on the back that I'd bought for fifty cents at a garage sale. I'd be taking delivery in a half hour of a big portion of the framing lumber on my materials list from Cardinal—their estimate had been just a little higher than the bid of another larger yard, but, as Howard had reminded me, it was a good thing to support your local lumber yard.

No sooner had the Cardinal flat-bed truck backed in and dumped its load in my driveway and I'd donned my tool belt than Howard meandered unannounced into the driveway in the beat-up and faded old Dodge pick-up he'd just recently re-acquired. I hadn't expected him, and, frankly, I wasn't pleased that he'd come by, although I didn't let on to him. That wouldn't have been at all hospitable or respectful. I'd rather hoped to take some personal and private time getting familiar with my hammer and the wood, taking some wild whacks and inflicting some dents, making as much noise as I wanted without attracting on-lookers. This was amateur night—I'd read my undistinguished library of two framing books for the fifteenth time, absorbed an atomic amount of the information I'd need to get the job underway, and I wasn't interested in showcasing my incompetence before an audience, particularly an expert one.

But Howard had come on a mission of mercy—we laughed about it as I retold the story to Gary in Howard's living room. He wanted to make sure that I got off to a plumb, level, and square start, and he'd come intending to demonstrate for me the basics of wall framing. And I'll be forever grateful. As I say, it was hot that Saturday morning, one of an endless succession of airless, blast furnace days, leaving one gasping for air, slapping at droves of little biting flies, cursing Gitcheegoomie for perversely locking the door of her icebox. Whatever faint breeze we'd be getting came from the south.

No relief for the wicked, as my mom used to say. Howard

belted up, loaded up with long and beefy "sixteens," grabbed his framing hammer, and invited me onto the twenty-four-by-twenty-six concrete dance floor. All that was showing around the perimeter were the heads of the J-bolts that Billy had installed according to my building plan. I'd already marked, measured, and drilled out the holes in the two-by-six pressure treated sections of boards that I'd be using as the bottom plates for the building.

Now a business-like, no-nonsense Howard was turning back the clock to 1996, except that now he was in mentoring mode.

He declared, "We're going to lay out a wall, and I'm going to show you the system that you should be using on all the walls you build, both first and second story, from now on. Ok?"

My lack of confidence and knowledge of what I'd need to be doing were transparent to Howard, but pride took a distant second place to attending to and practicing what Howard knew I needed not just to know, but to do competently. He was surprisingly generous and patient during the entire process.

"I'm sure you're going to do well once you get going, and you know that it goes without saying that I'm just down the street if you run into any difficulties that you can't figure out yourself. But I don't want you to get hurt—that's the most important thing—and I want you to use good, sound building principles. Do it right or don't do it at all. Plumb, square, and level. Studs nailed on center and stacked, along with joists, on top of each other. And it all begins with carefully measuring and cutting lumber and laying out, flat on the slab, all of the framing elements for your rough opening. Let's take a look at your building diagrams for the walls, and let's pick one to lay out the framing."

Pretty intimidating stuff. Put your hands up. Face against the wall. Now reach slowly into your back pocket for your wallet, drop it on the floor, and kick it over to me. Luckily, I had plans—boy, did I have plans. I'd been compulsively filling yellow legal pads full of them in the several weeks prior to the slab pour. The question was, which of these legal pads, stacked on the kitchen island that Howard had built for Linda several years earlier, contained the most recent plan of what I intended to build?

It's not entirely professional-looking to sprint off the job and into the house, with tool belt clanging against flapping hammer—sounds delightfully obscene, doesn't it? now there's a fantasy—to sort frantically for the right plan to race back with and to present breathlessly to Howard. My working persona was definitely not that of the cool, detached Jerry Tow wearing black Ray-Bans. My slip was showing. My hair was not staying up. My gown was puckering and gapping at the waist. I'd found a zit on my nose during my last look in the mirror. And I was surely going to be late for the prom.

My plans were highly amusing to Howard, but he did compliment me on their neatness and clarity. There would be a problem not readily apparent on those wall layout plans that he'd take me to task for later, and I'll get to that in the next chapter, but for now he could read what I intended, and noted that the north wall looking toward the Lake offered the most interest and practicality as a primer for framing all subsequent walls. I nodded dutifully, said something insipid like "Cool," and waited for further instructions.

That wall plan was pretty simple—a twenty-four-foot stretch containing an opening for a standard kitchen-sized double-sash window and an opening for a standard thirty-two by eighty-inch garage door. But Howard was astute in his choice. We'd need to lay out two rough openings of different proportions, each one occurring at the same height in the wall as the other. Not difficult—that's easy for me to say now—but essential practice for me in anticipation of the really big and daunting framing challenges ahead—the eight-by-seven-foot garage door openings in the front wall, a wall that would need all of the stiffening I could provide for it in the center, the corners, and the built-up headers above the openings; the seven-by-six-foot openings in the front and rear second-story gable walls where I'd eventually be installing a beautiful French door unit in the front and a large slider in the rear which would need to be perfectly square; and last, the huge rough openings, some five and a half feet high by four and three-quarters wide apiece, virtually floor-to-ceiling, to accommodate the enormous double-cranking casement windows that would look out from the second floor over Superior and be set into a shed dormer wall that would offer another adventure in framing entirely. Learning to lay out and frame those gable walls would occur within a set of circumstances in which I'd be hanging my roof on a sky-hook—I'd planned for a cathedral ceiling on the second floor, with my roof held up solely by a free-spanning pair of ungodly heavy and bolted two-by-twelves and the rafters running from it to the adjacent walls, with a four-by-eight post situated directly under it where the space bisects into two equal portions and directly over a four-by-eight post centered under the floor joists and on top of a rod drilled through the width of the concrete slab.

But here we were, man and boy, or a boy and his dog, ready to collaborate on some Stick-Building 101. First, Howard went back to the bed of the old Dodge Ram, retrieved a couple of old sawhorses—Howard would forever rag me about my Boston accent; "that would be sa-a-a-w-ahr hosses, Bill"—and shouldered them to the dance floor.

"These are yours now. I don't want to see them ever again. I'm donating them to the project. Use them in good health. And, lest you think I'm being overly generous, I'm not doing you any really big favors. Any fool can plainly see that they've seen their better days." And he was right. They were worn, covered with the scars of overly-deep blade cuts crisscrossing the cross bucks.

And, on top of that, they looked like the one-legged whore who gave the sailors a hell of a ride. I never asked Howard why both horses had a leg shorter than the other— whether he intended them for a slightly side-hill job or whether he enjoyed seeing the pieces of his work jiggling away from him toward the floor. But I've still got them. In fact, they are just as serviceable and reliable as when he made me their custodian. I used them to assemble my garage doors, and, on that same future Saturday afternoon, I cut lengths of soffit from them, blazing a few more creases in them as I always do.

Nearly worn-out, deeply scarred, wildly unattractive, stooped close to the ground, but built for the long haul—more than just a little like Howard.

So away we went. He'd be giving me the straight poop, and nothing but. First, Howard drilled me on the dimensions of the door.

"If its rough opening was set for eighty-two-and-a-half-inches, allowing for the pre-hung unit we'll be setting into it, how wide would the boards for the header above and supporting the opening need to be?"

"Why, an additional one and a half inches on each side," I stammered.

"Exactly. So what are you waiting for? Set that circular saw humming and cut two two-by-six sections to that dimension and wait for further instructions." Then, to pick up the slack of the five-and-a-half-inch wall dimension, since we'd be setting these boards on end, we'd need to trim off three two-and-one-half-inch widths of two-by-six to use as shims between each of the cut boards.

After I nailed that little box together and laid it on its side on the concrete deck, we consulted my plans for the lengths of the jack studs that would be placed directly under each end of the headers. Howard reminded me that we'd have to include the width of the bottom plate in that dimension. After cutting the jacks, Howard instructed me to lay each of those jacks on top of a full eight-foot stud and nail them together, after which I placed them in proper configuration with the header on the floor. We performed the identical operation for the construction of the header for the window to be placed in the wall, along with cutting the jacks and nailing them to studs to run from the bottom plate to the top plate. But this time those jacks were shorter, and a two-by-six was cut to rest comfortably on those jacks as the sill of the window.

It was time for marking the plate, along with a corresponding marking of a top plate of two-by-six from the straightest piece of lumber that we could select from the pile. As

Howard had said—and I vividly remember watching him do this during the early framing of the great room in the cabin—"I'm a visual person. I need to see things in my mind before I can build them." And scattering a bunch of studs and plates on the concrete floor served just that purpose, at the same time as it served an even more important one. Working a system, Howard emphasized to me, was everything. By spreading an array of studs to fit the number of wall studs that my plan had stipulated, I was better able to see how the wall would look and how it was going to come together.

More importantly—and even a novice like me could appreciate this one—I was able, with minimal physical expenditure, to mark the placement of every one of those studs on the bottom and top plates—because I was marking them both simultaneously, as per Howard's directions—draw a line followed by a "K" for every single jack stud that framed a door and window opening, mark with a line followed by a "C" the cripples, the baby studs that would support the empty spaces beneath a sill and over a door header, and mark two "X's" for the double studs that I'd be nailing together and situating at opposite ends of the plates. Pretty easy stuff. Mucho common sense. Very safe and effortless, unlike the terrific expenditure of energy required to assemble, nail, and locate on the "J" bolts a wall built vertically. Sure, I'd read about this methodology in my super-duper framing books, but Howard was leading me through that process in the only pedagogically effective way—by putting my hands all over it and doing it.

And what my framing books didn't tell me was the way Howard customarily made a wall of his assembly-line of double-studded ends, the door opening, and framing of the window. Step by logical step, full stud became nailed into jack, followed by slamming nails through our made-up header into those jacks and adjoining studs, with the perfectly cut cripples toe-nailed to the header. When the framed door and window openings had been assembled and the doubled-studded ends had been nailed together, our jig saw puzzle was almost complete. There was nothing left to do but set those framed and nailed pieces along with the regularly-spaced and standard-length studs against their assigned marks, cozy up the bottom and top plates to the ends of the two-by-six framing lumber to those marks, give the entire wall a quick walk-about in order to spot any outstanding irregularities that have become a hallmark of my lack of concentration and mis-measurement, and then, with the easiest and most natural of hammer-swinging motions, with one foot on stud and plate to hold them in position, nail those babies rhythmically together. Piece of cake. We're in bid-nez.

As any true master teacher will do, Howard took off before the wall was done. The Socratic method. Quintessential mentorship. Who was that masked man? I wanted to thank him. But his timing was beautiful. All he wanted to do was draw me into "the system," to give me a lesson in the efficiency of effort, movement, and use of materials. To introduce me to the natural "flow" of the work. From his perspective as a former field supervisor who used to school hundreds of framers to his system, anything more would constitute economic suicide.

I can't enumerate how many bazillion times my writing students have brought their work to me in conference and have bemoaned how their writing doesn't flow. We—the student and I—could both see and hear the roughness of the syntax, the phrasing, the inappropriate word choice, the lack of transitions, the unpleasing redundancy of word, the repetition of rhetorical elements or sentence patterns. Most of these problems, believe it or not, would evaporate the minute that writing student began to focus on a subject that she really cared and new something about, or was sufficiently motivated to want to learn enough about to do it justice. That step in the sequence *had to occur first*.

That's the way it is. Good writing is all about finding and expressing one's own voice. That sounds a little esoteric until one realizes that no voice—authentic or phony—can emerge unless one has something to say. And so students—even some of the most unpracticed and unengaged writers—begin to catch on to it, catch fire, in a different, more substantial way when an urgency seizes them, a need to communicate the importance of the subject they're writing about to an audience that may not include me.

That's what Howard did. There's a bit of the trickster, the charlatan, the confidence man, the swindler, in all teachers, and that goes for Howard. He wanted to test my skills, a base-line aptitude for the job I'd carved out for myself, but also the level of my commitment and my preparation for the task. I think he gave me minimal passing grades in those areas. He saw me as much like those "little better than average" writing students I've just mentioned. But he took it one step further. He equipped me with some "composing skills," a system for admitting a measure of "flow" into the expression of my total commitment and enthusiasm for the job. And, as any good teacher will do, he left me to pound that last collection of nails into that initial stud wall, infused with the belief that I could do it. *That* is *mentorship*. And, if, along the way, I forgot or confused the language of my subject, or admitted ugly or awkward or unsymmetrical structures into my "composition," I could always dismantle and revise them into correctness.

As he pulled the door handle of the pick-up vigorously with both hands to release the badly sprung door, he intoned insinuatingly, "Wood is a living thing, Bill." What a con. And then he was off, like "Bad Santa" exiting from the back door of yet another middle-aged spread, the old slant six straining loudly as he backed out of the driveway—I believe he backed into a tree again before he successfully exited—and the heavy plastic bed liner flapping like a loose tin roof in a storm against the entirely rotted tail gate.

I was ready to go, and, before the day was through, I'd cut, laid out, and nailed the opposing stud wall—not nearly as gracefully or as seamlessly as Howard and I had done it, but successful nonetheless. I was never going to be anything more than the roughest of rough carpenters working at a snail's pace, but I was, in my own way, moving forward. Thanks to the master.

CHAPTER 12

Externship II: From Master to Masterpiece

But there it was, just as the books said. You went in a circle, gave yourself endless trouble under the delusion that you were accomplishing something, and all the time you were simply describing some great silly arc that would turn back to where it had its beginning, like the riddling year itself.
--Mann, *Magic Mountain*

As I've already mentioned, D-Day occurred at Dyer Straits on the morning of Saturday, July 15, 2002, and ground operations went well after that, with steady advances. I never could have guessed that I'd move the project ahead so far, so consistent with my original purposes, and so free of serious personal injuries. And there have been lots of opportunities for me to become the fatty filling for a wall sandwich, do a triple gainer off an icy roof, or pitch from the top of a sixteen-foot ladder into a jagged pile of construction material. That nearly happened during completion of the last cornice return of my frustrating soffit job. Only a one-handed grab and some nifty footwork forestalled a broken ankle, leg, collar bone, or worse. I barely averted being squashed by a thirty-foot spliced two-by-twelve ridge beam I had no business lifting. And I nearly murdered Linda when a huge deck beam slipped out of the slot I was pushing it through, fell five feet like a guillotine blade, and glanced off her tiny hand. That one still flashes unsummoned on my mental monitor and makes me shudder.

Oh, sure, there have been a few near misses. My hands and wrists hurt sufficiently to impede circulation and a good night's sleep; forget the carpal tunnel—this was arthritis. And knives and hammers have always been nasty hazards for me. On a mid-July morning in 2003 I cut a deep gash in my thumb with a utility knife while working with Tyvek—I'd just changed the blade, so it was a nice clean slice. I flew down the ladder as quickly as I could, only to meet my wife blowing through the back door alerted to trouble by angry profanity I emitted when I injured myself. I was leaking blood, I'll admit, at quite a clip, but, ignoring my protests that it wasn't as bad as it looked and that a tightly applied bandage would do the job, Linda dialed 911 and summoned an ambulance. I was flattered at her concern, but also mortified that she'd told the paramedics we'd meet them on County Road C half-way across the long low hill to Washburn. And the way Linda was fishtailing up the road, I wasn't sure if the paramedics might be treating the both of us for more serious injuries. I remember repeating "this is crazy, and they're going to be mad as hell for being made to drive all the way out from Ashland with emergency lights flashing just to put a band-aid on me." It was unnerving to see how panicked Linda became the further down the road we sped.

And I was right for once. We met the ambulance. People passing us on "C" slowed and gawked as the paramedics led me into the back of the ambulance. I was already apologizing for calling them out for nothing, but they were wonderful, understanding, warmly solicitous of Linda. The three of them calmed her, telling me they were a hell of a lot more concerned for her than for me. I declined the ride and signed the release, but took them up on their advice that I proceed on to Ashland and the hospital emergency room. Well, it wasn't Howard's filleted digit, but I did get several stitches, a couple through the fingernail, and some interesting stories from the attending physician who happened to be a nephew of World War II's General "Old Blood and Guts," doing his bi-weekly stint at Ashland Hospital away from his home base in Michigan. 1 was back up on the building that afternoon.

And there was another reenactment of the Far Side "school for the gifted" cartoon when, just before supper a month later after a hot and rainy day that had kept me from working, I ascended the ladder into the loft with the intention of removing some nails in sheathing I'd used to cover the large rear opening. I wanted to get ready for the ledger board I'd be installing the next day below that opening and the deck I'd be hanging from it. It took me just about a minute to nearly knock myself out. Reaching up to hook the claw of my hammer over one of the rusted nails, I pulled down mightily. Since the nail didn't give, I moved closer and pulled harder.

The nail came out, alright. That's, at least, my partial recollection from a missionary position on the floor after the hammer head had hit me right at the bridge of my glasses. I hadn't been hit that hard in the nose in thirty-eight years. Absolutely centered. It's amazing that I didn't break it for yet a fourth time, and it was only due to Linda's smart suggestion that I ice it at twenty-minute intervals for the rest of the evening that I didn't end up looking like a raccoon. But it hurt. There was lots of blood. I put one hell of a notch on the bridge of my nose. And the band-aids I was forced to wear under the bridge of my glasses made me look even nerdier than usual. Serves me right. It doesn't get any stupider than that. I might, as Linda pointed out, just as well have foregone pulling the nail in favor of grabbing the hammer with both hands and applying it directly to my skull. Good job. Now it's your turn, Linda.

But, by and large, things had gone swimmingly, if not quite at the breakneck speed that I would have wished. And, except for the work I'd done the first couple of weeks framing the first story, Howard expressed approval at what I was doing. But there was no way for me to anticipate the negative reaction he'd deliver when he drove over to review what I'd done so far.

What I'd done, mostly, was the framing of the four first-floor walls. After the first one that Howard and I had made a solid and correct start on, I took it from there. Soon, I had the two adjacent side walls, the twenty-six footers, framed and laying on the deck. To get at the back and front walls, I'd need to find a way to raise the first two. Their weight was way beyond what I could lift, and, as I soon discovered, exceeded the combined exertions of me and a younger visiting teacher friend of mine, Scott. With no other options in sight, Scott and I piled into my car in search of a couple of burly guys. After trying the marina and Ehler's Store, I figured my last chance was the only bar in town, Fishlipps.

It was about lunch time when I wandered up to the bar and asked the bartender if she knew of anyone who might want to make a few bucks for a half hour's work. No takers. As I thanked her for trying, a large and unshaven young man who'd been sitting on the other side of the bar asked me what I needed the muscle for and where the job was located. When I gave him the details, he said there'd be no problem, he'd retrieve his brother as soon as he'd finished his lunch, and, with more specific directions, he'd be there in half an hour.

Scott and I found out shortly that these two guys, the Halvorson brothers, knew where I lived almost better than I did. Every morning for the past fifteen years, these guys and their dad had rounded Squaw Point on their way to Superior's deep fishing waters. The Halvorsons were the only commercial fishing operation still working out of Corny. These guys were almost too strong, not only succeeding in helping us lift the walls but moving them beyond the J-bolts and off the foundation. But eventually we lined them up, and, as those guys held the two walls in place, Scott scurried around to brace them securely with wedged two-by-sixes.

In a little discussion in the shop later, Howard told me that I should have employed "a couple of Mexicans" to make the wall-raising go more smoothly. Another rather un-PC interjection, to be sure. What he meant in this circumstance was a short-cut, one that would serve effectively when there was a shortage of manpower.

"Little pieces of two-by-six nailed vertically to the outside of a wall and extending below the bottom plate will prevent that wall from falling off the foundation and keep it in direct line with the J-bolts, Bill."

Duh. I should have been able to figure that out by myself. But Howard's long experience working alone and needing to discover techniques that would permit him to make progress without another set of hands had catalogued a small army of "Mexicans" like this. I'd respectfully defer from employing that term he used for time and work-savers, but, working alone over the period of two years, I would and did invent some effective devices for getting pieces of the job done and achieving progress.

I employed that "Mexican" that Howard suggested to raise, nail, plumb, line, and brace those other two walls, and, after a concession to my friend Scott's offer to help me sheath those walls with OSB, I was ready to request the critical presence of Howard for an inspection. I frankly felt great about what I'd accomplished so far and expected that Howard would applaud me. It was another Saturday morning visit toward the end of July. I kept my mouth shut as I followed Howard into roofless walled space. He walked around, looked closely, paid particular attention to the corners, said, "Yeah" and "Check" a few times to himself, and then stopped dead in his tracks a foot away from the back wall. His brow was seriously furrowed. Something was wrong. And he was miffed.

After a long silence, Howard asked me, "What have you *done* here?"

Jesus.

This was serious. I asked him what he meant.

Still looking away from me and at the back wall, he asked, as if he were formally grilling me, "What's your spacing on your wall studs?"

I said, simply, "Twenty-four on center."

He muttered to himself; quietly, but pretty clearly in disgust, "Twenty-four on center. *Twenty-four on center!*"

A little unnerved by now, I begged him to tell me what the problem was.

He shot back, moving his eyes away from the wall long enough to give me a side-ways accusatory glance, "Who told you to do that?"

My answer didn't please him: "Well, uh, I'd read a couple of framing books and a text on house construction that said that sixteen-on-center was a standard for framing two-by-four walls, but both authors said that twenty-four-on-center was an optional method for framing two-by-six walls."

No response. Nothing. Prolonged and uncomfortable silence. I pushed back against it: "What's the matter, Howard?"

He retorted caustically, "You don't want to know."

He was still avoiding eye-contact when I insisted, "Look, Howard, tell me what's eating you. I'm a big boy. I can take it."

Howard's response was frontal and close this time, and struck like a heavy slap in the face: "Because it's shitty construction, that's why."

I was feeling a little panicked as he walked away from me and planted himself in one of the framed corners. "Why, Howard? How shitty could it be if at least two published professionals have OK'd it?"

He was adamant on this one: "It's shitty because it's lazy, Bill. Think about it. Framing is all about stacking. If you're building 24-inch-on-center walls here, you'll need to do the same with your joists and your second-floor framing. Everything's got to be lined up. And what happens when you get a good wind from the direction of The Old Lady? What kind of protection against racking have you built in here?" Howard was referring to the kinds of forces on a building that could cause walls to move from side to side. "With 16"-on-center studs and joists, you'd have a nice tight structure to prevent racking, but 24's won't do that."

But that was only the beginning of the chewing-out from my mentor. Emerging from the corner and wearing a tight and mocking smile, Howard came back into my face and sneered,

"OK, Bill, so how much money do you think you saved by framing on 24's? Come on, let's figure it out right now. Do you think you saved a lot by taking this short-cut?"

Well, I hiccupped, coughed, and farted for a few seconds as my math-challenged brain started to struggle with the computation. But it was dead obvious even to me. On a twenty-four-foot wall, maybe four studs. Nothing at all. And hardly any extra time would have been expended in doing the job the right way.

There was little for me to do but throw my hands up in the air, abjectly confess my apostasy, and throw myself on Howard's evaporating mercy. "Can I save the work I've done so far? Do I need to rip out the studs, re-mark the plates, and make a real mess of things?"

Holding an erect index finger close to my face and then sweeping it toward one of the framed corners, Howard issued a directive I imagine he'd delivered often as a field supervisor: "What you've got to do is go back and do some serious bracing. I want you to run two-by-sixes from the top of each corner down to the plate to at least the mid-point of each wall, and I want you to angle them in and nail them to each stud along the way. That's the only way you're going to be able to build in the kind of protection against racking that this structure is going to need."

"And that'll do it?" I asked. "I'll be able to continue with the twenty-four-on-center framing that I started with?"

"Yes, but don't cut corners in an area where it really counts next time. I'll come by next Saturday to see if you've cleaned up your mess." And he was off in cloud of smoke and a wildly gyrating cancered pick-up bed.

I stood red-faced on the slab under the brilliant mid-morning sun, long enough for Linda to emerge from the house to satisfy her curiosity. "I don't think he liked it," I said, and then I told her about the serious verbal ass-kicking I'd just taken. Yeah, I was certainly rising and falling on Howard's approval this early in the project, and I cared tremendously what he thought about

Teaching Fools

Howard administers an instructive spanking

my work. But I found myself shaking my head and laughing about what had just happened. What the hell! After all, what did I know, and what were my expectations, anyway? And, most importantly, it really wasn't so bad, and I think that's one of the major points Howard was trying to drive home to me. Sure, it was tough to hear Howard singing his rendition of "Send in the clowns…don't bother, they're here" after all of the work I'd done, but he'd left me with the realization that it was all salvageable if I went back and used some basic construction principles to strengthen my walls. Shit, he was reminding me that I was working with wood; most of what I was going to be doing was repairable, and I needed to think things through carefully always with an eye toward safety, *sequence*, and the integrity of the structure.

I simply went back to those walls, applied forty-five-degree angle cuts to and then nailed the braces between studs from the top of each corner to the plates at mid-wall, and stiffened things. And Howard, arriving on the morning of the twelfth day, determined that it was good. A note well-taken, and, from that point, I started concentrating much more on the process, proper sequencing, and the implications that would come from following it than from blindly following a book's directions.

And that brings me to the flitch plate. That's right. *Flitch*. I'd never heard the word before, and, when Howard first used it on me, I didn't care to question him, thinking that perhaps this was carpentry's version of a malapropism. After all, through all of our discussions about language, we'd traded a number of beauties. Howard was particularly fond of the form of Texas shorthand that he'd grown up with. President Bush's use of the words "bid-nez" and "Amurk-ah" and "nuk-u-ler" come immediately to mind. But flitch?

The word came up while I was struggling over how to span the twenty-four-foot width of my framed walls with joists. Recalling the method that Howard had used to connect the front wall of the remodeled cabin with the window wall—four bolted thirty-five-foot laminated beams—I asked him if that might be the solution for the garage. I could see that I was going to need at least one post to support those joists, but, for the sake of the storage space in the garage and the prospect of running a car into a bowling alley of joist supports, I wanted to keep the space as open as possible. What about glue lams? And what about those ultra-light wooden I-beam joists that were being used in houses to span huge amounts of space—like the ones holding my daughter Karen's and my son-in-law Hunter's kajillion-dollar castle in Maple Grove, Minnesota? Could I use any of those?

I found out how little some folks knew about what I needed when I went to the local lumber yard. The advice was proferred, but it sounded misled even to me, if not downright wrong. Little Donny suggested that I turn my joists the opposite way—run them front-to-back instead of side-to-side, as I'd intended.

His thinking?—"to have a span of twenty-four feet instead of twenty-six for the beam that the joists would butt up to, allowing you to bolt together a pair, or even four, twenty-four foot two-by-twelves."

Well, it didn't feel right. I can't lay claim to any sophisticated sensitivity to engineering here—something didn't compute, though. I had this mounting fear (and I didn't air this out for Donny's consumption) that I'd be building a front wall with two nine-foot wide-open spaces that I'd be resting the ends of a bunch of very heavy joists—never mind the gable wall of the second floor and the full weight of the ridge beam—upon. Even given Donny's assurances that, "should you want to install one centralized post to position under that unbroken beam, you'd be home free," I didn't like it.

Donny said that, "if you don't like the two-by-twelve solution"—and I was appalled just thinking about how heavy four of them would be to get up in the air and bolted together—"I could order the glue lams for you."

My doubts about this "fix" drove me down the road thirty miles to Bayfield Lumber. Equipped with my drawings of the building and several earnest repetitions of what I was trying to accomplish to the wrong people in the shop, I finally was admitted to the inner sanctum, a naturally lit and crowded second floor loft offering an incomparable view of the harbor, breakwater, and sailboat moorings. There, the owner of the yard, who sucked on his pipe meditatively and smiled knowingly at me through the entire discussion, and an experienced builder patiently drew my story from me once more. They knew what they were doing, and they listened attentively even as I proclaimed my novice status. Discreetly, I conveyed the advice I'd received at the first lumber yard, expressed my reservations about it, and then prepared to take notes.

Their response was surprising. First, they liked the building I'd designed and applauded me for taking it on myself. "Welcome to the club, Bill," they said, "and to the land of self-reliance."

Secondly, though, they categorically eliminated from consideration the I-beam and glue lam solutions. "The I-beams are out, period. The loads are prohibitive, and the webs of the I-beams simply can't carry the weight you have in mind for them. People are just starting to realize that."

Thirdly, they said that my hunch about not running the joists onto the front wall was salutary, and they went one step further: "You can run shorter glue lams to a center post, attach them, and then run your twenty-four-foot joists to each side wall." They also suggested that bolted two-by-twelves, each thirteen feet long, could bridge the gap to the center post as well.

Nobody was trying to get me to buy anything. Incredible. Nobody was trying to delay my project or to suggest that I wasn't somehow up to doing it. They offered their advice, showed real interest in what I had in mind, told me to call for further technical or materials support if I thought I needed it, and sent me on my way with a very warm and fuzzy feeling.

After I transmitted those good feelings—it's been my experience that they're available up here in limited supply, with no shortage of bad advice—to Linda, I went to the shop in Herbster to query Howard. As always, he backed away from the cabinets he was working on, gave the chickens a mid-afternoon treat, poured me a cup from his thermos, and, fingering my building drawings again, listened to all the information that I had so far gleaned. His pronouncement came quickly and confidently—"You need to go to Ashland to have a flitch plate made up."

As I said earlier, I didn't at all get it. But this is what he meant, and the word actually carries an onomatopoetic sense of what he intended the flitch plate to do. A flitch plate aggressively opposes flitching. That is, it will allow no flitch to flitch before its time. Ok, then. If flitching is a tendency of an insufficiently stiffened but overly-long and particularly crucial beam to flex, give, and—let's think the worst—break, the creation of a beam from two pieces of two-by material surrounding a 3/8"-thick piece of steel of the same width and length will greatly strengthen it to oppose that tendency.

I should have known that. And I think I did, but I never affiliated the use of such a steel plate in the framing of a building. Howard told me that steel-fortified beams were common in the kind of standard construction he'd done in Maryland, and he was sure that folks in our area employed them as well, but probably called them by a different name.

All I'd need to do is determine the length of the beam I wanted to hang my joists from, pre-drill a series of holes in the two two-by-twelve boards that would compose the outsides of the sandwich, draw a true schematic of the two-by-twelve-by-three-eighths-of-an-inch steel plate replete with the locations of the holes I wanted drilled to correspond with those in the two boards, and place my order and schematic in the hands of the boys at Ashland Steel Fabricators, Inc. How supremely elegant!

But, with greatly enhanced tensile strength comes unliftable weight, and I hadn't quite banked on that. I was, as always, bound by the limitations of my own lifting capacity and anyone else in the neighborhood whom I could shame or bribe into helping. And Howard warned that I'd better have that help lined up. Howard's plan for the beam was simple but sound.

There'd actually be a pair of steel-lined beams, each thirteen feet long and running from the mid-point of the top plate of the back wall to the mid-point of the top plate of a beefed-up and posted front wall. These two beams would meet at the center of a four-by-eight-inch post in the exact center of the garage, mounted on a post cap and toe-nailed into the post. The three portions of each beam would, for the benefit of the weakling struggling with them, be shoved up onto the planks of a six-foot-high section of scaffolding situated directly next to the post, where I could assemble and then bolt the pieces of each beam with monstrous three-quarter-inch bolts. The monstrous bolts were my idea—I wasn't fooling around here.

Once assembled, each beam would then be pushed onto the platform of a wooden three-and-a-half-by-three-foot-wide tower that I built just for this purpose. This platform was my eight-and-a-half-foot-high version of one of Howard's "Mexicans." I will, from this point on, affectionately refer to it as 'The Lifeguard Station." Hell, it looked like the very device that I, during my misspent youth, used to see tanned, speedo'd, and raybanned young men and women lazing negligently from. But this one had no chair. In its place were two parallel two-by-six resting places for my beams at a height exactly three inches higher than the post that the beams would need to be slid on to.

The flitch plate was Howard's idea, and it was brilliant. The two three-piece beams would safely support a second floor, a roof over that, and, furthermore, would support the twelve joists that I'd be attaching to and extending from them to each adjacent side wall, providing in the process balance to the structure, some structurally correct "stacking" of those joists over the studs in those walls, and preservation of a sense of sanity in the length of the wooden stock I planned to use for my beams and joists. But the damned Lifeguard Station was all mine. I was beginning to think, to plan, to visualize what I'd need to make my job safer and easier—particularly to employ my imagination in creating a machine that could serve as another strong back and pair of legs and hands.

Chris sets the flitched beam sandwich

Dare I say that I was getting smarter? Perhaps.

Anyway, the job turned out to be every bit as perilous and physically taxing as Howard said it would. It took a yard worker and me to lift and place the beams onto the bed of Howard's pick-up, and we could have used lots more help. It was fortunate for me that Howard, by that time, had lost his pick-up bed to ferrous cancer and had built a very serviceable and eye-catching little wooden-posted and framed open stake body for it. I was able to muscle one of the beams up on the scaffold before my son Chris arrived on a Saturday morning to help. And, after we'd sandwiched and loosely bolted the beams, Linda jumped in the car and didn't come back until she'd rounded up two of our biggest neighbors to help us move things into place. It took, literally, ten minutes—one pair of us, Chris and I, on the Lifeguard Station and the other two guys stationed on the other end of the beam at the wall—to smoothly and deliberately shift the beams to the post. And the beer tasted especially good after that.

I was into August now, with little more than two weeks before "duty days," a battery of confounding committee meetings, and preparation for the beginning of fall semester classes. I could see that my vision of finishing the framing of the building before school started was seriously miscalculated. But there was still time for a couple of backbreaking jobs. I'll never erase the physical and mental torture of laying the 3/4-inch plywood sheathing over the joists I'd so neatly dropped into their hanger pockets. A wicked beast of a job designed for the Sisyphus I'd become, and it wouldn't have been possible during those breathlessly scorching two days without Chris' help loading up the lifeguard station with the 4-by-8 treated tongue-and-groove sheets.

Framing and lifting the second-story walls was the last process I'd be able to tackle before racing back to impersonate a college professor, and, as Howard reiterated, sequence and stacking were crucial parts of that process. The problems I'd encounter all revolved around the gable ends. I'd read the books and talked to Howard. But, would I be able to effectively implement a mathematical formula for framing the gable ends and decide whether it would be best either to build a bird's mouth at the top of each gable end or rest the ridge beam at the meeting point of the top plates of the gable walls? What I'd need to create here were a couple of construction "tools"—the first, three stanchions nailed at their base to the floor, with tall triple 2-by-6's extending to the computed height of the ridge beam with "bird's mouths" built into the top of each to receive and cradle the twenty-nine-foot scarfed ridge beam when the time came to lift it into place, and, secondly, a six-foot-high-by-six-foot-long-by-three-and-a-half-foot-wide working platform that I christened "the operating table" in order to get the job underway.

I'd also need to construct two side walls of different configuration: a four-foot knee wall on the south side to be opposed by a complex one on the side facing the Lake—a four footer for four feet on each end sandwiching an eighteen-foot section, eight feet high—designed to hold two five-foot-wide-by-six-foot-high double killer crank-out windows. This design meant that I'd need to anticipate how to hand-build a differently sloped roof on the north side—a 3-12 sloped shed roof looking out on the Lake and greatly complicating the efforts of a dumb guy who'd never built any kind of a roof beyond the small igloos he and his kids collaborated on after big snows in the back yard. Good luck.

Chris and I had great Sisyphean fun one weekend working on one of the gable walls. Chris had been hanging around our condo in Bloomington for no constructive reason that neither he nor his parents could fully fathom. Ostensibly, he'd moved in to perform his rendition of "Waiting for Godot." He'd graduated from college with his degree in Law Enforcement. He'd been waiting for a call from the Border Patrol, and, while waiting, he worked some forgettable temp security jobs, ate a lot, learned how to brew his own beer, slept away much of the day, polished up his computer game skills, and worked on his silent scowl and alienated persona. You had to love him—I mean, you really had to love him.

But soon he'd get the call from the Border Patrol and, within a month and a half be off to the Academy in Charleston. He'd become a happy agent on both borders. More significantly, he'd become a more confident, hard-bodied, generous, and once-again loving and lovable young man comfortable in his own skin.

Even though we made such a wreck of the framing of the rear gable wall that I had to reconstruct it after Chris left, it was wonderful to work with him. We had great fun up there, stumbling over ourselves as we marked and laid out and mis-cut and re-cut the gable-end studs and then nailed them into place. It was a cavalcade of errors—I'd found in the process of building this building that I worked better alone, without any additional distractions than the ones I provide all by myself. And I'd discovered that my effectiveness at working alone was due more to concentration and focus than it used to be about being self-conscious about displaying my incompetence to practiced professionals. But we did a splendid job of cutting and fastening the top plates to that gable wall, standing all of those second-story walls, and then squaring, plumbing, and attaching them to the floor and to each other. I truly couldn't have done this portion of the job without his great and good-humored assistance.

So, you see, my claim that I have constructed this building all by myself is somewhat of a bare-faced lie. The raising of the two-by-twelve spliced and bolted ridge beam that I built on the deck of the second floor revealed how much I'd been indebted to the wisdom, intrepidity, and patience of Linda to move the project forward. While taking advantage of her coaching and common sense, I can't do justice to the harm that I put her squarely in the way of in carrying out this crazy stunt. The stanchions were erect and nailed in place, based on my overestimate of what I thought I could, as a frail, 59-year-old, lift all by my one-zees.

That procedure was well-thought out, too. I blithely believed that I could carry the leading edge of that beam up my twelve-foot step ladder. And I did get that far, despite realizing that dropping that leading edge into the slot of the stanchion located nearest to the rear gable wall was dangerous all by itself. The damned 29-foot 2-by-12 ridge beam behaved like a hooked muskie, threatening to spin and whip at the slightest move. And its weight was enhanced by what it had been cut from. It was white fir of the toughest and strongest order, and slippery from having been treated, an awful combination when handled by two people, never mind only one.

I learned that lifting the other end to the same ten-foot level would be impossible, although I came within a couple of feet of my goal. Enter the redoubtable Linda, struggling sternly up the ladder to the second floor to size things up. Other reasonable solutions still existed, she reported after looking things over—the primary one being locating some really big guys who could be paid for the macho pleasure of tossing that beam like a twig into those three notches and then kicking sawdust in my face as I handed each of them a double sawbuck. No way, Jose.

Teaching Fools

Linda's 3-stanchion and pocketed solutions to setting the ridge beam

So Linda began to do what has always seemed so inaccessible to my one-dimensional mind—she got analytical.

"Dismantle one of those stanchions. Unnail the three-way braces on the one closest to the gable at the front of the building so that you can tilt it down enough to lift the beam into its slot, and move the middle stanchion out of the way enough so that beam won't be interfered with in the process."

Hmmm. That sounded way too reasonable. And, of course, it worked, with some considerable grunting and staggering up the ladder with the beam on my shoulder. While I held the beam up as high as I could, Linda inched the stanchion neatly into place, and I was then able, from my station on the ladder, to push the stanchion close to its upright position. It was dangerous—that was my fault, not Linda's, and my stubborn choice—and torturously slow, but the two stanchions, front and rear, supported the crown-up beam, and solidly enough for me to move the center stanchion back into place and to fiddle with the adjustment of all three stanchions until I had balanced the height of the beam equally from front to back and equalized the beam's overhang meant to carry the two-foot outriggers on each gable end.

What a battle! It was, once again, the myth of Sisyphus updated and enacted in real time. I'd still be up there, red-faced and sweating bullets, if it weren't for Linda's prudential superintendence. And then we staggered down the ladder, my legs like spaghetti, we ate supper, and I got drunk.

And then the hand-framing and raising of the rafters. This is where I felt I'd have the greatest difficulty, partly because it engaged my greatest proven incompetence— measuring and cutting, this time the rafters, using a carpenter's square in the process, marking the rafters for a ridge, bird's mouth, and tail cut. There'd be no gang-cutting of rafters here—I didn't have that kind of cutting equipment. Furthermore, there'd be some twenty-four of the damned things to stand against the building, pull up to the second floor, re-check for the crown edge, and then carefully cut. I don't use a circular saw often enough to feel real confidence in making consistently true cuts, and there was a lot riding on just that. I recollect making only one serious mistake—cutting one rafter with opposing pitch cuts for each end—unbelievable. But I took real care with the rest of them, cutting all of the 6-12 rafters first and preparing to set them into place against the ridge board before tackling the 3-12 shed roof rafters.

But to indicate that this process went quickly would be a lie. I was into September by now, and that meant school was in session once again. My schedule for enclosing the building had pretty much gone up in smoke. I was going to have to try to adjust to and master my new job as Humanities Program director at the university during the week and race north for a couple of days of work on the weekends before limping home completely lame from raising and swinging unwieldy 2-by-12's. It was pretty much a 9-to-6 second job on the weekend during that fall, some of it interrupted by foul weather, including an early October snow. And, since I had no wide umbrella against the weather and was plugged into all manner of electric power tools to get the job done, I needed some non-precipitating conditions to avoid lighting up me and the forest and ricocheting like an electrified pinball off my newly built walls.

A good deal of time on those fall weekends was wasted stopping by Howard's shop to pick up his slant-six Dodge pickup with the new wooden stake body, taking the slow and loud hour-long ride over the mountain and along the shore to Ashland to rent my three levels of scaffolding from the local A-Z rental place and load it onto the back of the truck. I'd need to keep one eye on my load to avoid becoming a one-man shrapnel machine for the cars driving behind me. I'd have to crawl along all of the backroads back to Corny, wasting nearly another hour in the process. Forget that by the first of a frigid November the manager of the rental joint and I had entered a laconic first-name relationship and that the thoughts of each of us were turning to my buying rather than renting the goddamned unwieldy and dangerous stuff. I needed it—that's what I told an increasingly skeptical Linda every time she demanded that I fork over the rental receipts, truly a record of pain and inefficiency. Of course, I still faced unloading and set-up after I backed my noisy collection of heavy and abused end pieces, X-frame connectors, feet, castors, and deck pieces into the driveway.

Well into the fall, I had the set-up and tear-down routines down to about a half-hour each way for the first two levels of scaffolding. It took more time and care for one guy to manage the erection—any kind of an erection (sorry, Linda) after a day of working with this stuff—of the scary third level. And that included leveling out and locking down the whole bloody mess on uneven and variably sandy and rocky ground. Better to spend time on this little task than to climb to the top only to activate a wild shimmy some thirty feet up that could spill me, my tools, and the whole mess to the forest floor.

Each weekend repeated still another unfortunate dance: a time-consuming, frustrating, and awkward realignment of my focus back to the previous weekend where I had last left the job in some stage of incompletion. I never got used to this. I had to recover my memory of what I'd last done, how I'd been doing it, the essential measurements I'd been working by, and some semblance of a normal working pace. It had to be this way. Shit, as Sisyphus, I was, in fact, creating my own rock with every task in the building process that I undertook. But it was particularly maddening when it involved a difficult part of the process like cutting, setting into place, and nailing rafters.

I didn't scrimp on the materials here—fifteen rafters got violently married to the ridge beam on the south 6-12 pitched side; there were four double rafters, as well, to accommodate the two four-by-two-foot skylights I'd be installing when the time came. And there were another six of those 6-12 pitched rafters nailed in on the two four-foot end sections of the north side roof, with another sixteen 3-12 pitched rafters set on the eighteen-foot double window wall to form the shed roof.

I was always faced with the same choice on these labor-intensive weekends. Since the damned rental shop closed at five on Saturday afternoons, would I work until 3pm, tear everything down, and creep toward Ashland with my unstable and ancient load, or would I hang on to it until the same time on Sunday, drop and stack it neatly against the building for anyone with a pick-up to steal until the shop opened at eight on Monday morning? More often than not, and with the manager's tacit agreement—Christ, I was his meal ticket!—it was the latter option. Exhausting and anxiety-producing stuff, that, and I still had the four-hour race home amidst an army of Ford F-150's, SUV's, and vehicles hauling big boats and small squadrons of four-wheelers going way the hell too fast, along with a feverish night of preparation for my real job. Thank God I knew more than a little about that one.

 I don't know if there's a story about the rafters, other than the way I used the "operating table" to set the rafters in place. For every couple of rafters, I had to dismount and haul the flat-footed table behind me to the position most propitious for hauling the next couple of rafters in place. That necessitated lifting the unwieldy apparatus over and around the many braces and cleats I'd nailed into the floor to anchor my three ridge board-bearing stanchions. And so it went. Sisyphus had nothing on me.

 It took me several weeks of this nonsense to finish hand-framing the roof, and then, around the first week in November, the application of the roof sheathing and the metal drip edge began. No fun, again, not because there was anything inherently difficult about these jobs, but because, as one of my all-time favorites, Gordon Lightfoot, noted before I'd ever seen Superior, the winds of November, indeed, came early for me that fall, turning my four-by-eight pieces of half-inch plywood into sails that threatened to carry me off the roof and into the trees.

 On one of the rare weekends that I was able to tease Chris with some prohibitively thick steaks and Irish beer to drive up by mid-day Saturday, he and I held on for dear life as we fired up the compressor and learned to drift with each fluttering sheet until we'd set it in place and secured it. Neither one of us feels anything but fear and loathing for heights, and the twenty-five-to-thirty-mile-an-hour gusts off the Lake only intensified those feelings, especially when we were crawling down the 6-12 pitched portions of the north side with the nailer and finding it hard to maintain our footing on the slick plywood sheets.

Enter Linda again with a very pragmatic fix. Working the north side wasn't that scary since we had that nearly level 3-12 big section to work on and around, but, with lots of open spaces below us and either an eight to ten-foot fall inside the building or maybe a terminal plunge of thirty feet to the rocky ground, Chris wasn't feeling any more comfortable than I was. Linda went downtown to Ehlers' and bought a fifty-foot length of their strongest nylon rope, along with three metal adjustors to attach the rope to ourselves, hook it to the ridge beam, and use the other hook to adjust the slack. Beautiful. It felt a little silly, but, with a rope with a two-hundred-pound test line tied around his waist and securely connected to the strongest beam in the structure, Chris was able to go about his business with confidence.

We didn't finish the north side. There simply wasn't time enough, and the ever-freshening northwest wind off the Lake was very difficult to buck. But Chris helped me move all of the half-inch plywood from the garage to the second floor by receiving and hauling up each piece that I lifted up to him. That saved me time and pain and positioned me for the much tougher job of sheathing the steeper 6-12 south side. I did that the following weekend, with intermittent flurries melting on the sheathing as quickly as they fell.

Three weeks into November, with the prospect of accumulating snow and much lower temperatures in the next ten days, I had a big decision to make. How important was it for me to completely close the building in by myself? How much was enough? At what point was I going to give pride over to prudence? With all of the delays and interruptions of weather, my own professional responsibilities, and cash flow, I'd managed to get the building to a pretty good stage. The roof was sheathed, some of the drip edge was up, most of the fascia was on, but, in my haste to finish the fascia on the shed roof, I'd made a sophomore mistake. I hadn't installed step flashing up each side of the shed dormer all the way to the point at which it met the roof peak. Stupid. Frustrating. And I'd also had no time yet to Tyvek the outside of the building—to body wrap it against the wet and the cold. And it was getting colder.

I stopped by the shop to counsel with Howard, and his professional read of my situation plus his understanding of my psychology were adept. "You've got nothing to prove, Bill. You've done the hard part. You've built a solid building. There's no shame in letting a pro step in to do the roofing. You need someone who does this for a living, who can set up and knock it out in a few days. It'll be cheaper in the long run. The most important thing here is protecting the building from the weather. If you don't at least get tar paper on the sheathing, a normal winter's snow, along with periods of freezing and thawing, will ripple every one of those plywood sheets. Let me make a call and see what I can do."

Well, he did, right then. And he got a commitment from a young independent general contractor that Howard had considerable experience with, and some regard for the quality of his work and his work ethic. Billy again. I'd known this guy from two former encounters. One, he'd helped me roof the cabin after Howard and Jerry had built the addition, and, most importantly, he'd done a professional job just a little over four months earlier of pouring and finishing the slab on which I'd built my building. What could be better? And, better still, the guy was newly married, intent on establishing himself in a competitive construction trade market, and, with winter coming on fast, needing to put together one more outside job before moving inside for several months. Great! It looked and felt like a winner. I thanked Howard profusely for reasoning me out of what was starting to feel, even to me, like a stupid and dangerous exercise in pride, went home, and called Billy to set up an on-site meet.

Billy and his bride drove down the driveway on a Saturday evening before sunset. After introductions, I explained to Billy what needed to be done—the front fascia and drip edge, a re-fit of some of the dormer fascia over step flashing, ice-shielding to protect against ice dams. I showed him all of the shingles I'd stacked at the roof's ridge and felt paper materials I'd stored in the garage, took him up to the second floor where I'd already transported the sky-light assemblies, and said, "what the hell, why don't you install those while you're at it?" I'd pretty much committed to a full, cowardly retreat. Thoughts of a warm living room, a full wine rack, a goddamned shower, for Christ's sake, civilized human interaction, all beckoned like Odysseus' seductive sirens' song.

Forget pride. Forget Emersonian self-reliance. Forget Thoreau's one-man cabin-building venture or his fucking bean field. It was quittin' time.

Billy stood with me on the second floor, looked up at the open sky, salved my wounded ego by telling me that I'd done a really nice job, and said that, after he finished a little inside job over the weekend, he'd be starting on my roof the following Tuesday.

End of story? Not nearly. This is the South Shore we're talking about here. In my momentary euphoria, I'd forgotten what Howard had preached to me so frequently and the phenomenon that I'd observed up close and personal. Too often, when the going gets tough on the South Shore, the tough go drinking. . .or fishing, or hunting, or whoring, or— who knows? Sometimes on the South Shore, the mere whiff of prosperity seems to cause many to run, bottle in hand, in the other direction. So I was about to get burned. But, much more importantly, I think, for Billy and Howard, so was Howard. As I said, Howard had a high regard for Billy, who'd done some good work for him. But, as Howard later informed me, he wouldn't anymore. Howard had stuck his neck out recommending him to me, and it would take a lot more than Viagra to jump-start that working relationship again.

So, when I came up a week later and saw no evidence of construction equipment or work having been started on the roof, I did two things. First, I called Billy, who was predictably unreachable. Secondly, I dropped by Howard's shop. Howard was a little concerned about Billy making the commitment and not showing when he said he would, but he said that he'd do a little investigating. By the end of the weekend, he reported back that Billy had underestimated his time commitment on the basement job he'd contracted to do, but that he'd be getting right to my job the following week. We were a full week into December now—I didn't at all miss the significance of the date of my disappointment occurring on Pearl Harbor Day—and Linda was already delivering her stern summary verdict on Billy's failure to communicate or show up, but I remained quixotically hopeful.

Finally, after another week passed without a whiff of Billy, I called him from the cabin once more. And this time I got him. I'm pretty passive and low-key during confrontations like this— I hate chasing people. I thanked him for agreeing to take the job and then, searching for a shallow breath, expressed my respectful concern about the date on the calendar, the rumors of snow the following week, and wondered bashfully in his direction if it looked at all possible that he might be starting up soon.

The response I got was most unexpected—"I thought I told you that I was finishing up a job, Bill. I can't really tell you when I'll be getting to your roof, but you'll just have to be patient."

But I knew by the brusque tone that I'd caught him. I was probably not the guy he wanted to hear from unexpectedly. He wasn't ready with a really good response, kind of like an adolescent doing something behind a bathroom door that an aggressive knock from the outside had taken him away from. I found out the next day from an angry Howard that he'd been offered another job after the basement job was done, and he'd gotten a little greedy, perhaps thinking that I'd let it slide to him anyway when the weather really got bad. Hell, he'd probably be able to begin the next spring season on my roof before he started in on more profitable jobs.

But I already knew when I hung up the phone that I was done with Billy. I remember thinking as I dialed up Linda down in Bloomington that there were absolutely no hard feelings on my end. Howard had educated me well about how business in the building trades is conducted up here, and, although I wasn't ok with it—why the hell couldn't he have just answered one of my phone messages, *communicated* what he planned to do, and shot straight with me? How tough would that have been?—I'd had two weeks off to heal some of my dings and scratches, and I was resigned to get going again. Suddenly, it was all about controlling my own destiny, trying to beat the weather, seizing ownership over my own building, and getting it done.

It surely wasn't about the money. Even though Billy hadn't actually estimated the job for me, I figure, with a helper on the roof with him and absolutely everything he needed already up there, the whole thing would have run not much more than $2000. And, while we're at it, what price would I be able to place on my own safety for not having to wrestle with a tarp and tar paper in full furl and avoiding a fall from an icy roof? It was about what it's always about—pride, self-determination, with an admixture of stupidity. And all of them came into play when I came up the following week with a couple of inches of new powder on the roof and the temperature hovering at four below.

Terror settles in around me when faced with the prospect of stepping off and above three levels of scaffolding to a pitched roof. I hate heights. I'll never get over it. Hugging the inside wall of the Toronto Space Needle to my kids' uncontrollable laughter many years ago comes sharply into focus here. My imagination works overtime in such circumstances to replace real sight with jagged little moving pictures of me sliding off the edge of the roof with fingernails scraping up shingle grit and impaling myself on a small birch stump below. Perfect. But that feeling worsens when enriched by the inertia a driving north wind and sub-zero temperatures bring. There's no getting warm, ever—one must simply ignore feet still cold despite two pairs of wool socks, legs still frozen despite a good set of long johns, and the pain caused by the smallest collision with hard metal or wood. And, even though working fast can't really happen because of the awkwardness of too many layers of clothing and gloves that must be continually pulled off and on, the idea is to move as fast as one can.

The lifeline that Linda had rigged up for me continued to work well. I had to be careful to avoid getting tangled up in and tripping over it, but, with the roof getting even more slippery the more I climbed over it, it was all that separated me from frozen ground. As difficult as it had become to move, dismantle, and reassemble the scaffolding by myself, and as unwieldy as the aluminum flashing material, rolls of tar paper and ice shield, and drip edge pieces were to lift to the top level of the scaffolding, the more grateful I was for the freedom the life-line had given me to lift, carry, and resituate bundles of shingles to precisely where I needed them.

It took me three grueling weekends to complete the roofing task—probably three times what Billy would have needed if he'd deigned to dog it with a helper. But that's ok.

Because the bulk of my clothing made hurrying impossible, I concentrated on doing the job correctly. And it was, like every other stage of the construction job, an integrated and systematic process. First, there was the step-flashing of the small eaves of the shed roof, along with the need to seal the top of the flashing with roof tar.

After installing the rest of the fascia board running from the roof peak down to the pieces running the length of the dormer, I began to roll out and cut the three-foot-wide sections of ice shield up the entire 3-12 dormer roof and six feet up the 6-12 roof on the other side. I'd had some nightmares about working with the ice shield, remembering how, several summers previous, I'd been driven mad by turning long sheets of the expensive and highly adhesive stuff into sticky wadded balls. But not this time. The frigid weather dampened some of its adhesive tack, and, with a construction stapler, it went down smoothly.

So did the tar paper, except that the wind occasionally made it difficult to cut and hold on to at the same time. I nailed the remaining pieces of drip edge just prior to the shingles, a task witnessed only by a mature eagle that had situated itself atop a trunk of a dead birch between me and the water. Savage amusement.

The shingling process became an enormous pain in the ass. With the shingles on the roof and located where they're supposed to be, it's normally just a mindless job. And, one would think that, with the help of a power roof nailer, it would go like greased lightning. But I'd already become fully initiated into my nailer's chronic dysfunction. Generally, it would fire two nails, if I was lucky—before it would jam and require me to manually feed the coil of nails into the firing chamber. It didn't always behave this way; sometimes, I'd get ten nails in a row before I'd have to stop, open the plastic nail coil retainer, hand-feed the coil, close the retainer, and fire, But, too often, I'd have to reset every nail after a string of misfires. There are procedures more frustrating than pulling off gloves to readjust nail coils and then pull them on again, but I don't know what the hell they might be when a gusting northwest wind fans the wind chill to thirty below. Forget Murphy—Sisyphus had usurped control of every mechanical operation on the job!

I'm certain that the nailer required only a professional adjustment to work efficiently. However, that would have meant a trip to Superior or Duluth and the loss of an entire day of work. And so I plodded on, leaning against the wind and the nailer like that gifted kid in the Far Side cartoon. In retrospect, that loss of a day's work in the worst of circumstances seems the wise choice.

But, as routine jobs go, this one eventually got done, too. Surely, it didn't help to combat several bouts of snow and ice over the two and a half weeks I was on the roof and repeated lugging of shingle bundles to different locations so that I could install the two skylights on the south side, finish the rest of the shed roof, and install the ridge vents and cap of trimmed shingles. By this time, my patience had worn out from many forced untetherings from my life-line and descents from the scaffolding to re-trip a circuit breaker because of the surging of the compressor. But the really big snow and, worse yet, sleet, stayed away. And, even more important, it was *done*.

Sometimes, that's all that counts. I'd been working against my own deadline of sandwiching half the roofing job around two restful, wound-healing weeks in a nineteenth-floor condominium overlooking the warm gulf waters of Florida's Sand Key. Always more challenges for the acrophobic! But, now, that idyll had passed, it was three days before the beginning of spring semester, and, as I returned the scaffolding to A-Z Rental in Ashland yet another time, I could feel some small measure of satisfaction at a job not done quickly or efficiently, but well. True, the windows hadn't been installed yet, and no building paper protected the exterior from the weather, but the roof was done and pieces of plywood and OSB covered the openings. Until early spring, to paraphrase Hamlet's final words, the rest was silence.

I can't say that I derived a lot of solace or chest inflation from the roof job. It felt a lot more like some weird act of penance. Like most things I've gotten tangled up with—including teaching; my purposeful assault upon my wife's fortress of virtue when we were no more than kids; my blunderings through parenting; my long unrequited love affair with the Boston Red Sox; the rounds of golf I've been playing endlessly in my head since I was old enough to blow a tournament—I'd allowed myself to get way too invested. I'd pretty much allowed the carriage house to consume nearly every waking thought for a little over six months. By my own impossible expectations, I was two months behind schedule. Hell, the windows should have been in by the first of November, and, if I was still working in the first two weeks of a cold Wisconsin winter, I should have been slapping on the Tyvek.

Slow as molasses. Dyer's warp speed is glacial speed. Incompetent. And I had lost my perspective on the rest of my life. No balance.

It's lucky for me that Linda knew me for the monomaniacal and stubborn extremist that I am—well, not lucky for her, perhaps. Her greatest concern through all of this was that I'd cut off my nose with my chain saw to spite my face or carve myself a new asshole with my chop saw. It occurs to me that I managed, until late 2004, not to cut the cord of my chop saw. When I informed Howard how I cut that cord with my circular saw in the midst of a chaos of cords and pieces of cedar siding I'd been applying to the building, he just laughed: "What took you so long? Welcome to the trade. That's an occupational hazard. I never considered myself truly into a job if I didn't slice a cord."

But, as usual, I was being too hard on myself. As I stepped away from the building after hanging the OSB over the window and door openings and stowing my tools, the enormity of what I'd been able to create so far began to settle in on me. I remember thinking, "Jesus. How the hell did that building get to this state of nearly being constructed? How the hell did I do it? The thing looks pretty damned good. It could fool a lot of people most of the time." I was tempted to conclude that I'd gotten lucky, that I really didn't know anything, that there was plenty of wasted time invested in the building, and that there was plenty of time yet to parade my incompetence.

But more than luck had gotten me this far. The biggest part of it was the continuing mentorship of Howard, the initial carpentering "tips from the top" that he confided to me, the visits to the job site, the endless patience he bestowed on my dumbest questions and most indecipherable drawings while always gently encouraging me to figure things out for myself, his lending of his tools and his truck any time I needed them.

Howard, without question, was my Zen Master, although he'd never admit it.

And lest I forget, my insanity has pollinated from Howard's. Though mine isn't nearly as pure and informed by ability, Howard's dedication to the craft was unrelenting and uncompromising. I'm crazy, and, very frequently, I'm more than a little stupid, but some of the more positive craziness that gets expressed as focus and concentration on the task and anticipation of the next logical step in the building process I owe to Howard. No question. I looked at it, and it was good.

But there were other wondrous things to look at besides my insignificant little project. I'd never forgotten about looking up from my work to notice the rich and variegated life around me and to hear it all breathing, from the rhythmic booming and boiling of swelling ice flows filling and retreating from the sea caves nearly under my feet and the angry chittering of the red squirrels in nearby pines warning me to abandon their neighborhood to audible unfoldings of leaf buds over my head.

Let me flash ahead to the summer of 2004 to provide a bracing example. I'd been agonizing to the point of Hamletian immobility over how to finish the cedar siding job in the gable area above the little balcony I'd built that made it nearly impossible for me to get at without a hovering helicopter. And, on the evening of July 20th, a particularly chilled evening with the wind blowing from the northeast off the Lake, after just having finished my second gin and tonic and thinking rather hazily how good it would be to have one more little bottle of tonic water to splash over just a little more Blue Sapphire, I incidentally glanced toward the diverse collection of hummingbird and seed feeders hanging over the holding tanks on the west side of the cabin. I'd been glancing that way frequently since dinner a couple of hours earlier, having taken only a short break from such habitual glancing to run up the stairs of the carriage house to close the skylight windows before the storms that MPR meteorologists had promised would arrive.

I'd only been back inside again for a couple of minutes, again ensconced in my thirty-five-year-old Lazy Boy and monitoring the clusters of gold finches and cedar waxwings that jockeyed for space at the feeders when I suddenly realized that a part of my view of the woods and the Lake was being occluded. A kind of black hole seemed to be forming, as it were. As I stood shakily in front of my chair, the black hole began to move and sprout arms, large paws, and a large and tan-colored snout. And those paws and snout, as well as the impossibly endless tongue that emerged from it, were enveloping a Baltimore Oriole feeder. What the hell...fair is fair. I'd had my gin and tonics, and the black hole with arms, paws, snout, and tongue that had now grown a pair of erect ears and a vertical height of about seven and a half feet was determined to suck down his.

In a moment of unreflective imbecility, I strode out the door and onto the deck, confronted the black hole, and shouted loudly and sternly that it should get the hell out. I didn't think then how stupid that must have looked to the black hole —a sixty-something grey-haired dude a couple of feet shorter than itself and nearly hairless in comparison— or why the people next door might have thought I was yelling at Linda like this, but a wonderful, magical moment followed. The black hole very gently released its hold on the feeder and fell back down on its haunches. Its ears—it's possible—grew even more erect, its head tilted slightly to the side as if it were looking at an entirely different kind of black hole and, for what seemed like a very long minute, its blank black eyes locked onto mine. For a moment, it seemed to be entertaining a tentative approach on me—so much for those assholes who say the sure-fire way to send a bear into retreat is to scream bloody blue murder. But, with the assistance of another very stern rebuke, it turned its back, elicited a few low guttural grunts, and retreated ten feet off the holding tank hill. Then it turned abruptly, did a complete sit-down, and stared at me with a look somewhere between befuddlement and betrayal. Crestfallen, that's what it was. Priceless.

I wanted to go over to him and tell him that I hadn't really meant it, to deliver the oriole feeder to him with an invitation to come inside and join me in a gin and tonic. But, just as I'm spending way too many words trying to recapture our encounter, I'd waited too long. The black hole—a rather young, sleek, and beautiful one, I might add, probably only a teenager as black holes go—rolled smoothly up on its feet and meandered ever so slowly through the long thick weeds and birches to the property next door, with only an occasional rueful side-long glance back at me. And, before I knew it, the black hole had evaporated into the gloaming. My favorite word. Use it every chance I get, particularly under the influence of a couple of gin and tonics.

But so much for black holes. And, from the perspective of an impatient retired couple next door who'd won the prize of living in the dark shadow of the big box I'd built, I'm sure that's what they were thinking, too. To their credit, they never complained, although a couple of times, after having just pulled into their driveway and hearing me play some murderous riffs on my circular saw from the roof, they beat a pebble-strewn retreat back to Duluth in their big Suburban with nary a word.

To my credit, I continued to be sensitive to the inconvenience I'd borne them, not to mention the total eclipse of each day's sunrise. Because I wanted to respect their early morning solitude, I played unplugged until about 9:30 on the weekends. That approach to the work hampered my progress when the spring of 2003 came and they began to use the cabin regularly again. By then, I knew that I had one full summer season and a partial one left before the outside of the building was completely buttoned down.

Each job that remained for me to execute was totally new to me. Let's see—there was the dreaded fashioning of the soffits and fascias; the nightmarish mystery of constructing the cornices; the installation of the windows, downstairs side door, and the huge rear slider and front French doors; the assembly of the redwood doors for the garage openings and the installation of the tracks they'd need to be mounted on; the hanging of the six-foot deck that would run the twenty-four-foot width of the back of the building plus an additional six that would step down another six inches along the north wall and give way to a flight of stairs that would descend to the side door opening; and a strange little seven-foot-long-by-three-and-a-half-foot-wide balcony that the French doors would open on to.

No big deal for a real carpenter, with a real crew, and real equipment to facilitate the ease and safety of their execution, but a really big deal for me of meager skills, less common sense, with only two hands and legs who tended to make things up as he went along.

And, just as importantly, most of these jobs were going to

put my inconsiderable ass right in my neighbors' faces. If I'd been them, I would have been equally appalled.

All of these jobs required lengthy consultations with Professor Bowers. About this time—late April of 2003—Howard had decided to build his own garage. Hell, why should he be different? Everybody, it seemed, up and down scenic 13, was embarking on a garage project, the most ambitious of these begun by the obsessive-compulsive guy who'd solely crafted the little one-story house set away from the road on the Lake side just a mile outside of Herbster—a work of art that remains unfinished. Howard wouldn't be doing the garage himself. Unlike me, he was intelligent enough to know when his time for climbing over building frames was past, and, besides, doing the job himself would take him away from work that would turn a profit.

Howard gave the garage job to "Hammer Dave," a carpenter with a huge capacity for work as well as several other unhealthy addictions, a fearsome anger index, and a pathological insistence upon working alone. And, when he was working, he proceeded with break-neck speed and yoga-like concentration. I have yet to actually meet "the Hammer," a nickname which he disdains and the use of which is an invitation to a fight. I've been told how he came to acquire that trademark by the person who said he bestowed it upon him. Based upon the extreme animus that now exists between this man and Dave and Howard's very knowing take upon how that man came to earn Dave's violent rebuke, I'm not going to share that story. It's enough to say that Dave prefers to keep his own counsel, just as he prefers to work alone at his own frenetic pace, and that, as the name implies, Dave sometimes resides along the ragged edge of sanity.

But no contesting the high quality of his work. Examples of it have sprung up all over the South Shore the past ten years or so, a couple of these pretty little structures situated just adjacent to Herbster's tabernacle of grease, Tracy's-by-the-Lake. Both were once used as gift shops, but one of them I dearly love—the one-room sawed off shot-gun affair with a tiny upstairs gabled storage area and walk-out deck ringed off with rope attached to four-by-four pilings. A beautifully weathered example of the waterside buildings scattered from Hyannis to Provincetown. He built it with the speed and noise of a piliated woodpecker. I still lust after it.

When Billy left Howard in the lurch, Hammer Dave was right there, at Howard's service, contracting to do exactly what Howard outlined—to frame, side, and then install a steel roof over a garage connected to Howard's main house. Howard's building was to be even wider and deeper than mine, with an entry door located between the nine-foot garage doors to provide a separate and, in the winter, even more practical entrance into the house. Even though Dave was respectfully fitting Howard into his already overcommitted schedule of house and cabin building, he delivered the goods, just when he promised he would so that Howard's garage would be closed in early enough to allow him to have his way with the insulation and the set-up of his wood stove.

And a truly imaginative approach to the insulating Howard took, first filling the cavities between the studs and then laying furring strips over the insulation prior to applying sheets of plywood to finish and insulate the interior. Howard had, indeed, left me and my little project in the dust—just a little unintended kicking of sand in the face of an amateur to illustrate how a professional job is done with efficiency.

As I stood in that garage and wondered at the beautiful job that Dave was doing in invisible hit and run swipes—I'd still never seen him doing any of the work—I told Howard of my schedule for the summer and asked for his criticism. Pouring himself and me a cup of coffee, he reminded me that everything hinged upon "sequence." "Don't get ahead or in the way of yourself, William. Remember where you are in the job and what needs to happen before the next stage. Think it out before you get into it, and keep retuning your schedule. You'll save time, expense, material, and frustration in the long run."

This was Howard's oft-repeated "om," and it came in handy at a time when I was getting anxious about doing the soffits and finished fascia. Howard reminded me that doing the rear deck next would provide a safe platform for doing the soffit and fascia work in the rear of the building. And, as difficult as it was to set that rear deck in place by myself— digging the post holes, sinking and filling with concrete the sonotubes on which the posts for the deck would be hangered and nailed, leveling those posts the best I could, and then, after bracing the posts from two directions, assembling pairs of two-by-twelves sandwiched around a layer of plywood and using my twelve-foot ladder to jockey them into position between the post caps—I got it done.

All of this sounds well-reasoned and thought-out. However, I'd acquired little of the resourcefulness and imagination that both Howard and Hammer Dave had developed over their many years of working alone that led them to create time-saving as well as life-saving tools and jigs.

This is as good a place as any to sort out the "Mexican" issue, as applied to my finishing up the job. I need to define the term respectfully, and with some apologies, while putting into relief what Howard might have meant by invoking it. He noticed how I cringed when he used it the first time in his shop, while he was doing a glue-up job on a set of cabinets. He'd set in place a number of clamps to hold the job while he glued and called them "Mexicans." I knew I had to be careful here, but I couldn't let it pass without a protest. I blew a very loud and critical "What?" in his direction, like, "what the hell are you talking about?"

Howard then laughed and backed away from the table to explain. "The term comes from my west Texas beginnings."

Now, he knows and I know from having lived in the same region for a couple of years about the unofficial caste system that everyone who lived there back then acknowledged as real. Poor Mexicans weren't the lowest on that caste totem pole, but they were down there. But, besides acknowledging the redneck associations with his use of the word and how politically incorrect it is, he meant the word positively.

"These are really hard-working people," he said, "people

who, unfortunately, often had to work for much less money, and for longer hours, to put bread on their families' tables." From his experience, "these folks were friendly, hospitable to a fault, generous, uncomplaining, reliable, hard-working, and quick studies at the craft they were learning and practicing." These traits made them effective, competent, and, more often than not, nearly invisible on the job, for better or for worse. "Good hands, too often obtained far too cheaply, that showed up and did more than two hands might be expected to do."

That was the culture of the southwest back in the '40's and '50's, and, from what my Border Patrol son has told me, not much has changed to make Mexican Americans in the southwest more visible or appreciated.

So, in Howard's unfortunate professional parlance, "Mexicans" were work savers, invented tools or jigs or strategically placed pieces of wood and nails that provided the strong, reliable, and invisible hands to allow Howard to perform tasks while working alone. They were time and money-savers that, rather than compromising the quality of the work he was doing or his personal well-being, freed him to apply his best skills to it. I'm talking about the huge Trojan Horse that Howard constructed out of two-by-sixes to provide the necessary support for the thirty-five-foot glue lams that the old boom truck he brought on the job for $50 carefully swung through the window opening on the second floor of my cabin. Ingenious.

There've been so many I've seen Howard employ in his shop and suggest to me during the cabin remodel that, just like in the *Bhagavad-Gita* when Krishna opened up his garment to Arjuna and displayed in himself all that will ever exist, I've forgotten most of what he's shown me. But I'm ok with that. Howard's "Mexicans" were the result of a great accumulated wisdom, experience, and pragmatism, a lot of which he absorbed from working with older craftsmen sufficiently patient to transmit that wisdom to him.

I didn't like Howard's use of the term "Mexican." He was far too much of a political "lefty" to allow himself to be trapped in such a pejorative use of the word. But I celebrate the specific meaning he'd attached to it. And, if I've forgotten ninety per cent of what he'd taught me, Howard had gotten me to employ a cadre of "Mexicans" on my own project to great effect, stripped of that unfortunate term.

Let me make a brief list here. I've already mentioned the lifeguard station and the operating table. They qualify as invisible helpers because they fit Howard's criterion that they be tools or jury-rigged machines or nailed or screwed-on wooden assists. It took some time to slap together both of these workstations, which supported me anywhere from six and a half to nine feet off the ground. Because of the feet I'd attached to them, I could push and pull through brute strength both of them to the portion of the building I'd been working on. And both, though reminiscent of medieval machines used to storm walled towns, have been multi-purposed, enabling me, in the case of the operating table, to frame the roof at eye level, install the skylights, work on various portions of the roof sheathing and shingling, and eventually hang the roof insulation and the cedar plank ceiling.

As for the lifeguard station, I'm not sure that I'll ever tear it down—it's just too useful. In addition to the many services it's rendered me, I'd undergone my humiliation during the soffit and fascia and cornice work on it. I'd done the exterior caulking on it. Without it, I couldn't have held the three $3/8$"-thick-by-five-and-a-half-inch-wide right angled fabricated pieces of angle iron that I sandwiched and bolted between a pair of treated two-by-sixes and then bolted directly to the rim joists underneath the French doors in the front. Flitch this.

This was my answer to the question of how to hang a three-and-half-by-seven-foot balcony over the garage doors that could safely support mature adults of ever-widening girth sitting comfortably in deck chairs with drinks in their hands. Using the raised platform of the lifeguard station to take the weight off the wood-clad steel triangles and hold them firmly against the building while I ran long lag bolts through the 90-degree angled plates and into the building was a day at the beach.

And "the catwalk" was the product of one of these brief moments of creativity. It was July again— two years almost to the day from the time I'd closed my eyes and swan-dived into a project that was way beyond my depths. I'd been siding in a leisurely fashion for parts of a couple of weekends during the crunch of an exhausting summer session of teaching. Ten-inch cedar—gorgeous, fragrant stuff. Not my first choice.

I'd finished the back and south sides of the building, and had run up the front and north side as far as my twelve-foot step ladder would safely allow. But, in the process, I'd discovered that I'd seriously gotten in my own way. The problem?—in erecting the rear deck that swept six feet around the corner of the north side and the stairs that ran down from it, I'd inadvertently blocked access to almost half of the second story. No way to get scaffolding anywhere close to the windows that I'd need to side between and over, no way to hammer home the nails with which I'd be fastening the eighteen feet of freeze board under the soffit, and no way to caulk any of it. My first thought was that I'd violated Howard's constant warning about sequence—not only within the individual tasks that I'd need to do on various portions of the building, but in the logical relationship that should obtain among the many individual processes that would result in a completed structure. But I knew that the rear deck and stairs *had* to be built when I'd built them. I absolutely did not want to apply the ledger board for the deck over the new lap siding.

Those boards needed to be affixed directly to the rim joists, and I'd determined to flash those rims in anticipation of the siding I'd be applying above and below the ledgers. All of this seemed logical to a bumbler like me, and, besides, the siding on the back as well as the construction of those dreaded soffits and cornices had gone more smoothly because I'd built myself such a strong, safe, and wide platform on which to work.

As I looked at the north side from the back deck of the cabin, I could tell that using even a twenty-foot construction ladder was out of the question. And, although I toyed with the idea of running some long, nailed-together, and braced two-by-twelves from the top of the second level of scaffolding to the top of the deck, doing so would, at best, guarantee a violent pirouette into the hospital. None of this speculation was appealing given that it was mid-week in the middle of the woods, about quarter to three and no one in the place except the black hole and me. I wasn't even within healthy screaming distance of the nearest resident, and, if I went down, it'd be me and the wood ticks until Linda pulled into the driveway late Friday evening.

I then experienced one of those moments of pure luminosity that visit me so seldom that, like UFO sitings, I rarely believe them. Why not build a catwalk from the midpoint of the scaffolding's second stage to the farthest and highest point of the deck and support that point with a little platform of nailed two-by-sixes to the approximate height of the catwalk on both ends? I was a little worried about the height of the catwalk—about twelve feet off the ground—and the span of the thing, which I'd calculated at about sixteen feet. Would it be strong enough not to need support at its midpoint? I'd remembered that, back when the remodel of the cabin was in full swing, Dan and Howard had fashioned an eighteen-foot catwalk from the top of the loft to the front wall so that we could assemble the four huge glue lams that Howard had guided through the rear window opening on his Trojan Horse, drop them in the slot where the front wall joined together at a prowed angle, and bolt them together. This would be a lot higher than that, but that catwalk was strong enough to carry three of us at a time. Hell, I was still using it as a walkway to the gazebo!

I wasn't going to fool around, given my anxiety about working at heights. Even if I didn't intend to build a little railing for the thing, I'd make it plenty wide—thirty-four inches, broad enough to perform an Easter promenade with a parasol. I'd need a pair of strong sixteen-footers to lay on edge and serve as the base for it, and that meant hitting the lumber yard once again to purchase a couple of pressure-treated two-by-sixes. And I had a sufficient cache of framing lumber to brace and deck it. I even planned to run legs and feet down from the sides of the catwalk to the stairs below for added support.

But, I was, after all, Hamlet. I needed some professional confirmation that what I was doing was safe and sound. This would be one heavy mother when built and set in place. I figured that, working with my usual glacial speed, I'd need a little more than three hours to slam it together. Kind of like building my own coffin. And I don't think that I can take it, 'cause it took so long to bake it, and I'll never have that recipe again. Oh no… Perhaps Howard could save me from myself.

Before I made another small investment in Cardinal Lumber, I stopped by Howard's shop. Big doings. Howard had just moved out the huge set of floor-to-ceiling bookcases that Gary Davidson had ordered for the palatial log "cabin" that he and Karen would be wresting away from the carpenters in the next week and was spraying varnish on two small cabinets to the point of asphyxia. When he finished the job and unplugged the gun, I asked him what he thought of my monumental "Mexican." Howard immediately shot back, "You're not cantilevering the goddamned thing, are you?" It took me a moment to absorb what he was suggesting. Yikes! No way! It was a little sobering that Howard might even consider that I'd walk off a heavy and unsupported plank of my own design. But he was right to ask. It was me, after all. What the hell did I know? And it was bracing to be reminded of how little I actually did know, how much of a serious danger I was to myself, and how fortunate I'd been so far in not maiming or killing myself or anyone close to where I'd been masquerading as a carpenter.

When I responded with a defensive "no" to his question, Howard simply said "well, it sounds fine to me. Just make sure that you've got plenty of overlap on both ends of the catwalk so that it's absolutely stable."

"How about the legs and feet, Howard? Do I need 'em?"

"Do what you want, Bill, but that thing's going to be plenty strong for what you're using it for. Just be careful and don't go jumping around on it."

And, so, there it was. The Catwalk. Once built, it placed

all of my work at eye level. No possibility of putting my big hammer through one of those beautiful double-cranking windows. No straining or stretching. Flashing over those windows was a pleasure, even though I nearly forgot to do it, and even the nasty job of caulking went smoothly. So quick that I was able to finish up, dismantle the catwalk, and carry the pieces of it down to the shore for reassembling the final piece of the walkway I'd built through the woods to the gazebo.

There was nothing unique about this latest or all the other time and body-saving tools I'd built to finally finish the exterior of the carriage house, even though all of it was new to me. Linda was fond of telling me and anyone else who'd listen that I look directly at things without ever seeing them, and that I hadn't heard ten consecutive words she'd aimed at me for over fifty-five years. *Hello.* Is anybody home? I'm great at turning intended dialogue into soliloquy. And I'm certain that many of the tricks I gleaned from Howard—and many that I didn't because my brain was on screen-saver—weren't his, but had become a part of his repertoire from having observed or been instructed to use them by his *own* mentors. But that's a part of what wisdom entails—the ability to fit the knowledge one has acquired through contemplative study and active engagement into the larger web and woof of understandings that have come before his.

Another attribute possessed by a truly wise person is the patience to transmit those personal and historical understandings to another. A wise person need never proclaim himself a teacher—Socrates pronounced himself unequipped for such a task. He didn't need to talk loudly or impress himself on students. He was too busy expanding his understanding and perfecting his application of it. But one will surely know a teacher when one finds one. Such a person engages the student in dialogue, includes him with subtle—unless it's the real Socrates—questions in the collaborative resolution of a problem. A wise person counsels that there's no doing without reflecting, and proves Shaw wrong by demonstrating that one not only can but must talk and chew gum at the same time.

Yes, Howard's use of the word "Mexican" to refer to time, work, and ass-saving devices, even benignly intended, deserves a little quality time with a shock therapist. It comes from another very bad time and place—or does it? Turn on the nightly news or the loud and despicable talk radio crowd and you'll hear it still. But, whatever he calls them, they helped me finish my project solo. If what I've done so far depended on my proficiency to pound a nail straight or to follow a set of directions, I'd be totally screwed and wouldn't have gotten beyond framing the first floor. That I'd graduated to the point of standing back at difficult points in the job, problem-solving, and recruiting wooden and steel pairs of hands and feet when I needed them speaks volumes to me. Good, inductive teaching earns my admiration every time, regrettable language notwithstanding. "Howard University."

Here's looking at you, Howard

Teaching Fools

Bill flitch-plates the balcony supports

The balcony takes shape

Sleeping on the job: The balcony and Life Guard Station

CHAPTER 13

Commencement (Or, Let the Real Games Now Begin)

"A.M.F."
--Professor Howard Bowers

I was thinking this past Mother's Day weekend as I celebrated the exquisite motherhood of my daughter Karen while continuing to grieve the absence of my one-and-only Linda, now that the weather had really turned the corner and was spinning a succession of perfect sky-blue brilliant over-70 degree days up here, about what the hell I could have possibly been thinking nineteen years ago when I originally embarked on this insanity.

Which insanity? Writing about Howard? Building this carriage house?

That's "carriage" pronounced with one's tongue rolled up against the back of one's lower teeth so as to produce a snooty-sounding "d" in place of the double "r" in the truly high-falutin English manner. The elevating of one's nose as if to avoid an objectional stink, the arching of eyebrows and squinting of the eyes, and the inserting of one's boot up one's ass while thus pronouncing "ked-didge" are optional.

Well, it's the building project, of course. It was a glorious 6pm on a Sunday evening, and, as I was watching five hummingbirds fight the Battle of Britain in and around the tall pine on the edge of the deck, I was doing the two things that I do most proficiently: drinking and contemplating. Hamlet. There were still another two good hours before the sunset beckoned me to desert the two-person pine rocker facing the west for a seat in the gazebo along the cliff to watch it.

As I perched on the rim of my third margarita and prepared to plunge into it, I stared in semi-wonder at the north wall of the carriage house and asked myself two questions: how, in Sinatra-esque fashion, I had done all that (and, may I say, in a very shy way); and, while I was at it, why did I, in fact, do it? The first question really has no answer. It's like any other major project that one commits to, with real but fuzzy expectations and major self-doubts—one sub-process followed another until I was confronted with the application of the final boards and fasteners that led to seizing success from the jaws of defeat. It just happened, perhaps in my case explicable because I had to budget time and money over a longer than normal span to realize the finished product. But, although I can summon up a memory of the myriad sub-processes that caused the building to ascend to its finished height—two years after it was done, I'd graced the top of it with a home-made cupola and copper sailboat weather vane that Linda helped me pick out in a Bayfield shop—I still can't believe I actually built that building. Magic. Divine mystery. Me? Unbelievable. But contemplating an ambitious and successful piece of writing you've labored over for quite a while can work the same effect. I'll get over it, particularly when the first roof leak occurs (no problem—I was up on the roof re-shingling a year ago March). Whatever.

But it's the second question that three drinks made me confront with some honesty. I've said all along, and shared the view with friends, colleagues, Linda, children, and, most importantly, Howard, that I built the garage for the following reasons: (1) we needed storage space; (2) I wanted the cars to stay warm in the winter; (3) I wanted to award Linda with her own personal space for doing her crafts—how gallant...how chauvinistic—high above the ground with virtually panoramic views of Gitcheegoomee; (4) a building that needed to be built on our property had to be built by me because contracting it out would be cost-prohibitive and inconvenient. Oh, and it would make the world safe for democracy. Solve the debt limit crisis. How about preserve the ozone layer and slow global warming. Right. Bullshit.

In another moment of luminosity, I looked at the building with a smirk and admitted that I did it because I wanted to know if I could. It was, I saw, all about me. It would make me feel good if I could do it. Silent bragging rights. Personal ownership. Hell, Linda had sat down at the coffee table with her strong box stuffed with every receipt that I'd accumulated from the pouring of the concrete pad, dragged out her calculator, and, in a couple of hours, read me the irrefutable bottom line. If it was money I'd been wanting to save, I had probably saved a goodly amount. But the twenty-odd thousand I had into it without saying anything about the two years of part-time inside finish work (a little bathroom with shower; a six-inch aspen-planked ceiling from front to back; an alternating 6" oak and Brazilian blood-wood hardwood floor; a six-foot-deep large knee-walled storage room running the length of the south wall all the way to the bathroom; railings for the front balcony and rear deck) was considerably beyond what I'd budgeted.

That's saying nothing about what my time or the wear and tear on my aching, ageing body might be worth. I left a lot of me in there. All of this was good to know. Self-revelation is a good thing.

But, as I drained the last sweet green chips of ice from my glass, I knew none of that other stuff mattered. I wasn't going to brag about any of this. Quite to the contrary, I'm still amazed that I wasn't watching some other guy finishing the garage from a wheelchair. It's still inexplicable how I didn't seriously hurt myself somewhere along the way. As Howard well knew, this is a craft fraught with peril, and, if it's possible, my last thought before I staggered in from the deck and away from the mosquitoes and biting flies was that I was humbler now than before I started. Chastened. Murphy had bedeviled me from the outset as he would any underprepared and underskilled rookie, but we're both Irish and he must have taken pity on the afflicted. Fools rush in.

But what about Dan? He'd rushed in to rescue me some twenty years ago. As competent a carpenter as he was, he'd proven way too human. But what had happened to him? I'd lost track of him almost immediately after he'd left the project. One little accidental contact on a late fall evening twenty-four years ago on the plaza at the university—I'd nearly collided with him on my way to a big lecture series event, and I was late, as usual. Dan, on his way to the library, strode head-down into me. Bouncing away and recognizing me, he grinned his broad, toothy, mustache-framed grin and asked me how things were going. I wanted to talk to him—find out how he was sorting out his professional difficulties—and I invited him to join me at the lecture. But Dan politely begged off, noting his need to get after some research. We promised to keep in touch.

But we didn't. I'd nearly forgotten about him when, maybe two years later, the phone rang. It was the middle of a late spring evening, but this time I was at home, laying across my bed and trying to concentrate on correcting a set of papers. I hate phones on general principle, and I never answer them at home after supper. But I had no choice this time— Linda was out in the neighborhood sniffing out next-day garage sales.

I was more curt than usual with my "hello." And there he was. I knew immediately: "How have you been, Bill?" My lungs empty, I managed a "Dan! How are you! How've things been going for you and the family?" Wow. I'm in English. What a wordsmith.

Dan's voice was quieter than I remembered, distant. I could have sworn he was calling from a phone booth. He evaded my pleasantries and bore gently in on what clearly was his purpose for calling: "How have things worked out at the cabin, Bill? Did the remodel come in the way you wanted? Did Howard and Jerry get things all buttoned down for you and Linda?"

I told him how happy I'd been with the person who'd taken over for him, about the volcano that erupted between Howard and Jerry when Howard caught him undercutting him, doing intentionally bad work, about the call I'd gotten from Herbster about that whole mess and Howard's promise to carry things through to closure by himself before the snow flew.

Dan betrayed no surprise about Jerry's failure, and he responded to Howard's professionalism with warmth: "I knew Howard wouldn't let you down. He's old-school. He saw a real challenge in your project, and he had the stuff to sort out all the difficulties."

His approval—it felt good. I remembered, before Dan had ever appeared at the cabin, that his specialty had been building decks—elaborate ones with hemispherical fronts and stairs cascading down the length of them. "When we get done with this, Bill, I'll come back and build one of those for you next summer," he'd said. I told him I'd just finished building a deck like that, surrounding the cabin's sides, moving toward the Lake in two levels, and giving way to stairs as wide as the deck.

Dan's response? Gentle, generous: "Good for you, Bill. You've come a long way with your skills. You really own the place now, and this is just the beginning."

We talked a bit more, but awkwardly. He wouldn't open up about his studies except to say that money had gotten tight, Louise had taken a secretarial job at the university, and he'd taken a semester or two off from his studies to build decks and privacy fences and work at a nearby cement plant. And that's where he was calling from, he said. But the numbers didn't compute—he should have been done by now, both at the cement plant and at seminary. I filled the silence by urging him to take me up on my offer to use the cabin in the fall, do some hunting, take a retreat with Louise. Just ask. Anytime. "I will, Bill. You can count on it." And he was gone.

But not nearly as gone as he would be two years later. He never called back, and what follows is all second-hand information. At break time during a spring night graduate class, I struck up a conversation with a young man named Leif. It turned out that Leif now taught classes at Bethany.

I asked him if he knew Dan. "Yeah. I've never really met him, but I've heard a lot about him."

"Is he still at Bethany? Does he have his own church now?"

Leif was unclear about the details, but "he never finished. Some serious academic difficulties. A nice guy, serious and sincere, but a little over his head."

I asked if Dan and his family were still living in Mankato, across from Bethany. And then the bomb dropped. "He's gone."

Gone? Back to the San Juan Island area? "No. Just gone. Disappeared." Shit. In the couple of minutes it took us to walk back to our classroom, Leif spilled the little he knew. Dan had left his wife? His family? Without explanation.

Vanished.

Howard was disappointed to hear about Dan's meltdown. But he seemed to understand, and identified a bit. "Perfectionists are their own worst enemies. I was. Most alcoholics are perfectionists. When failure and stress over it tapped me on the shoulder, I opened the bottle and crawled in." All of Dan's enthusiasms, all of the impossible pressure he'd imposed on himself. Confronted with his own shortcomings, even his excruciating love for Louise wasn't sufficient to prevent him from jumping off the edge of the world.

But what about Howard? I was finished with my project by 2006, but where was he so late in his career? If I knew nothing else, I knew that he'd never quit if there was anything he could do about it, any more than Sam Maloof in California who made that furniture that Howard admired so much—the guy was by then way into his eighties, with so many concepts he wanted to move from abstraction to concrete realization. Nonetheless, there were obviously some further limitations to face. He was still as strong as a bull, and twice as ornery. He was so independent in his thinking, working, and living that confronting some physical or mental curtailment of that independence would be catastrophic. And it was nearly upon him.

A couple of weeks later, I watched him painfully extricate himself from his chair. Here he was, having apparently battled and whipped prostate cancer, almost unable to stand up because of arthritic back pain. Suddenly he was musing to me about possibly having to reorganize his shop and to build more back-saving "Mexicans" so that he could continue his work. Luckily, due to a competent doctor's analysis and some codeine, he soon returned to work under nearly full steam with a positive prognosis.

But we're not talking about someone who's pursuing a hobby—he needed to work. It's not that he didn't get social security or medicare or the rest of that good stuff; but, as much of a wildly left-swinging Democrat as Howard was, minus the ethnic incorrectness, he was also a radical little capitalist of an entrepreneur. Old Blue Eyes' declaration about New Y-a-w-k that if he could make it there, he'd make it anywhere, didn't apply to Howard's situation—he could've gone somewhere else as he'd done so many times before, but he didn't want to. A congenial hermit, maybe, but he was way past resuming the life of a nomad. It was either here or nowhere.

The business coming through the rough set of double doors on the side of his shop would determine, as it had since he'd been working out of it since about 1988, what Howard and Sally ate, how they lived, and paid their bills. Howard heated his shop and house with wood most of the time, maintained an ugly portfolio of road relics, and salvaged all the windows and electrical and plumbing components he could store on speculation, but he still needed the business.

And the South Shore, probably no less than the North Shore, was a merciless environment for any but the most wealthy who could afford to open up barely-researched stock-in-trade based on no demographics and gaily piss their investment into the wind until boredom overcame them.

The best example of a business that might have stood up

against the realities of too few clients was the new bread baking shop that had just opened up in the beautiful little balconied shop built by Hammer Dave and sold by the couple who'd failed to make a go of it as an antique shop. The couple who bought it both practiced medicine in Duluth; both still worked at their professions but were nearing retirement. They both loved to bake bread—they didn't even bake it in Hammer Dave's little shop; it's too small for that—and they'd come to love the South Shore enough that they'd begun their little operation with a limited repertoire of breads and rolls, all prepared organically, with no real concern for making a profit. We're talking "hobby" here.

I asked the female member of the partnership what they'd do in the winter when things got snowed in and most folks disappeared into the woods, down 35 to the Twin Cities, or down to the Tex-Mex border to enjoy the very mixed pleasures of trailer park life.

She blithely said, "We'll be coming up to cook our bread on Friday nights. We're going to advertise to all our customers and anyone else interested in knowing that they can place their bread orders with us during the week, and I'll open up the shop on Saturdays so that they can come and pick up what they've ordered."

Definitely not concerned about keeping the wolves away from the door. What a way to run a business. If you're rich and your momma's good looking. And, Howard, of course, failed that test on both counts. The bread shop disappeared in little more than a year.

This is where I got concerned about Howard. Three weeks back I'd dropped by the shop to announce that I was taking up semi-permanent residence now that summer school had ended. When Howard had finished ripping on everyone who wasn't ever going to be as lucky as he because, as the resident Peter Pan promoter of the South Shore's natural gifts, he never had to leave like the rest of us, we got to talking a little about the flow of the work that Howard had been doing.

Since the previous December, Howard had been busy as

hell, happily turning down the jobs he didn't want because he didn't like the attitude of the people who offered them to him. Gary Davidson had contracted with a Minnesota log-home builder for his huge manor house-by-the-sea, and that meant a very big kitchen and island for Howard to build. Gary Perkins, the former co-owner, with his wife, of the Village Inn in Corny, had virtually adopted Howard as his personal furniture maker, and there wasn't enough time in the day to anticipate the hutches, the tables, the office cabinets, and counter tops that Gary continued to dream up and kick out walls of his house and barn to make room for. There was at least one other potential kitchen contract mixed in there, along with a huge armoire and other pieces that Howard had taken on for an electrician over in Bark Bay.

It didn't look like the work would ever run out, and, since I'd known Howard, it never had. One needed to get on Howard's "list" maybe six months ahead of when one actually wanted to see a piece or a kitchen in one's house. But, this time, Howard and I were jawing about his work flow around an empty shop. Yeah, he'd been putting the finishing touches on a set of dining room chairs done in his rough-cut rustic style—and pretty neatly, too, since he'd rigged a lazy Susan platform for spinning each chair around as he spray-varnished it. But there was no mistaking the concern he was voicing about the sudden lack of work. He'd been through some fallow times before, but, as he looked out beyond summer into the fall when he expected to begin his major work, there was, for the first time in his memory, not a single contract for a kitchen. And Howard was a cabinet maker. His bread and butter.

We both bemoaned the stark realities of the current stagnant economy. Both of us were able to see through the smoke that was being blown up and around our asses about how the market was recovering, how more than a million burger-tossing, chimney-sweeping, and toilet-scrubbing jobs had been created, and how corporate entities were opening their mail at their Bermuda post office boxes and high-fiving over their obscene profits. Yeah, they'd gotten theirs, but, up until now, neither Howard nor I had seen anything but a continuation of the same old squeeze on our resources.

Pondering over what might have happened to stop the steady flow of kitchen jobs into his shop, Howard settled upon two possibilities—first, maybe he'd built all of the kitchens the South Shore would ever need, and, second, maybe things were so tight on a clientele that, economically, was so very much like him that folks had determined to postpone for greener times anything that wasn't a necessity. The latter made sense, while the former didn't. Little more than a steady trickle of newly retired residents, seasonal vacationers, and well-healed second home builders and buyers was making inroads into Herbster, Port Wing, Corny, and, of course, the little jewel in the South Shore crown, Bayfield, which was beyond Howard's reach.

Howard had been doing exemplary work in the area for more than fifteen years, with all kinds of glowing referrals to speak for it. He had, it's true, disdained hauling his wares to regional craft venues to showcase his skills and "product." Once was enough for that nonsense, he told me. Very little return on the investment of way too much dead time, and Howard would much rather be working than standing around looking like a benign Russian lawn troll. A frightening prospect. The good word had long been out on Howard's uncompromising craftsmanship and his ability to do custom work that made tangible the most complex designs. All Howard needed was a photograph. It didn't even have to be a good photograph.

No, I was convinced, on the basis of nothing concrete or provable, that Howard was a victim of trickle-down economics and was in the midst of an empty bubble that would soon burst with the arrival of a spate of fall projects. Hell, the South Shore doldrums could even be partly ascribed to the slow rebuilding of two washed out bridges west of Port Wing and the widening of 13 between Port Wing and Oulu, both of which had sent summer traffic away from 13 and into the boonies, way across County Roads F and FF and over to A, some ten miles south of Port

Wing leading back to 13 and that word-defying view over the hill's crest of the Big Lake. Dangerous roads. Narrow and populated by hundreds of headlight-frozen road rodents licking the salt off the road's faded center line. It would all work out for Howard, I was sure, provided he wasn't particularly ornery to prospective customers and wasn't so damned cavalier about rejecting jobs on the basis of customer character.

But there was something else on Howard's mind, something I hadn't heard him talk about in anything but a disparaging tone. Teaching. Hmmm.

It was another indigo-skied Sunday, this one made paler and more desolate by the chill of approaching autumn and the looming specter of my return to the university for "duty days" and the start-up of another fall semester. Shit. Syllabi. Books to read and re-read, articles to get started on. Bowels roiling and bubbling in delirious anticipation. And I wouldn't be going for another two weeks yet—some things never change! I'd asked Howard the evening before if I'd be imposing by dropping by the shop on mid-Sunday afternoon to ask him a few final questions for this disreputable manuscript. No problem, he said, no matter what my reason for coming.

After Linda and I had spent our usual Sunday morning in Bayfield buying the Sunday paper, a couple of huge and thickly-frosted buns at the little bakery on Exchange Street, and then positioning the car next to a boat ramp overlooking the lazy Lake traffic with Madeleine Island in the hazy distance, I called Sally at the shop to find out when Howard would be done with his afternoon nap. "Any time after 2 would be fine, Bill." She told me to check by the shop first to see if he'd be coming back to work or spending the rest of the afternoon with his roses.

I pulled up alongside the shop a little after 2:30 to find the double doors open and Sally and a female client discussing a little job with Howard. I could tell that he was a little out of sorts. I'd purposely left the tape recorder home this time and wanted to concentrate on a discussion of a few important issues connected to where Howard was with his craft, and I sensed that this might,

Teaching Fools

indeed, not be the best time for broaching the questions. But Howard insisted.

And he also insisted that we'd be much more comfortable back at the house than talking amid the interruptions that would occur in the shop. He spoke briefly about how, though it may not have looked like it, he'd spent large parts of the last few days rearranging things in the shop—really cleaning things up and "organizing." Most everything he'd been working on had been moved out. The only article looking remotely like a job-in-progress was a large three-inch rough-cut pine slab that he'd be fashioning into a rustic coffee table. He'd done many like it before.

It took a while to get on to the track of the interview. Howard wasn't ready; he was restless, maybe even preoccupied, or just reluctant to confront a couple of hours talking about himself again. But after a fashion, we eased into it, and it began with some backtracking into what had become a familiar line by now—this new bee in his bonnet about taking in interns. I challenged Howard on something he'd told me a couple of years back—that he'd never take an apprentice— because doing so would impinge so much on his ability to get his own work done. I also shared my recollection that offering courses in woodworking at the local community college had no appeal to him—too little money, too much preparation, too much distance to travel, too much hassle.

Howard quickly noted that I had gotten only a portion of what he'd said about these matters right. So to correct my misperception, I asked him to return to the origins of his real teaching experience. The dates of Howard's engagement with King Associates, a large construction outfit in Virginia specializing in malls and apartment complexes, were vague, but, for approximately a year and a half Howard was employed as King's primary "teacher." As Howard put it, after he'd been doing contract work with them for a while, "they asked me to break a bottleneck." King had come to know through long association with Howard that "I was well-versed in the full spectrum of construction work." What King was then faced with played into Howard's particular skills, temperament, and people-management. King's huge projects involved a ballet of trades and skills to get the job done. If one of the parts of the assembly line fell behind, or if a single subcontractor on the job wasn't performing efficiently to permit the other parts of the process to function smoothly, the contract would be broken.

So, hired on with the same salary as a project superintendent, Howard became the all-purpose "bottleneck-breaker." With about 160,000 square feet of flatwork to be poured on one project, a lot of the bottleneck-breaking involved concrete, but, whether the bottleneck occurred in the area of structural steel work, carpentry, or elsewhere, Howard told me that his approach was simple and direct: "a sub got behind, I came in and fired the whole crew and hired a new one." The idea was to bring on a bunch of young men who "didn't know much," who hadn't already set in stone their ideas about how to do their job. "I wanted a clean page to write on." His approach to teaching these guys had to be personal and accelerated, because the job was huge and needed to progress quickly. Howard noted that, in relation to the structural steel work he was intervening on, "these were among the first apartments to be piggy-backed (i.e., one one-story townhouse was constructed under two two-story townhouses, thus requiring large quantities of structural steel).

Each one of these "bottleneck interventions" was "a dynamic thing. You'd start with a fucked-up mess, and it was a lot of fun straightening it out." There was absolutely no time to provide any classroom work for the groups of blank slates Howard was bringing in off the street: "the company made it clear that this [Howard's training approach] had to make money. A lot of con-ing" was necessary to get these new guys to the point of feeling that they could work competently, and on-the-job directions were the rule. Howard might bring on twenty new guys within a particular subcontracting area, and, quickly, "the cream would rise to the top."

Not only was there little initial turn-over in these green

crews that Howard hired, but "it didn't take long for these neophytes to become productive." He employed what he called "the leaning principle": if, as Howard put it, "you use a steady unyielding pressure against an immovable object, finally it will move." Obviously, part of the "leaning" required "constantly con-ing people, for the good, and I used to feel like I was looking behind their eyeballs. I kept asking myself what is there in this man's mind that I can appeal to that will get him to do what I want?"

Howard wryly recalled that he had to accelerate the learning curve of these men. In order to get them to respond to that pressure to learn and immediately perform and produce, "you have to psyche them up to get the most out of them, and so sometimes they would think more of themselves and what they thought they knew and could do than they should." Consequently, a good number of these guys would, not too long after learning their new skills, go off on their own and start their own contracting businesses. Clearly, there was considerable variability in the levels of competence that members of his crews developed, but he would entice the "cream" of the crew with the prospect of becoming a foreman and running his own crew.

All this adds up to—and as a classroom teacher, I'm vaguely familiar with it—crew psychology. Howard was a master of it—you had to be in order to know how to motivate new hires. But the key to his bottleneck-breaking enterprise was finding the sufficiently skilled and motivated person that he could ask "how would you like to learn crew psychology?" When he'd identified the person that he could train to be a foreman and run a crew, he was ready to step into the next bottleneck. And that's teaching, par excellence—getting a class to operate efficiently whether you're there or not and, in a sense, to put yourself out of business.

Howard told me lots of stories that exemplified his "leaning principle" of teaching and the psychology he employed to get his inexperienced crews to perform and to believe they could. One little anecdote will suffice. We'd spent maybe an hour exploring his method, but I was still skeptical that someone like me, if hired off the street with a bunch of other Greenhorns to do house framing, could perform that task with anything approaching efficiency. Howard recalled a time back in Virginia when he was contracting framing. Leading his new hires onto the job site, he told them they were going to frame a house where they stood. Everyone became noticeably anxious. But Howard told them to settle down because he and they were going to do "some old-fashioned planning, and then they could get excited!"

Bingo. I've been there during a similar kind of planning session—careful, patient, calm, methodical, hands-on. By the end of it, I felt there was no way I couldn't do what he'd shown and engaged me in. Let me at it. I'm all over it. And I could understand how using this method on a group of young guys, however rough or uncut, would have the same effect.

Howard didn't need to tell me that he was, "by nature, somewhat of an impatient person." But he always tried to maintain "a veneer of calm and patience, even when I've been absolutely furious." He said he was known in all his superintending jobs as "a son of a bitch," and he was probably understating the case. But he could always inspire confidence and well-being. He was the Zen master for the untutored. And, as he said on that Sunday afternoon and many times before, "it's all planning," whether the issue is teaching someone how to perform a task, contracting a portion of a job, superintending a complex operation, or executing a set of custom cabinets.

Most of Howard's professional life had been spent solving problems, putting out bushfires. That's the way it was. There was little time for congratulating oneself on having built a perfect piece of carpentry because it happened so rarely. It was all about getting beyond difficulties. As Howard said, "bushfires are caused by not knowing what the fuck you're doing." That little piece of profane wisdom translated into "planning is everything." In teaching. In practice.

I vigorously nodded my agreement. Hell, my biggest continuing problem in everything I do is an almost willful lack of planning—if it didn't eventually kill me, it would at least threaten to under-bankroll my retirement.

Then Howard leaned forward to finally trump my earlier impression about his intention never to take apprentices on. He'd worked mostly non-union jobs or contracted himself out to other outfits, he reminded me. In those situations, "there was never an organized apprenticeship program, but, nevertheless, I was always teaching." As his employers at King Associates informed him, "you've got a training program, whether you like it or not." Whether one is talking about an actual apprenticeship program or the kind of creative on-the-job accelerated operation that Howard conducted, "it costs money to train people." The main distinction between the two, Howard said, was that, while no one really expects an apprentice to contribute substantially while being paid to learn for five or six years, he was expected to make his young men immediately productive so that the portion of the contract that they were contributing to would turn a profit. That's pressure.

The discussion quickly gravitated to the teaching enterprise that Howard had been considering most recently—the idea of taking a person or persons into the shop. When I asked him to be more specific about the profile of student he had in mind, he smiled and retorted "preferably mature people. My mental image of an ideal client is a guy at least 55 years old, probably but not necessarily retired, solvent, sober—at least during the day—who loves the idea of doing woodworking. He wants to have an accelerated program and experience of learning shop woodworking." Like an apprenticeship, "it'll be one-on-one," not a crowd of variably tuned-in students, and that, he said, is "a big difference."

Why now, I asked? Howard fired back that "I have the physical facilities for it. I foresee some hard times coming. I think our economy is in serious trouble. And maybe I've mellowed enough that I can do it." I was still trying to wrap my mind around the concept of Howard, a guy who works alone exclusively, who, by his own description, operates with his switch either off or on with no dimmer, sharing his shop and his own precious work time with a stranger.

But Howard offered this rejoinder: "I never had the idea formed just like this before. If you're still thinking about me taking a part-time job teaching woodworking evenings at Northland Community College over in Ashland, it's about putting up with some mediocre bullshit in a situation with no continuity. And, as for taking on an apprentice—what a pain in the ass, and they cost me so much money."

Wagging a forefinger nearly as big as a baby's leg at me for emphasis, he said, "Now, it's time. I never had the time before. And, at $750 a week, I can afford to give someone as much time, six to eight hours a day, as he needs, and I might even be able to get some of my own work done in the process. It's the reverse of the cash flow that would have to go to an apprentice that makes this possible."

Howard went on to tell me that, for years now, a number of people he'd gotten to know in the area had asked him for some help in moving their projects forward, and one even said that he'd be happy to bring his project, no matter how mindless, over to the shop for a little clinic, with the use, of course, of Howard's equipment. He shook his head in exasperation: "he doesn't realize how much my time is worth."

The recollection of such thoughtless interruptions got Howard on to his two favorite topics: rhythm and sequence. "When you break that rhythm, you ruin the efficiency of the work you're doing." Wow. Howard's comment jolted me like a live exposed wire to my nose. I told him that I'd experienced that special euphoria of rhythm only several times while building the carriage house. Most of the time I'd be spilling the nails out of my tool belt, dropping and picking up my hammer fourteen times, continually mis-measuring and short-cutting boards, or whirling around like a dervish trying desperately to find my ass to save my life. But then, I told Howard, there were those occasions—never during the first or last hour of performing a procedure—when the awkwardness and self-consciousness about one's movements gave way to an unrushed ease. When it happens, if you're even conscious of the zone you're in, it's almost like hovering outside and above while watching yourself perform. There's no hurry, no undue application of force with the tool you're using. And the work moves ahead with competence and efficiency. The mind seems to play no part—the movements are intuitive, automatic. Howard nodded knowingly. Om.

I grieved about how these rare periods of competence and productivity lasted so briefly—the longest I'd ever been able to sustain one while framing, building decks, roofing, or siding was about an hour, beyond which everything began to go straight to hell. Howard again nodded silently. I speculated to Howard that these little yoga-like windows closed for me because (1) my skill level at carpentry wasn't high enough, (2) I had the powers of concentration of a springer spaniel in heat, and (3) carpentry wasn't my predestined end. And getting tired from performing the task played its part in breaking the rhythm, too. I thought about the 71 years of golf I've played, how I used to expect to break eighty at least one of the several times I play each summer, and I wondered at those several holes during a given round when the mind shuts off and the club and body become extensions of each other. Total confidence. Until it all goes away. Timing. So fragile. Taking on an apprentice necessarily disrupts rhythm.

But, if rhythm is essential for productivity, then sequence is "absolute king in construction." If you get out of sequence, "you've cost yourself time and money. There's no way you can maintain rhythm if you jump sequence." To clarify what he meant, Howard recalled superintending the building of a batch of houses that were nearly ready for the painters to "go inside and go." But the painters didn't show up when they were supposed to, and, since "the resilient floor guys were ready to go, I let them go in the kitchens and bathrooms, and they promised not to fuck up and make a mess, but, of course, they did."

Howard told me that he was looking forward to the prospect of transmitting some of those hard-won lessons about rhythm and sequence to a receptive intern. And, as to the question of whether an intern could survive a week or a month with Howard in a relatively small space, that chivalrous southern manner broke through again smilingly: "When the need is there, I can be a charming son of a bitch." No Bad Santa in what he termed Bum Fuck, Wisconsin, here. Quite to the contrary.

But what Howard optimistically envisioned was never going to happen. Almost immediately, his prostate cancer returned with a vengeance. There was no chance to fight it. The many trips to Marshfield clinic and a hospital in Duluth over the next few weeks of the fall of 2009 left him a pale, inert shadow. It happened so quickly. I visited him only twice at his little house located just a block away from the shop he would never enter again. He was able to talk haltingly but alertly to me from his living room lazy boy during the first one. But, only a week later he was silent, glassy-eyed, and enveloped in a morphine fog.

He'd be gone in another seven days.

* * *

I'm certain that Howard couldn't have sketched out his passing more perfectly on one of his contractor's story boards. When Socrates counseled his friends not to grieve his impending death in prison at his own hands, he explained that to escape prison to live in exile would be to contradict who and what he had always been—a constant and constructive irritant to the state, even at seventy and beyond. He *was* his interactive and inductive work. Just so, Howard had repeatedly told me that, when one stops doing the work he loves and is compelled to do, that person is dead without knowing it. True to his credo to the end. And I'd be a fool not to emulate him.

Erasmus had it so supremely right in his *In Praise of Folly*. To be human is to be foolish—to be driven by enthusiasms, obsessions, delusions, and prejudices but very little by rationality. To be mad, a little or a lot. Teachers are fools, too, but truly wise teachers enthusiastically abandon rigid and rote "professing" in favor of engaging their audiences in an inductive journey toward self-knowledge—like Socrates; Erasmus; Montaigne; Thoreau; MLK; Christ (Erasmus' ultimate fool because he sought to convince his followers of a reality that could not be seen). The epitome of fooldom. The wise fool. The fool in motley. I'm left holding Howard's cap and bells. And the pleasure has been all mine.

Teaching fools.

Seventeen year-old Howard

AFTERWORD

A Post-Doc Reflection

Tomorrow, and tomorrow, and tomorrow,
Creeps in this petty pace from day to day,
To the last syllable of recorded time;
And all our yesterdays have lighted fools
The way to dusty death. Out, out, brief candle!
--Shakespeare, *MacBeth*

On a hot mid-July Sunday afternoon in Avon, Minnesota, in 1981, Linda and I sat on a pair of intentionally uncomfortable Adirondack chairs and stared out into a ripple-less little lake. Yes, it was, in fact, Lake Woebegone, named that by the regrettable host of "A Prairie Home Companion" with whom I'd spent an awful weekend *not* celebrating his sixtieth birthday many years later. Linda and I had stepped away from an end-of-the-year barbecue for the English faculty at the College of St. Ben's to engage in some deep reflection. I was done at St. Ben's—a non-renewable one-year contract following three one-year contracts at Indiana State—and, although I'd been frantically searching for another teaching job, I'd come up empty. It was getting late. Although I still had unanswered applications out in the ether, it was time to put our heads together on a back-up plan. This was a bad job market for young faculty. And university teachers who'd gotten long in the teeth weren't retiring at a time of sky-rocketing inflation.

"Where should we go to look for work, Linda?" She, who had logged several years of successful teaching, in addition to her crafting and artistic skills, was the likeliest of the two of us to find work, wherever we decided to go. And we weren't just planning to stick around in rural Minnesota—this was going to be a big move.

"We've got family back in the Boston area," she offered. "Maybe a few connections, too. And I've got a Mass. teaching license and elementary school experience in western Massachusetts. I'm ready to go if you are. Kids, cats, and cars."

Not I, though. "I cast my vote for New Mexico." My last two years of undergrad work occurred at New Mexico State, with a huge assist from Linda's elementary school teaching job. It took us an entire year to get used to living in Las Cruces in what seemed then like the windy surface of the moon. But we'd found friends during our second year, settled in, and loved it as a base for traveling all over the U.S.

"Nothing doing," said Linda. She still remembered our first year there when she cried herself to sleep every night from homesickness. We knew that neither of us was likely to get a teaching job wherever we went so late in the summer. We'd need to be creative in marketing ourselves, and that's what we spent the next three days brainstorming about.

But suddenly came a potential embarrassment of riches. Well... not quite. The two jobs that I'd suddenly been invited to interview for—one on the edge of the Allagash Wilderness on the border between northern Maine and New Brunswick and the other just down the road apiece, as my mother used to say, at Mankato State University—offered very small money. The former was a tenure track position, but with the tiniest of salaries amidst a total number of faculty (26) that made me afraid to accept it for fear the university would blow away for lack of students.

So it was Mankato. But that meant still another one-year

contract that came with a sobering wild card. On the day of my interview, I was invited into the department chair's office to discuss my official duties. Until then, the interview had been remarkably unchallenging, more like a wake than an academic exercise—and fast. There seemed never to have been any question about my being offered the job or turning it down. Once they confirmed that I had a Ph.D. and a pulse, they knew they fairly had me.

And I soon found out why. The stern department chair laid her cards on the table. We wish to start a teaching assistantship program to support the development of a larger student audience for our M.A.-Literature program, she declared. If you accept the position, it will be your job to create the new T.A. program, recruit and hire prospective T.A.s, train them to teach one Comp I section per quarter, visit their classes and evaluate their work, and develop any and all materials to support the endeavor.

Yikes! And I thought that I was interviewing for a World Literature and Composition job! This looked and felt like Falstaff's enlistment of cannon fodder. Spear-carrier. A one-year job almost guaranteed not to end well.

So... everyone raise your hand if you know why this job was still open at the end of July. And raise them again if you have a hunch why no currently employed faculty in the department had volunteered to take on this challenge. And, if your arms aren't too tired from waving them wildly to respond to the first two questions, raise them a final time if you have a clue why the job was being offered to someone *not* a Comp Specialist, and for a one-year contract! That last one was guaranteed to leave a mark.

Well, of course, I took the damned thing. Not for the challenge, but because I had so few choices. But taking it would make all the difference in the kind of teacher I'd become. My recruitment "con" started almost immediately by interviewing anyone I could find who might be remotely interested in teaching a Comp class (no experience needed—will train) while taking at least six credits of graduate-level English courses. And what a motley bunch that first group would turn out to be. Besides the more traditional types who'd intended to do an M.A.-Lit degree with no coaxing, some fringier folks wanted to pursue Women's Studies, History, a way to get out of the house, or the small stipend the T.A.-ship would offer. Others hadn't thought it through. And there was the guy who'd fallen drunk off an apartment building roof in full Bat Man costumage and had to be bailed out of jail by a sympathetic faculty member. I didn't accept everyone who applied—but almost. And Bat Man turned out great.

But what happened after that con was akin to what Howard would do for the King Associates in Virginia and, eventually, for me. Out of self-defense, I boot-strapped a two-week end-of-summer course that collaboratively had the eleven of us defining the teaching task; understanding the organic steps in the writing process; designing and sequencing assignments; developing strategies for "conferencing" with their students; using good and bad papers I'd received in classes at other venues to practice grading, constructive commenting, and establishing criteria for great, good, fair, and awful writing; demonstrating the importance of revision and how to incorporate it into their courses; and developing each of our syllabi, to be shared and critiqued on the final day of the workshop.

The long and short of it was that I didn't get fired and my recruits of varying ages and no experience did increasingly well for themselves by their students, if unevenly. In the course of what would be my six-year "tenure" in this position, we got better. Lots of visits (by me and each other) to their classes to see how everyone was progressing, meetings twice a week to trouble-shoot teaching problems and techniques. The gradual development of a real and mutually supportive cohort and camaraderie. And, by the end of the fourth year, we'd composed our own practical text that we kept under constant review.

I learned enough about teaching from that experience to change the way I thought of myself as a teacher. Besides incorporating significantly more collaborative work in all my classes, I began to use student interns in many of them. My thinking?—I wanted to foster more active, student-centered learning, with less emphasis on me as supreme authority. I intended these internships to mean much more than a student wheeling a cart full of pre-loaded slides into a classroom, closing the lights, and flipping a switch. I wanted to enlist talented, interested students into a full buy-in. Over my thirty-three years at MSU, each of the twenty-five or so undergraduate and graduate interns I selected met with me to plan a syllabus and carve out an area of interest that the intern wanted to ply. That might include tracking a theme or trope through course material and finding space for those findings and students' questions about them as the course unfolded. It could, for most interns, involve committing to "owning" one of the course texts, right down to the researching, teaching, and developing assignments related to it. I insisted, though, that every intern would join me in regular planning and critique sessions before and after each class, share grading of written assignments, and maintain a continuing journal through the course.

Almost without fail, the interns did remarkable work for and with me while other students in those classes became accustomed to looking toward the both of us for direction. In some memorable instances, the in-class interactions between me and a few of those interns were magical. So many of those internship experiences resulted in interns collaborating with me in conference presentations on what we had done at the regional, national, and international level, and just as many of these collaborations ended with the publication of their work. I learned so much more about myself, my craft, and my subject matter in those situations than I ever could have alone.

Over the last twenty years at MSU, one continuing collaboration with a small cluster of faculty from different disciplines taught us all how to constructively "con" other faculty from across the university to incorporate writing into their courses. Of course, we bribed each group of about twenty participants with a tiny stipend to join us in one of our many

Valley Writing Workshops that occurred after Fall Semester had concluded. Our mission?—to convince every faculty member of the importance of making room in their upper-division and graduate classes for students to write—not just in an exam or a course-concluding formal paper but in an assignment or interlocking group of assignments that each instructor would provide some time during their courses to develop in an unfolding process, from beginning to finished product.

Lots of initial resistance from older faculty, and not just those in math and the sciences. But it became great fun to engage these faculty where they were, with the goals they needed to fulfill within their courses, and to find natural spaces for that student writing to germinate and prosper in a planned and economical way. Lots of modeling by the workshop presenters on what good disciplinary writing looked like and how to model it for their students; some hilarious (they were to *us!*) skits about the writing process and how the product shouldn't be prioritized over the process. Those workshops worked for the largest percentage of participants because we got them to use our workshop to choose one course, re-acquaint themselves with their goals in it, select a portion of it where writing should/could play a vital part in the teaching component, and hone in on the articulation of an assignment and its constituent parts that would help them and their students get where they needed to go. At the end of Spring Semester, we would meet once more in a several-hour "symposium" of their individual presentations, replete with handouts, with the assignments they'd developed, how those assignments had meshed with their course goals, and their assessment tools that gaged how effectively all of this had gone. Nothing like seeing teachers re-imagining themselves, the geography of their courses, and the relationships between their assignments and the goals of their courses.

Only two days ago did I fully realize what Howard had done with me mirrored so closely what my students and I had done together. Classic mentorship. Howard would never have called himself a mentor, but he'd been doing his work in a practical, mentoring way at least since the day at King Associates when he fired their carpenters and replaced them with untrained men off the streets that he could shape into a collaborative and productive force. And King Associates would *never* have acknowledged nor understood that they'd hired him to be a mentor, just as I didn't know that I'd been doing something very similar for the bulk of my career, intuitively living and breathing it in my work.

As I've said earlier, all teaching is a con. It's about getting someone you're charged to work with to do something that they don't want to do, don't think they can do, see little value in doing, or think they know how to do already. Somewhat like my having taken for granted Howard's generous invitation to me—a rank amateur and potential liability—to step out on the floor, dance with him until my small repertoire of basic steps had been exhausted, and be allowed to stay on the floor with him because of the new steps he was willing to take the time to teach me on the fly. Trickery. Charlatanism. Performative subterfuge.

When I grabbed my legal pad and tape recorder to ask Howard questions about his history in carpentry and began following him around on site visits, I thought *I* was in control of the process, but it was actually Howard who was doing the interviewing. Much like he did with Dan at the very beginning of the remodel of our cabin, Howard was testing my interest and seriousness in what he knew. In the end, Howard would be leaving it entirely up to me whether, after a year of watching him do what he did and asking questions, I was prepared to take a little of what he'd inductively taught me and make it my own. I didn't know that I was auditioning for a part in his play, but, when he finally expressed confidence that I now had done and knew enough to take on a big project with his continuing support, I knew I'd pass the audition. On-the-job training that never felt *at all* like on-the-job training.

Ultimately, through my reflections on what I'd done with and learned from Howard, I understood the meaning of mentorship and that I'd spent a career doing it with students and faculty I'd worked with. I'd just never thought—nor, probably, had Howard—to put a name to it. So good mentorship knows no disciplinary boundaries, no academic sphere, to prosper in. Nor does it require the mentor to have completed a formal program of study, never mind a high school degree. Expertise, experience, a willingness to share it, and a commitment to provide support for as long as it might take—those are the qualities of real mentorship. And Howard's was a university without walls.

Bill Dyer
May 2023.

ABOUT THE AUTHOR

William D. Dyer III (or IV, but who's counting?) spent forty-two years in the teaching wars, thirty-seven of them in fulltime positions, and his final thirty-three years at Minnesota State University, Mankato (it will always be Mankato State to him!). His career took him from Western Massachusetts and a Ph.D. in English from the University of Massachusetts at Amherst to Fitchburg State, New Mexico State, and Indiana State University at Evansville to the College of St. Benedict before settling in at Mankato State to teach everything he'd dreamed of teaching: World Lit; English Lit surveys; writing-intensive courses; a slew of Humanities courses including one in Russian literature, history, and culture; the Latin American Novel; Dickens and Dostoevsky; Shakespeare's Tragedies and Shakespeare's Comedies and Histories; and a number of on-site courses associated with his three-and-a-half week Summer Sessions in England, Scotland, and Wales, with a side order of Ireland. He lives now in St. Louis Park with his two Siamese cats, who, as Montaigne so astutely observed in his own case, deign to play with him rather than the other way around. And the fire still burns hot in his continuing love affair with his cabin and the South Shore of Superior.

Printed in the USA
CPSIA information can be obtained
at www.ICGtesting.com
LVHW011554210823
755837LV00001B/1